THE FILM DIRECTOR

THE FILM DIRECTOR

SECOND EDITION

Updated for Today's Filmmaker, the Classic, Practical Reference to Motion Picture and Television Techniques

Richard L. Bare

IDG Books Worldwide, Inc.
An International Data Group Company
Foster City, CA • Chicago, IL • Indianapolis, IN • New York, NY

To Gloria

IDG Books Worldwide, Inc.
An International Data Group Company
919 E. Hillsdale Boulevard
Suite 400
Foster City, CA 94404

For general information on IDG Books Worldwide's books in the U.S., please
call our Consumer Customer Service department at 800-762-2974. For reseller
information, including discounts and premium sales, please call our Reseller
Customer Service department at 800-434-3422.

ISBN 0-02-863819-0

Cataloging-in-Publication Data can be obtained from the Library of Congress.

Manufactured in the United States of America

04   03   02   01   00   4   3   2   1

Second Edition

Book design by Holly Wittenberg

CONTENTS

FOREWORD

The day I met Richard Bare changed my life. Before that, nobody knew my name outside of Norman, Oklahoma. A little after that, my name became fairly well known as a contract player at Warner Bros. and very well known after I was cast in the title role of *Maverick*, a TV show that garnered (excuse the pun) more viewers than I thought a western ought to. Of course, *Maverick* was not the usual western we'd all grown up with. I wouldn't go as far as to say that Bret Maverick was a coward. He was more like a gambler who only bet on a sure thing. A typical script would have a pretty girl run up to me on the street and say, "Mr. Maverick, I need your help!" and I would point and say, "The Sheriff's office is right over there, Ma'am."

But enough about me. Dick Bare got me started at Warner Bros., and I'm going to let him tell you the circumstances in the following pages since I would not want to rain on his parade, or anything like that. All I know is that after directing the first TV show Warners' ever made, he's still going strong. He has always been a capable director who got the work done on time. He wrote this book for aspiring directors, and when I directed my first show it came in mighty handy. Up to that time, I'd always thought a TV director was the fellow they sent down to the set to keep the actors from bumping into each other. *The Film Director* is a must read for those who want to learn the ins and outs of the director's craft.

Aside from all that, Dick has had an amazing life, and his accomplishments as well as his heartbreaks make up a thoroughly engrossing story, told in an entertaining style as only the man who has lived it can relate. He tells it like it is. Richard Bare has made a name for himself in the movie and television business. The only place some folks make a name for themselves is on a tombstone.

James Garner

INTRODUCTION

No aspect of our society has escaped the flood of do-it-yourself books that have poured onto the market in recent years. Although many of them have served useful purposes, books on motion picture—and most particularly motion picture directing—have left something to be desired. *The Film Director* is a welcome and needed exception.

Dick Bare is not only a professional and highly skilled director who is fully qualified to discuss his craft, but also an articulate spokesperson for his fellow directors. As a result, *The Film Director* is both instructional and entertaining reading.

The point has often been made that film is an art form, and in order for it to develop to its fullest, directors should scrap existing rules and make free use of their own creative abilities. The obvious comparison is to painters who have broken with tradition, developing new techniques, even new schools of painting, to broaden the horizons of art appreciation. But while the comparison is valid, what should always be borne in mind is that only an artist who has mastered all of the rules can break them properly and make the fullest use of the medium he or she has chosen.

The value of *The Film Director* to the student or fledgling director is that it emphasizes the basic rules (not only of camera techniques and the use of film, but also of helping actors create the needed emotion) and points the way to the free flight of creative imagination that breaks the rules to provide exciting new uses of film and camera. In doing so, Dick Bare has made it clear that, like any other art form, film is constantly changing in both technique and content, and the creative director must constantly strive to improve his or her skills, since yesterday's innovation may well be tomorrow's cliché.

This should not mean, however, that an idea once used must be discarded. When I was first handed the script for *The Sound of Music*, I questioned the opening because it was patterned after my concept for the opening of *West Side Story*, and I was reluctant to open my second musical with another high-angle helicopter sequence. But we were unable to come up with another opening that was as good—and I'm glad we couldn't. Nothing else could have set the mood of *Music* nearly as well, and, despite my preopening apprehension, even those critics who disliked the film did not contend that the opening was an attempt to copy a previous success.

These are the things, of course, that must be learned through experience. But the growing number of schools for aspiring filmmakers provides a solid groundwork that can hasten an understanding of the various factors on which experience is based. In past days, many of us started in the business as messengers and gradually worked our way through various crafts to reach the status of directors. Today's routine is different. The blueprint as spelled out in *The Film Director* indicates far less time is consumed—but the novice comes to the medium now with far more understanding of the basics than we had. To paraphrase an old Hollywood joke, "To be interested in film is not enough—one must also have an understanding of it."

The Film Director goes a long way toward providing that understanding.

Robert Wise
FORMER PRESIDENT
DIRECTORS GUILD OF AMERICA

Editor's Note: Mr. Wise received Academy Awards for The Sound of Music *and* West Side Story.

PREFACE

preface

This is more than a textbook. It is a chronicle of one director's viewpoints and experiences set forth to illustrate the requirements of a fascinating but exacting job and to provide hope and inspiration to those who would like to crack the movie or television business.

Time and time again, film directors have maintained that directing is an art, not a science, and have consistently taken the position that there are few rules or other criteria that can be successfully passed on to a newcomer. This is true only to the degree that Leonardo da Vinci was able to pass on his particular genius to his students, some of whom, I am sure, turned out to be reasonably proficient painters.

Veteran director William Keighley believed that certain basics of film directing *could* be taught and, accordingly, conducted a class in this subject at the University of Southern California. I assisted him in this course, which spanned an eight-month period, and much of the material in this book is based on the approaches to teaching that were formulated at the time. Keighley made one point worth underscoring: He could show students how to make pictures, but he couldn't guarantee that they would be good pictures.

Although this book covers the rudiments of film directing, the mechanics and techniques of staging and handling the camera, as well as the dramatic and emotional processes involved in handling actors and telling a story, it also cites my own experiences in *getting to be a director*.

Admittedly one of the world's toughest professions to break into, film directing can be one of the most rewarding, not only in financial terms but in terms of doing work that is fulfilling, exciting, sometimes important, but always *fun*.

Richard L. Bare
Newport Beach, California

Kevin Costner on the set of *The Postman*, which he directed as well as starred in. His first stint at directing, *Dances With Wolves*, resulted in an Academy Award for Best Director. Photograph by Ben Glass.

CHAPTER ONE

THE IMPORTANCE OF
THE DIRECTOR

Never before in the history of motion pictures has there been such a wave of genuine interest in the making of motion pictures. At last count, 691 colleges and universities in the United States offer courses in film education, and more than forty-five of these currently give degrees in the subject. Even some high schools provide classes for aspiring filmmakers. Film is fast becoming the art of the present generation.

THE EMINENCE OF THE DIRECTOR

To understand fully the subject of cinema is to delve deeply into the inner working of the one person who shoulders (today more than ever before) the greater responsibility for what reaches the screen. And this, most experts will agree, is the director.

From the 1930s to the 1970s, most moviegoers, before deciding to see a film at the theater, asked first, "Who's in it?" Unless the reply was Cary Grant or Clark Gable or some other superstar of the day, the waiting line outside the theater was not apt to be long. The perpetrators of the star system had done their work well; the world had been mesmerized into believing that the biggest single ingredient of a picture's worth was the actor. Many moviegoers still identify a film with its stars, yet the trend

1

now is to find and separate the one person who can be held accountable for the result of the total product. *Film* has taken its place as the chief cultural topic on the campus; the "new director" has been substituted for the latest novelist at social gatherings.

This eminence accorded the director received its impetus from an article in the French magazine *Cahiers du Cinéma* in 1954. François Truffaut, a popular film critic who yearned to make his own films, wrote that movies were not group art, but rather the result of a single authority over story, acting and photography. The maker of a film brings to his or her work the same personal creativity as the artist does in painting, the sculptor in sculpture or the author in literature. Truffaut proclaimed the director as the true "author" of the finished film, hence the *auteur theory* of filmmaking.

Since the thirties, millions of serious film devotees have rallied to the support of a favorite director, seeing in the director's films the indelible and, to them, the unmistakable stamp of the auteur. Suddenly, film festivals were springing up on both sides of the Atlantic; films of Hitchcock, Huston, Ford and Wilder were gathered together and studied like some newly discovered set of Dead Sea scrolls. Even Don Siegel, a competent but never previously acclaimed director of such films as *Coogan's Bluff* and *Madigan*, had several of his films shown at a Siegel festival in Paris. When Siegel was asked to address the group, his opening remarks clearly expressed his surprise: "Where were you when I needed you?"

Perhaps a less lofty description of the auteur, and one that is gaining favor especially with the newer breed of directors, is: the *total filmmaker*. I can think of no director who is more worthy of that title than the late Charles Chaplin. From the time he broke loose from Mack Sennett, he assumed total control of his films; he wrote the scripts and then directed, edited and produced them (with his own money). In his later films, he composed the music as well. No one can deny that Chaplin was the "author" of his films.

Of course, anyone who has a dream, puts it on paper, raises the necessary money, produces and directs the film, and then edits it can rightfully be labeled a total filmmaker. Steven Soderbergh broke into the

. . . .

Charlie Chaplin had a penchant for falling in love with his leading ladies, but that didn't interfere with his creative juices. He owned his own studio and financed his own movies, ensuring that he had total control. Shown here is a scene from *The Circus* costarring Myrna Kennedy, circa 1928. The next year all studios had turned to sound pictures, but not Chaplin; his films were silent until he made *The Great Dictator* in 1940.

film industry by doing all of the creative jobs on *Sex, Lies and Videotape*. He has since turned out ten films, though he cannot claim to be the auteur for all of them.

Although the auteur theory has gained favor with many moviegoers in the United States, and film companies find themselves giving directors complete autonomy, there remains one area in which the director is not the dominant figure. This is in series television, where week after week a program must perpetuate its original look and format, as well as its established characters. Some television shows have as many as a dozen directors during a season's programming. Each brings a different style of shooting, but the actors' characterizations must be constant from week to week. The person who molds all the elements of the show is the producer, who is also usually a writer and often the creator of the format. The producer must supervise the writing, making certain that the various writers conform in style. The producer also must make sure that the show is edited according to the form established in the pilot film. With the chores of story collaboration and much of the editing taken away from the director, there is only one place left for the director to display his or her craftsmanship, and that is on the shooting stage.

Whatever the arguments, pro and con, appear to be, the idea that a director "authors" a piece of film is true only to the degree to which the director conceived the original idea, shared in the writing, took over the producing chores and then went on to overcome the infinite obstacles that lay ahead. All directors must master complex technicalities; the great director has something more—the talent to mold the complexities of human emotions into an inspired whole.

THE FORTUNATE 400

It seems that practically everyone connected with the motion picture or television business harbors either secretly or openly a desire to be a director. Sometime ago the word got around that this job is the most gratifying one in the motion picture business. For years the writers and the actors obstinately maintained that this wasn't so, but lately even they have come around.

Frank Capra once opened the annual banquet of the Directors Guild of America with these words: "Good evening. I wish to welcome actor-directors, producer-directors, actor-writer-directors, writer-producer-directors, and just plain director-directors." Of course the crowd laughed,

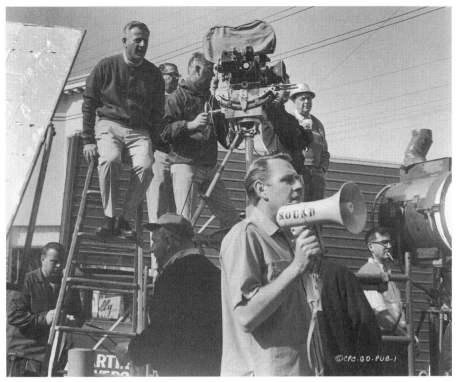

On location in San Francisco for *Guess Who's Coming to Dinner,* producer-director Stanley Kramer takes a high perch to watch the action. Kramer is one of the few producers who turned director, liked it and stayed with it. (Columbia)

and the business of the evening went forward: The handing out of the coveted Directors' Award for Best Director of the Year, which incidentally was won by William Wyler, a director-director.

According to the latest count in 1999, there are 5,152 director members in the Directors Guild of America (DGA), an organization that represents all theatrical, television and commercial directors in the United States. Many of these members are retired and protecting their pensions, which are considerable. In addition, the roster contains the names of persons who have directed only one or two films, actors such as Kevin Costner, Mel Gibson and Barbra Streisand.

Many directors on the list are either retired or working in other fields, holding on to their coveted membership card on the chance that one day they will return. Of the entire Hollywood director membership, no more than 400 or so are regularly engaged in directing. Approximately 100 members make only theatrical films, and the rest are divided between television programs and commercials.

Cameraman Laszlo Kovacs (left) and director Dennis Hopper check the camera angle for a scene of *Easy Rider,* starring Peter Fonda and Dennis Hopper. Hopper is an actor who made good as a director. (Columbia)

The preceding statistics are provided to illustrate the fact that the job of director is as highly competitive as it is coveted, and many persons seek and obtain the opportunity to direct their first film on a commercial level, only to fall by the wayside in favor of the "fortunate 400."

But those who would seek entry into this exclusive group can take solace in the fact that its membership, by the nature of the demands of the business itself, is a rotating one. Nowhere in the world are there such opportunities for the young newcomer to reach the top in so short a time as in the film industry—especially if that newcomer has chosen directing as his or her life's work.

THE LOW-BUDGET DIRECTOR

Not all directors have the luxury of 100-day shooting schedules, two cameras on every setup, a private office on the set, a mobile dressing room or a chair with his or her name on the back. The low-budget director, who typically operates on a financially precarious budget, must forego these expensive perks.

The director may be too broke to come up with the initiation fee to join the prestigious Directors Guild of America. Of course, there is no law that says one has to join, but not joining will mean denying oneself residuals when the film goes to TV. Furthermore, it will be difficult to avail oneself of a top studio production manager and assistant directors. The film will be going nonunion all the way. However, the Guild now has a special contract for low-budget productions that is completely negotiable.

Rick Schmidt, author of the book, *Feature Filmmaking at Used Car Prices*, gives practical advice to the newcomer and shows step by step how he made a feature film for $6,000. He offers solid evidence that such a thing is possible and gives details of his experiences making *A Man, A Woman and a Killer*, and his slightly more expensive follow-ups, *The Remake* and *Emerald Cities*.

Schmidt advises all low-budget filmmakers to "get as many charge cards as you can *before* you start making the feature." And, he adds, survey the various foundations for funding, such as the National Education Association's Media Arts Program. In Schmidt's case, his first film was self-funded with a little help from family and friends. And it doesn't hurt to establish credit with a film laboratory that will hold the negative until you are able to pay their bill. Schmidt paid everyone in his cast and crew $20 per day, plus a generous 60 percent of the profits. In the case of *A Man, A Woman and a Killer*, the film reached a break-even point with one sale, and the investors, to their surprise, were paid back.

Another budgeting trick practiced by some low-budget directors is to use all available funds to shoot the picture and assemble a rough cut. If a distributor likes the film, in many cases the distribution company will provide the cash to take the project through post-production and scoring. It is much easier to raise funds when the investor can see the quality of the story, acting and direction, rather than having to rely on only a script.

Of course, few films of commercial quality are made as cheaply as Rick Schmidt's was; the majority cost from $100,000 up to $2,000,000. The average cost of a major studio release is about $40,000,000, and the Directors Guild considers those costing below $6,000,000 as low-budget films.

George Romero, who broke into mainstream pictures with his scary *Night of the Living Dead*, is a pioneer in low-budget filmmaking. The horror movie of all horror movies cost under $100,000.

Wes Craven's *Last House on the Left* cost a meager $90,000. He made his second film, *Nightmare on Elm Street*, as a low-budgeter but broke out into the big-time with *Scream* and *Scream II*. A good horror flick has a strong shelf life and can earn many millions more than its production cost.

While codirectors Daniel Myrick and Eduardo Sanchez were shooting the uniquely different *The Blair Witch Project*, they had no idea that their $35,000 film would make the covers of both *Time* and *Newsweek*. Nor could they have imagined that their modest little film would mesmerize moviegoers and gross $108 million in the first three weeks of exhibition. Of course, these young filmmakers were not the only ones to be surprised. Most of Hollywood's distributors were shocked to witness such an unusual blockbuster during the film's opening weeks. The consensus is that the mildly spooky film will ultimately gross at least $150 million.

Running only eighty-one minutes and shot in black and white, the film breaks tradition with contemporary, slick horror films. Its grainy images and shaky camera work would normally turn off audiences but, because of its clever premise, these "flaws" seem to have worked. The greater part of the film comprises a tape of a documentary supposedly left behind by the story's victims.

In 1998, over 1,000 mostly low-budget films were entered into the Toronto Film Festival. The New York Film Festival garnered more than 1,200. The Telluride Festival has a "student program" and, from the hundreds of applications it receives, invites between fifty and seventy-five young filmmakers to show their best work. The primary goal of all new directors is to get their work shown at a film festival.

Even though the number of small features being produced is large, adequate financing is apparently available. The availability of financing notwithstanding, it's arguable whether these films have a market. Paul Bartel, director of *Eating Raoul*, which was made for less than $300,000, pooh-poohs the idea that if a film is in focus it will find a distributor. The truth is, laboratories are full of unreleased film negatives, the final prints of which, upon screening, had received high praise at the festivals.

Even Orson Welles was known to leave the negatives of his partially finished movies scattered about in European film laboratories. Near the end of his career, he contacted me and said he needed $25,000 for postproduction on a film called *Dead Calm*. I looked at the rough cut and assured him I would help him out. But when I talked with his lawyer in New York, he laughed and told me that $25,000 wouldn't come close to paying all the encumbrances against the negative, which reposed in a Sarajevo laboratory. Needless to say, I declined Welles's generous offer.

Steven Soderbergh, an unknown kid filmmaker looking for a sale, brought a print of *Sex, Lies and Videotape* to the Sundance Film Festival. When he left, he had a distributor and an advance against film rentals— and a rosy future. Not so with 28-year-old David Cunningham, who produced and directed *Beyond Paradise* on the Big Island of Hawaii. It was well-produced and had a theme that Cunningham thought would be of interest to all teenagers: interracial conflict. He had experienced similar tensions as a minority white kid in a Hawaiian school. Although the young director managed to get play dates for his movie in Hawaii and even Guam, signing a U.S. distribution contract eluded him, and he found himself up against a stacked deck. Without the impressive studio budget and actors with star power, Cunningham could find no distributor willing to finance the considerable cost of prints and advertising. Hopefully, by now *Beyond Paradise* has attracted the right distributor and been released as it is an interesting and well-made film.

The cinematic rainbow does not always end in a pot of gold. Ex-bartender Phillip Creager, with no previous experience as a filmmaker, raised $80,000 and shot a 35-mm feature called *Face Down in the Family Pool* about an AIDS death in his family. The Edwards Theater in Irvine, California, booked the film for one week in June 1999 but did not extend the run, as each showing averaged only four viewers. Undaunted, within days Creager was already planning his next venture into filmmaking.

Robert Redford is the modern-day extoller of the philosophical adage, "Hope springs eternal in the human breast." Every summer since 1981, the famous actor has given his time and energies to his Sundance Filmmakers and Screenwriters Lab. He explains his reasoning: "The summer lab gets the least attention, but it's the most important thing we do."

Each year, several thousand applications flood the little mountain town of Sundance, Utah, and eight or so young hopefuls are selected to chin, chat and pick the brains of professional directors. They even shoot test scenes from their own scripts, acted by such established performers as Ally Sheedy and Martha Plimpton, all under the eye of accomplished directors such as Gus Van Sant (*Good Will Hunting*).

In a month of challenging twelve-hour days, the lucky learners have the opportunity to display their talents and hear the sometimes harsh criticism that follows. The 1999 seminar included Michael Canton-Jones, who directed *The Jackal* and *Rob Roy*. He worked closely with the "fellows" as they are called.

A Few Film Festivals

Aspen Film Festival
601 E. Bleeker
Aspen, CO 81611

Atlanta Film Festival
75 Bennett St., #M-1
Atlanta, GA 30309

Baltimore Film Festival
10 Art Museum Dr.
Baltimore, MD 21218

Chicago International Film Festival
415 N. Dearborn St.
Chicago, IL 60610

Denver International Film Festival
999 18th St., #1820
Denver, CO 80202

Florida Film Festival
1300 S. Orlando Ave.
Miami, FL 32751

Hawaii International Film Festival
700 Bishop St.
Honolulu, HI 96813

New York Film Festival
70 Lincoln Center Plaza
New York, NY 10023

Palm Springs International Film
  Festival
P.O. Box 2230
Palm Springs, CA 92263

San Francisco Film Festival
1521 Eddy St.
San Francisco, CA 94115

Santa Barbara International Film
  Festival
1216 State St.
Santa Barbara, CA 93101

Seattle Film Festival
Egyptian Theatre
801 E. Pine St.
Seattle, WA 98122

Sundance Film Festival
P.O. Box 16450
Salt Lake City, UT 84116

Telluride Film Festival
P.O. Box B1156
Hanover, NH 03755

USA Film Festival (Dallas)
2917 Swiss Ave.
Dallas, TX 75204

Washington, DC Film Festival
Box 21396
Washington, DC 20009

Montreal World Film Festival
1455 Boulevard de Maisonneuve
West, #H109
Montreal, Quebec H3G 1M8

Toronto International Film Festival
70 Carlton St.
Toronto, Ontario M5B 1L7

Vancouver International Film Festival
410-1008 Homer St.
Vancouver, BC V6B 2X1

Among former fellows are Quentin Tarantino and Paul Thomas Anderson, the latter of whom directed the provocative *Boogie Nights.* Mike Hoffman, a 1984 attendee, went on to direct *A Midsummer Night's Dream* and continues to live outside of the mainstream in Boise, Idaho.

While Hollywood's goal is to produce only that which sells, the Sundance Filmmakers and Screenwriters Lab aims to instill in its fellows the passion to make films that haven't been seen before, films that *stretch* the imaginations of their creators. Redford admits that "the whole focus here at Sundance is the story," and the fellows are selected on the quality of their scripts.

Former fellows Walter Salles and Tony Bui created two films, *Central Station* and *Three Seasons*, that were lauded when they were released. They, like all achievers, never gave up hope.

A word to the wise: The obvious is still true. Choose your subject matter carefully, and write what you know about. Don't aspire to loftiness; let the big studios gamble with the blockbusters that are loaded with special effects, explosions and car chases. Do simple stories that either tug at the audience's heart or make them laugh. Set dramatic limitations for yourself and then keep within them.

WHAT MAKES A DIRECTOR?

Unlike some gifted artists, actors and writers who are born with their talents and can often succeed on their own, the director must learn the art from others, acquiring knowledge and skill through observation and practice. As an aspiring director, you can learn from watching the films of good directors and also from watching directors at work. Reading cinema books and taking cinema courses are other ways to learn, but the best training ground for the would-be director still remains the motion picture business itself. At least this has been the avenue most-used by the better accredited film directors in New York and Hollywood today. One exception in this respect is my own experience, which will be related in subsequent chapters and which attests to the fact that serious academic schooling in the fundamentals of filmmaking, when combined with practical experience in making films, can lead to a creative position in the movie or television industry.

Some directors have apprenticed as script clerks. If they were lucky enough to work with a James Cameron (*Titanic*) or a Steven Spielberg (*Saving Private Ryan*), they would have kept the records of the shoots while quietly observing first-hand the working of the director's sometimes harried mind.

There are other jobs on the movie set that, because of their proximity to the director, are time-honored steppingstones to the director's chair. The film editor normally enjoys a close collaboration with the person behind the megaphone—otherwise known as the director. Incidentally, although the megaphone is a relic of the silent era, it is still used at times on large sets. It continues to be the most effective means of communication between the director and the actors at the far end of a large set. The film editor, who prefers that title over the one that he or she is most often called—cutter—learns how to be a director through years of handling film that has been turned in by a variety of directors and ranges from excellent to not-so-good. The editor vows that when he gets *his* chance, he will never make *those* mistakes.

John Sturges, director of such films as *Bad Day at Black Rock* and *Ice Station Zebra*, started as an editor at RKO Studios and edited Air Force training films at Wright Field during World War II. Sturges became friendly with William Wyler and codirected *Thunderbolt*, an outstanding war documentary made while the two were in the service. When the war was over, Wyler dropped a few words of praise in the right places; Columbia placed Sturges under contract, and he never cut another film except his own. He got his break and went on to direct many box-office hits.

Robert Wise, two-time Academy Award winner, started at RKO as a messenger and worked his way up to film editor. After he edited Orson Welles's masterpiece, *Citizen Kane*, he never looked back and was soon directing *Curse of the Cat People*, a low-budget film that has become a classic.

William Fraker made the leap from cinema student at the University of Southern California (USC) to still cameraman to head cinematographer on three top pictures in one year, *The Fox*, *Rosemary's Baby*, and *Bullitt*. When his ex-agents decided to turn producer, they hired Fraker as a director on the big-budget film *Monte Walsh*, starring Lee Marvin. He, in turn, elevated his camera operator to director of photography.

The late James Wong Howe, Hollywood's only Chinese cinematographer and a top man in his field for thirty years, tried his hand at directing. George Stevens, who piloted *Giant*, *Shane*, *The Diary of Anne Frank* and scores of other blockbusters, started as a cameraman on Hal Roach comedies years ago. Somewhere down the line he realized how easy it was to direct the actors, since he knew what to do with the camera. Rudy Mate, the director of *Miracle in the Rain*, gave up his job as a cinematographer when he decided that directing wasn't all that hard. He had spent many years at the elbows of the industry's top directors.

Many cinematographers have "directed" at times when a new and uncertain director has faltered or become confused over the staging of a scene. It seems appropriate to mention here that cinematographers, or "directors of photography" as they prefer to be known, will almost always come to the aid of a new director, offering solid counseling at a time when others may be waiting for the novice to fail.

John Milius, who directed *Red Dawn* and *The Wind and the Lion*, came from the USC Film and Television School, where he directed a short called *Marcello, I'm So Bored.* Apparently, the audience wasn't, and John was soon directing important pictures, some of which he wrote himself.

The prolific Randal Kleiser also graduated from USC, where he made the 16-mm film *Summer Days Don't Last.* He has since directed seventeen movies such as *Grease* and *The Blue Lagoon.*

Robert Zemeckis directed two short films at USC and attracted an independent producer who signed him to direct a low-budget film. He made the leap to high-budget when Michael Douglas was impressed with the young man and signed him to direct *Romancing the Stone.* His three *Back to the Future* hits solidified Zemeckis' place in the industry; and when *Forrest Gump* came along, he was ready for a departure. He never

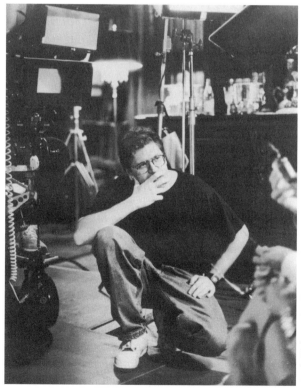

Robert Zemeckis came out of the University of Southern California's film school with two short films in his portfolio. His first low-budget feature attracted the producer Michael Douglas who signed him to direct the actor Michael Douglas in *Romancing the Stone.* A few years later, Zemeckis won the Oscar for directing *Forrest Gump.*

thought, however, that a simple, character-driven story could become the blockbuster that it did. Zemeckis was interviewed by Ted Elrick, who said that some critics have compared him to Frank Capra. Here was his reply: "I guess you can make a comparison because the issues are life issues. The villains aren't psychotic axe murderers, and there aren't any terrorist bombings. The Capra films dealt with what are perceived as realistic life issues. The villain is the banker in the town. In *Forrest Gump*, there isn't a villain of any kind. Capra is one of my favorite directors, so I am flattered by the comparisons."

Haskell Wexler, a top director of photography, made the leap to director with *Medium Cool* and *Latino*. In my own case, my first real job in Hollywood was as an assistant cameraman on a cheap movie called *Narcotic*, which I managed to keep in focus.

There has been a recent assault on the director's ranks by actors, and at least three have won Oscars for their work: Kevin Costner for *Dances With Wolves*, Warren Beatty for *Reds* and Clint Eastwood for *The Unforgiven*. In television, many stars have gone on to try their hand behind the camera. Tom Hanks, for instance, has directed episodes of *Tales From The Crypt*, *Fallen Angels* and *A League of Their Own*.

Logical, you might say, for actors to go into directing. They have had close contact with the best and worst of film directors over the years. They have watched, studied the director's technical problems, and waited. Many were sure that, if given the chance, they could do it better. Some have and some have not. On average, the degree of success among the actor-turned-director group has not been any more spectacular than for other groups.

The screenwriter has, perhaps, shouted loudest in criticizing the director, and it is understandable why so many screenwriters have joined the ranks as directors. Their too common complaint, "I turned in a beautiful script, but between the producer and the director it was hacked to pieces," says it all. The writer often dreams of the day when every word, every nuance, every bit of delicately written dialogue will find its way to the screen, unadulterated and tamper-free. A screenwriter's solution to the problem is to take on the role of director.

One of Hollywood's most notable examples of the writer turned director is Blake Edwards. His creations include *Victor/Victoria*, *The Great Race* and six versions of *The Pink Panther*. Garry Marshall, who started as a writer of sitcoms such as *Happy Days* and *LaVerne and Shirley* (starring his sister Penny) and who subsequently directed both sitcoms, finally got his first feature assignment at age 47 with the mildly successful *Young*

Doctors in Love. As Marshall put it, "I was petrified. At the end of the whole thing, I told Penny 'I'm never going to do this again.'" But he did, and the result was the giant hit *Pretty Woman.*

Hollywood has always been the end of the financial rainbow for people from the New York theater. Stage directors who have become outstanding in their field have had little trouble finding work in films. Mike Nichols sailed into Hollywood and made his name bigger than ever with *Who's Afraid of Virginia Woolf?* Warner Brothers assigned a top cameraman, film editor and script clerk to help him adjust to the technique of filmmaking.

An important new breeding ground for mainstream directors is the field of television commercials. Obligated to tell a story in a minute or so, the commercial director has, when moving up to full-length movies, brought with him a staccato-like rhythm that can, in some instances, become annoying. Much can be said in favor of allowing a camera shot to be appreciated for its composition and artistry, to say nothing of valuing the time and money that went into making a shot that may be as short as eight frames or one-third of a second.

Cost-conscious studios, however, hire commercial directors for important pictures because they bring a fresh look to the big screen as well as a low price tag for their services. Kinka Usher of the "Got Milk?" and Taco Bell Chihuahua campaigns was assigned the $75,000,000 *Mystery Men* as his first Hollywood movie.

"A commercial director is more likely to look at things from the audience's perspective because we're used to doing that," he says, adding that he favors pretesting his film in focus groups. He completely changed the ending of *Mystery Men* as a result of the input from a test audience.

Mark Pellington, a commercial director, made *Arlington Road* in 1999 and completely broke a sacrosanct rule by having evil prevail in a quick twist at the end: Jeff Bridges is accused of the crime he was trying to solve, while Tim Robbins (the real villain) goes off scot-free.

With commercials becoming the farm system of Hollywood, and commercial directors having more time and money per foot of film to hone their skills, it is obvious that ad films are an easy route to major productions.

The late, great Stanley Kubrick (*2001: A Space Odyssey; Eyes Wide Shut*), while in high school, decided to take his still photos to *Look* magazine. Mistaken for a messenger boy, he managed to see the editor, who promptly bought all his pictures and asked for more. At 17, Kubrick

Mike Nichols came to Hollywood after a successful series of Broadway hits and started out at the top directing Elizabeth Taylor and Richard Burton in *Who's Afraid of Virginia Woolf?* Although his background was largely in comedy, he made the transition to dramatic director with flying colors. (Warner Bros.)

was a full-fledged staff photographer. While still working for *Look*, he conceived an idea for a movie documentary about a prize fighter on the day of his big fight. That was in 1951; and once he had taken hold of the movie camera, Kubrick never relinquished his grip. It was a short road to Hollywood, where he directed *Paths of Glory* at the age of 28 and established himself as the most promising of the postwar generation of filmmakers. *Dr. Strangelove*, *A Clockwork Orange*, and *The Shining* have all contributed to his versatility. He died in 1999, a few months before the premiere of *Eyes Wide Shut*, his final film.

Directors can come from any place. Dick Moder was a wardrobe man just a few years ago, and he worked on one of the pictures I directed at Warners'. The next time I saw him, he was a director and probably giving the wardrobe man the same trouble he himself used to endure.

Dialogue directors often evolve easily into directors, undergoing little strain during the transition. After all, many a dialogue director has put the polish on a performance while the director was concerned with the physical problems of staging and camera angles. When I directed the first TV show for Warner Bros., *Cheyenne*, my dialogue director made life much easier for me as he coached a performance out of newcomer Clint Walker. I asked him why he didn't strive to become a director himself.

"I don't know," he said, "I just couldn't handle all this cutting and camera stuff and get the picture done on time."

I told him we should meet nights; I would show him about cameras, lenses, movement and production shortcuts, and he could tell me all he knew about actors. We never got together, but less than two months later he got his first chance to direct a television film. Incidentally, he made it on schedule.

Until the 1960s, no major Hollywood films had been made by black directors. Then Gordon Parks, a famous still cameraman, was given the opportunity by Warner Bros. to direct his own book, *The Learning Tree*. Ossie Davis was handed the directorial reins on *Cotton Comes To Harlem* for two reasons: Ossie knew Harlem, and he had written for the screen and television. A fine actor, he settled into the director's chair like a veteran.

Melvin Van Peebles, although born in Chicago, had to go to France to get his break as a director. In Paris he wrote and directed a few short films. A writing award, a job as a French journalist, and four published novels led to his directing *The Story of a Three Day Pass*, which he himself had written. The picture was a hit, and he was consequently named the French delegate at the San Francisco Film Festival, where his picture was critically acclaimed. Then Columbia signed him to direct *The Watermelon Man*, a job that he attributes to his success in France. "It certainly didn't happen because I'm black and that I'm beautiful," he says, half kidding, half serious.

Perhaps the most successful black director is Spike Lee, who exploded on the scene with the ultralow-budget *She's Gotta Have It*, made in twelve days. His recent *Summer of Sam*, about the Son of Sam killer in New York during the summer of 1977, is a deviation for the director in that it is more about Italian-Americans than blacks. Lee selected Ellen Kuras as director of photography. Interestingly, Lee always shoots with two cameras simultaneously, claiming that it not only helps the schedule but greatly helps the actors as well.

Most people outside the entertainment business have the impression that the job of producer, not director, is the pinnacle of success in Hollywood. Too many top producers, however, have moved over to become directors to give credence to this story. Stanley Kramer had many fine pictures to his credit before he tried his hand at directing. Joseph P. Mankiewicz (*All About Eve, Cleopatra*) was a top writer doing only the most important pictures when he became a producer. He apparently found that being behind the desk was as frustrating as writing, for soon he was telling the actors and crew what to do on the set.

Strangely enough, few assistant directors make the leap to director, or even aspire to directing. Since assistants are more production manager than director and are seldom concerned with the aesthetics involved in making pictures, it is understandable that they do not move upward in this fashion. There have been a few exceptions, however, and former assistants like Robert Aldrich and Howard Koch have distinguished themselves as directors. In Koch's case, he moved up to producer and then to production head of Paramount studios.

Among the current crop of directors who started in the business as assistant directors, Alan Rudolph is perhaps the most famous, having directed fifteen feature films, including *Dorothy Parker and the Vicious Circle* and *Afterglow* (all low- to medium-budget pictures). He worked as an assistant under Robert Altman. Rudolph cannot say enough good things about his association with the maverick director, his mentor.

In an interview with Tomm Carroll for the *DGA News*, Rudolph says: "When Robert Altman became my producer (on *Dorothy Parker*), I was very happy. Altman is the only American filmmaker whose films you can come into after missing the titles and yet you still know whose film it is." When asked what he learned from Altman, Rudolph said, "He teaches you to trust yourself, to go after what you think is your own truth and your own art and that there are no rules."

I have to say here for the record that when I was directing a series of shorts for Warner Bros., a young Robert Altman stood around on my set. He watched how I worked, though I'm not sure if my style had any influence on him in looking back on his prolific body of work.

Actually, there are not many instances in which a director has coveted any other job. A few have moved upward and onward into that much maligned realm known as producing, but they usually hang on to the director's chores as well because the director, with all the headaches, continues to have the most personally rewarding job of all.

A LIFETIME PURSUIT

There is a doctrine among the powers that be in the film industry that the making of films should only be entrusted to the younger generation. The rationale: Young directors understand what appeals to young audiences. However, this narrow perspective has caused the studios to make the serious mistake of turning away from the huge and now untapped resource of what was once the mainstay movie audience—those moviegoers over forty who have consequently turned to cable TV to satisfy their appetite for more substantial film fare. A few older directors have defied the current youth-oriented system and continue to direct major films.

The film *A Fish Called Wanda* was considered a success and especially appealed to younger audiences. Yet, it was directed by Charles Crichton who was seventy-six at the time—a testament that directing can truly be a lifelong endeavor.

John Frankenheimer came from live television, where he directed more than fifty episodes of the memorable *Playhouse 90*. His most noteworthy films include *Birdman of Alcatraz*, *The Manchurian Candidate*, and *French Connection II*. Today Frankenheimer is in his seventies and still goes from film to film, most of which are seen on the better cable channels.

The late Stanley Kubrick was seventy-two when he directed Tom Cruise and Nicole Kidman in *Eyes Wide Shut*, proving that a director of any age who has the necessary physical stamina can continue to direct movies.

In 1999 two-time Oscar winner Robert Wise at age 85 directed a feature-length film, *A Storm in Summer*, for Showtime Productions, proving that directing is like riding a bicycle.

The irrascible Budd Boetticher, who is eighty-four at the time of this writing, is Hollywood's only director who started out as a bullfighter and then parlayed his experiences into the renowned *Bullfighter and the Lady* has this to say about the subject: "There *is* a gray list in Hollywood and it is horrendous. How can movies be a young man's game? You don't know what you're doing at first. You're like a rookie quarterback who doesn't know what signal to call. They don't think anybody over forty knows how to make pictures."

As for my own "twilight years," I recently signed a contract to direct a film for a new company. It seems that once one has the passion for making movies, it never fades away.

WHAT IS A DIRECTOR?

A few years ago I was asked by the Academy of Motion Picture Arts and Sciences to write and direct a documentary short subject to be entitled *The Film Director*. This was only one in a series of public relations films they were producing in an endeavor to enlighten the public about what went on behind the scenes in the making of a motion picture.

I tackled this assignment with proper dedication, knowing that here was the opportunity to make a visual statement concerning the importance of the director, one that might serve as a testimonial to a somewhat misunderstood profession. I was sure that the audience as a whole still had a mental image of the typical Hollywood director as a rather noisy, flamboyant character who wore loud sport coats, a beret, and jumped around the set with his hands held before him in the time-worn gesture of framing the shot. Here was the perfect chance to depict the movie director the way he or she really is, more often than not working in casual attire with no attendant hysterics or personal theatrics to awe the onlooker. Here the director could be shown as a hard working, responsible individual who was often first on the set in the morning and the last to leave the studio at the end of the day. At night, it would be explained, the director worked over the script and organized the next day's shooting, and many times devoted weekends to rewriting scenes with the producer or writer. Here was the opportunity to show the infinite problems that face a director during the shooting of a picture.

The film was made and was exhibited in theaters all over the country, and it answered to a great degree the question, What is a director? However, even today the question of who does what in the making of a motion picture is one of perpetual mystery to those who view the finished work. And the reviewers seem to be more mystified than anyone else when it comes to writing the notices after a preview.

For instance, a reviewer may comment, "Brilliant camera angles and dynamic camera movement by cinematographer Richard Roe." In most instances this credit should have been assigned to the director.

"George Spelvin's directorial touches far surpass anything he has done in the past." Those touches, in this case, were written into the script by the author.

"Producer John Henry has shown extreme taste and judgment in casting a black actor in a Caucasian role." Again, this was the director's idea, since he brought the whole package to the producer.

William Wyler in his heyday was a superb craftsman, but he got his start as an assistant director. His most famous films were all Oscar winners: *Mrs. Miniver, Best Years of Our Lives* and *Ben Hur.*

Despite the protestations of the proponents of the auteur theory, the contributions to a motion picture are many and overlapping; sometimes even those who worked on the picture aren't sure who contributed what. That is why we so often hear the winner of an Academy Award say, upon accepting the Oscar, "Thank you, but this award would not have been possible without the help of everyone on the picture. It was a team effort."

Directors function in a unique and all-embracing way. They pre-conceive a motion picture as it will appear in its entirety and vitally

Director John Schlesinger lines up a shot with the last of the reliable workhorses, the Mitchel Reflex. Almost all major pictures today are shot with an array of Panavision cameras.

participate in all phases of its preparation and execution. Since they are also in command of others, directors must know something of their functions. They must know the rudiments of acting, writing and photography. They should be able to physically edit films. They should have a working knowledge of architecture, costume design, makeup and music; else, how can they communicate with those whose job it is to provide these ingredients? Above all, they must indelibly stamp their personality, their style,

. . . .

As Clint Eastwood approached middle age, he realized his days as a movie star might be numbered, so he turned to directing. His first effort was *Play Misty For Me*, a limited success; but he gained his stride again when *The Unforgiven* won Best Director at the Academy Awards.

their *touch* on the film they create, and the measure of this success is the extent to which they enlighten, uplift and give pleasure to the audience.

WHO CASTS THE DIRECTOR?

A maxim has long existed in Hollywood that says a good director, with talented performers, can raise the level of an ordinary script to such a point that the public accepts the production as being extraordinary, at least commercially. Seldom does this work in reverse; an incompetent director cannot turn out superior screen entertainment even though he or she has an exceptional screenplay from which to work.

In the old studio system, directors were under contract and, like the stars, they sometimes balked and rebelled, refusing to take on a particular assignment. Of course, this was in direct proportion to their bank accounts. I know, I was there as a contract director at Warner Bros., and

I helmed several pictures I was not enamoured with. But I was a studio director and glad to have the assignments that limited the "layoff" periods during which I didn't get paid.

Today, the important director is typically "packaged" by a talent agency, along with the script, the producer and a major star. This happens long before the studio is approached for financing and distribution. However, the director sometimes finds the literary material that becomes the cornerstone of the package.

During one of my many layoffs while under contract to Warner Bros., I read a *Reader's Digest* condensation of a book called *The Saga of Pappy Gunn*, by George C. Kenney. This true story of one man's amazing exploits in World War II was truly amazing. On December 7, 1941, Pappy Gunn was a middle-aged civilian running a small commercial airline in Manila, with a wife and four children. General Douglas MacArthur commandeered Pappy's single engine Beechcraft and made him a Captain in his valiant, but as yet unproved, Air Corps.

When the Japanese entered Manila, Pappy was on a mission, flying plasma to MacArthur's beleaguered troops holed up on Corregidor. The Japanese army entered Manila, captured Pappy's wife and children and interned them in the infamous Santa Tomas prison camp. From that day on—for over three years—Pappy Gunn rampaged up and down the Pacific islands in a wild, daring and highly personal campaign to get his family back.

Impressed by the story, I contacted the author and arranged to tie up the rights to the book. I decided to save time and money and write the screenplay myself. Once that was finished, I presented it to Warner Bros., who promptly stuck a pin in my balloon. It turned out that they, too, had optioned the basic rights but had subsequently abandoned the project, finding it too hard to cast.

My friend and former boss of Warners' TV department, William T. Orr, had left the studio a few weeks earlier. I sent him the script, he read it and shared my enthusiasm. I had begun to build my "package" with a talented executive producer.

We began to think about who could play the leading role. According to Bill, there was only one bankable star of the right age to play the cantankerous Pappy Gunn. Fortunately, Bill knew John Wayne personally and had the script delivered to the star's Newport Beach home.

Within a day or two, Bill and I sat in Michael Wayne's office and negotiated a deal with the venerable actor's son. John Wayne would star, Bill would coproduce with Michael, and I would direct, provided the elder Wayne approved. I felt confident that after I got to know the actor, I would get his approval.

What made this package unique was the fact that there was no talent agency taking 10 percent off the top of all the talents' salaries and that Paramount Studios would automatically be brought into the deal as financier and distributor because of Wayne's commitment with them.

Unfortunately, a month later Bill heard from Michael Wayne. Sorry, but his father would have to withdraw from the project. Bill and I were devastated as we watched John Wayne stride across the stage to accept an Oscar for *True Grit*.

Two months later Michael Wayne announced to the media that his father had died of cancer.

The script, now called "Tiger in the Sky," went back on the shelf. I still would like to see someone make the story of Pappy Gunn.

Although the days of the studio-produced films seem to be past, occasionally a hit Broadway show or an about-to-be-published novel is acquired by a major film company. The first consideration once the property is acquired is who will direct the picture. Invariably the studio will insure its oftentimes astronomical investment in a new property by using a top director.

Pictures were once scheduled for production as soon as the stars were set; today it is usually the director who is given the first consideration. The wise producer knows that a film's success, after the script has been written, lies in the hands of the person selected to mold the physical and emotional elements into a single tangible strip of film. A slow, indecisive director can run a picture hopelessly over budget, and an insensitive, mechanical director can turn out a film that is listless and unalive. But if the director is someone of taste and talent and if the story is sound, the actors are competent and the producer has the resources to give the director the necessary time and production values, a successful film should result.

Sometimes, independent producers develop scripts and then seek directors who they feel will help get the picture made. Other times, it is the director who has a story idea and convinces a writer to write the screenplay on speculation. The next step in completing the package is to bring in a major star. This is where your best-laid plans can go astray.

I was once preparing a movie that I was producing as well as directing, and had made a deal with a distributor. I had my heart and soul set on a certain young actor for the leading role; but, when I told his agent how much money I had in the budget, he laughed and refused to send the script to his client, whose career at the time was at a standstill.

Convinced that the young actor was the only one for the role, I called a friend of his and got the actor's phone number. Since we had worked together in the past, he was happy to speak with me. I told him about the picture and how his agent refused to submit the script to him. He rankled at this disclosure and asked me to send him the script. The next day, he called and invited me to his Beverly Hills home. When I arrived, he started berating his agent and told me how much he liked the screenplay.

"What do you have in the budget?" he asked. I explained that his agent had quoted a standing price of $250,000 and that I had only $100,000 for the role.

"Well screw him—I'll take the job," he exclaimed, "When do we start?"

I told him we would head for location in a week. He told me later that he fired his agent the day he accepted the role, accusing the agent of pricing him out of the market.

When the producer, the director and a star are attached, the rest can be relatively simple. After all, the hard part has been accomplished, and the studio merely has to "green light" the production and supply the money and distribution. Some studios, like Paramount, will finance a picture only if the filmmakers bring in at least one-half of the money.

Bette Davis, a temperamental star who in her long run as a Hollywood legend had more than one disagreement with a director, admitted, "In films it's the director who's the supreme artist, who in the final analysis is responsible for the success or failure of the picture, who shapes the material, inspires the performers, controls, juggles and fits together all the pieces. We players are merely puppets a director dangles."

Charlton Heston wrote an article in the Directors Guild magazine *Action* and said the following about directors: "In a film, how the scene plays on the floor isn't necessarily all that important. One of the first significant things you discover in acting for films is that your best performance of an entire scene may not be the one that is used. A scene doesn't even exist in the dailies. It doesn't exist until long after the actors are off salary. The vital 15 percent (that will find its way to the screen) is made in a Moviola with the director running the bits and pieces back and forth. Thus, who the director is, is of vital importance to you."

Sometimes the star has final approval of the director, and it is always the actor who selects the director when the picture is being produced by the actor's own company. This usually results in a "cooperative" director being assigned to the production, since the superstars like to call their own shots and important directors will have no part of that. George

John Frankenheimer started his career as an actor, but soon he was working as an associate director in live television. In 1954 he got his chance to direct, and he turned out such shows as *You Are There* and *Danger*. Now firmly established in feature filmmaking, Frankenheimer has directed such stylized pictures as *The Manchurian Candidate* and *Burning Season*, for which he won an Emmy, one of four. (United Artists)

Stevens has said, "It is most difficult to direct an actor who owns the company. I am not about to direct any actor who insists on telling me how I should do my job."

Hollywood long existed on the star system, and pictures were sold to the exhibitors mainly through their stars. Cary Grant, Clark Gable and Marilyn Monroe had their fans at the box office; today's films are making their own stars, such as Sandra Bullock and Leonardo DiCaprio. But through it all, we find some directors with as much "box office" as many stars. For over thirty years, the name of Cecil B. De Mille on a marquee ensured success for the pictures he directed. Alfred Hitchcock used to be the best-known film director in the world, largely because of his television appearances and the fact that he played a small bit in each of his movies.

There are still a handful of directors who are bankable, no matter the other ingredients of the package. They bring to the project a comfort level for the studios that are financing the pictures. If you were in charge of "green lighting" films for a major studio, would you not embrace the likes of Steven Spielberg, James Cameron or Martin Scorsese? Wouldn't you throw out the red carpet for Francis Ford Coppola, Robert Zemeckis or Barry Levinson? Of course you would, because when you're on the line for $50,000,000 or so you're counting on your director's story and casting judgment to protect yourself. Securing a top director is the cheapest kind of insurance you can buy.

Sydney Pollack graduated from filmed television shows to feature pictures with *The Slender Thread*, starring Sidney Poitier and Anne Bancroft. Since then he has directed *They Shoot Horses, Don't They?*, a grim story of marathon dancers in the 1930s with Jane Fonda, as well as the wild comedy *Tootsie* with Dustin Hoffman, and the stylish *Out of Africa* that starred Robert Redford and Meryl Streep. Producers have learned that their investment will be secure with Pollack in charge.

Many directors, through their individuality and characteristic viewpoint, bring a distinct trademark to the screen, one that is recognizable from picture to picture. Pioneers like Ernst Lubitsch (*Ninotchka*) and King Vidor (*The Big Parade*) brought an unmistakable stamp to their pictures, as did Orson Welles (*Citizen Kane*) on his initial visit to Hollywood.

King Vidor, the first president of the Directors Guild and whose earlier films were infused with serious themes, maintained that the movie director

has a strong and articulate voice, and he or she should use it well: "In my opinion, the motion picture is the greatest medium of expression ever invented. The films that have expressed the greatest unity, and given the most satisfaction to the viewer, have been those in which the guiding hand has been imposed on every section of the film's many divisions. Story, casting, settings, photography, acting should all bespeak *one* mind."

Vidor was obviously referring to his belief that the director is the most important single person in the creation of film entertainment—a doctrine formulated over thirty years prior to Truffaut's conceiving his auteur theory.

THE DISTAFF SIDE

The strides that women filmmakers have made in the past ten years are nothing short of phenomenal. As of June 1999, the number of female director members in the once all-male DGA was 741. Not all made a living, of course, but more than a few have distinguished themselves.

When Dreamworks was seeking a director for *The Peacemaker,* their first feature production, they looked over the availability list and selected Emmy-winner Mimi Leder. Although *The Peacemaker* was full of raw action and foreign locations, Steven Spielberg was confident that a woman director could do the job as well as a man. For Leder, the job was even more demanding because she elected to take her small daughter with her on locations that included Slovakia and Macedonia.

In *The Peacemaker,* using only a storyboard for the action sequences, Leder got her feet wet with blue screen and CGI (Computer-Generated Images), but she insisted that the railroad scenes and explosions be real.

"Steven gave me great respect in all aspects of this movie. He let me make my movie, my way," she says enthusiastically. "I did my cut, and then Steven came in and went over the cut. He gave me great notes, and we worked together to finish it."

Until that time, Mimi Leder had been directing for over ten years, starting as a cinematographer and moving to a script supervisor. Her short film *Short Order Dreams* caught the attention of Steven Bochco,

· ·

Mark Rydell, a former actor, directs a scene by long distance. He looks through the 250-mm lens at the action and then shouts instructions through an electric megaphone. (Cinema Center–National General)

Who said women can't direct action-adventure films? Mimi Leder proved that she could by directing *The Peacemaker,* a thriller shot on foreign locations and starring George Clooney and Nicole Kidman. Her second film, *Deep Impact,* has grossed over $370,000,000 to date.

and he gave her an episode of *L.A. Law* to direct. She subsequently did shows such as *China Beach,* as well as nine TV movies and *ER,* for which she won her Emmy. After her first feature was released, Leder was besieged with offers. She accepted the big action thriller *Deep Impact.*

Another successful female director, Martha Coolidge, has over a dozen films to her credit. A fifteen-year veteran director and a current board member of the Directors Guild of America, Coolidge (*Rambling Rose, Valley Girl*) has established herself as a multifaceted filmmaker with a hands-on approach to her craft. She started making short films as a student in Rhode Island and then enrolled in film classes at New York University, where she got her master's degree.

Her first real job was as an assistant editor for a commercial company. Straining at the leash, with her head brimming with creative thoughts, she raised enough money for two documentaries—*Old Fashioned Woman* and *Not a Pretty Picture,* an apt title for a date rape film. Those efforts got her an interview with Francis Ford Coppola, who had left Hollywood for San Francisco to form his Zoetrope Studios. Although nothing came of that introduction, she did manage to turn out a film called *City Girl* that brought her the chance to make the mainstream *Valley Girl.* The film established her as a Hollywood major-studio director. Her advice to newcomers is to go to film school. "Film school gives you the opportunity to be part of a community of filmmakers in which you'll be functioning for the rest of your life."

But when Coolidge applied to film school, they told her she couldn't be a director—she was a woman. She replied, "Oh, is that so?" Martha Coolidge showed them.

Not only are more women than ever becoming directors, but women are also entering the academic arena as deans of film schools. Take Elizabeth Daley, for instance. She has been dean of the USC School of Cinema/Television for eight years. She was selected over many applicants because she had professional filmmaking experience, having produced and directed a number of highly reputed television productions.

THE FLAP OVER SCREEN CREDITS

There have been many squabbles between writers, production companies and directors over the past few years. They are inevitably over the "possessory credit," the one that usually reads "A Film by _____" during a movie's opening. This grabbing of credit in the vein of the European auteur rankled the Writers Guild of America. For a time the Guild had a nonpossessory ban written into its agreement with the studios. But the DGA bargainers were able to strike the offending clause from the Basic Agreement with the Motion Picture Association, which represents all the major studios. All parties agreed that if the director was important enough to demand the credit and if the studios agreed, the credit should read "A Film by _____." Personally, I consider this a bit ostentatious and unnecessary, since the term *director* is as important a credit as can be given.

A separate, but no less dire, situation occurs when, after previewing their movies, directors decide they don't want their names associated with "the disaster" they believe it to be. Enter Allen Smithee, who will gladly allow his name to be used as a director. He cares not one whit as to the quality of the movie and even seems eager to grab the credit since he seldom works these days. Not only that, he has the reputation as the worst director in Hollywood, although he has directed all genres, from comedies to westerns.

Smithee will never be assigned to an $80,000,000 blockbuster. Nor will his footprints be stamped into the forecourt of the Chinese Theatre on Hollywood Boulevard. The reason for this is that Allen Smithee does not exist. He was created after Robert Totten was replaced by Don Siegel on

This could be—and then again it may not be—the only photo ever made of the elusive Allen Smithee who eschews all publicity. He thinks it's too ostentatious to have his name on the back of his chair, preferring the generic term.

Death of a Gunfighter. When the picture was finished, neither wanted his name to be connected with what they felt was a disaster. The DGA, which adjudicates squabbles connected with screen credits, wrestled with the problem and came up with a solution. As long as the director, or directors in this case, kept mum about it, they would allow a pseudonym to be placed on the credits. But the directors would have to forego all future residuals. Both Totten and Siegel were happy to let Allen Smithee take the blame.

The irony was that most reviewers lauded Smithee for his sensitive work. The *New York Times* said: "This film has been sharply directed by Allen Smithee. He has an adroit facility for scanning faces and extracting sharp background detail." *Variety* reported: "Smithee's direction keeps the action taut, and he draws convincing portrayals from the supporting cast."

When the very expensive space fiction movie *Dune* was completed, director David Lynch appealed to Allen Smithee to take the fall for him. With good cause, too. One reviewer, Roger Ebert, growled: "This movie is a real mess, an incomprehensible, ugly, unstructured, pointless excursion into the murkier realms of one of the most confusing screenplays of all time."

But Allen Smithee could care less. He's always available and has a batting average of .500 when it comes to the reviewers, the audiences in general and the studios' bottom lines.

chapter two

CHAPTER TWO
THE DIRECTOR AS
PSYCHOLOGIST

TEMPERAMENT AND TRICKS

William Keighley (*The Man Who Came to Dinner* and *Each Dawn I Die*), one of the first important directors to conduct classes in film at the University of Southern California, placed a high degree of importance on the psychological factors involved in directing.

Keighley had been under contract to Warner Bros. since the early days of sound and had risen to the position of director via the route of dialogue director, having originally come from the theater. In his early days as a full director, he had the occasion to direct many temperamental stars, including Bette Davis, and was forced to devise unusual, if not devious, techniques in directing.

On one such occasion, Keighley was attempting to get a performance out of a particularly high-strung and nervous leading lady, an important star of the day. After several takes, it was apparent that the actress was not doing the scene correctly and tension was mounting. Each time, Keighley would ask for the scene to be done over and she would ask why; *she* thought it was good. It took all the diplomacy and expertise that Keighley could muster to persuade the actress to make another take. Finally on the ninth take, as the scene was nearing the end, Keighley knew he would have to shoot it again. But how would he tell her? Spotting a bucket lying near the camera, he slowly moved alongside it and with a furtive movement kicked it against the camera dolly.

"Cut! *Cut!*" he cried, turning around to face the crew. "Who did that? You spoiled a perfect take!"

The astonished crew looked from one to the other while Keighley walked up to the actress, put his arms around her, and expressed a profound apology for the clumsy idiot who ruined the scene just when it was going so well. Now they would have to do it again . . . . In this way, the director got what he wanted out of a star who, because of a feeling of insecurity in her own work, was not giving a performance equal to her reputation.

Often a director casts a leading actress who has passed her prime, and is faced with the dilemma of how to make her look the age of the role she is playing. The cameraman, of course, can do much to bring a flattering and youthful look to the actress by careful positioning of the lights. Adding diffusion filters to the lens, the purpose of which is to wash out the wrinkles and sagging chin lines, can also work miracles. But the director can add the finishing touch to this metamorphosis, and a good way is to keep her laughing. There is nothing like a touch of humor initiated while the camera is starting to roll to bring the lady's face up to her former levels. By the time you say "action" and the scene starts, she is relaxed and smiling; and this youthful expression will many times hold for the entire scene.

In Norman Lear's first try at directing, the writer-producer turned director handled a difficult crowd scene like a veteran. The location was a small town in Iowa; the picture was *Cold Turkey*, starring Dick Van Dyke. The scene that Lear was shooting called for Van Dyke to exhort a large crowd of townspeople into signing a no-smoking pledge. But the crowd's lack of professional acting ability marred the scene; the proper reactions to Van Dyke's appeal were not forthcoming. Finally, in desperation, Lear started screaming at the top of his lungs at Van Dyke, calling him stupid and incompetent for the way he was playing the scene. Van Dyke, in on the ruse, hurled insults back at the director. The crowd buzzed and reacted with proper realism while the cameras slowly panned over their astonished faces. After the scene, the director explained to the townspeople that he had wanted a shocked reaction from them and that fooling them with the temper tantrum was just a director's ruse.

During the run of *The Rockford Files*, James Garner was confronted with the news that the director who had been assigned for the episode had suddenly become ill. The producer wanted to know, could he take over? After all, no one knew the characters and situation better than Garner. With some misgivings, the actor agreed to finish the episode, which had three more days to shoot.

The next morning, the cast of regulars, Noah Beery, Jr., Stuart Margolin and Joe Santos, were waiting on the set, wondering how their star would handle them, since Garner had never directed before.

A little late, but with characteristic bravado, Garner entered the set attired in riding breeches, boots, red scarf around his neck, a tam on his head and a lens finder around his neck. Everyone howled with laughter, and the filming continued in relaxed fashion. To cover his own nervousness, Garner had decided on the ploy that would allay any apprehension his fellow actors might have had about his ability to direct them.

THE OVERZEALOUS ACTOR

The art of directing is an extension of the actor's development. A good director does not run a school of acting, but rather guides the performers along in their own interpretations. The director must be sure that these interpretations fit correctly into the overall tone of the script as the director has envisioned it. I have seen actors so charged up with their own delineation of a character that they completely failed to coordinate it with the other characters in the story. This usually happens when an actor, who has been used to more important roles, accepts a small part, intending to make it "memorable." The director, whose job it is to de-emphasize the overzealous actor, sometimes calls on various psychological techniques. The one I find most helpful is to explain to the actor that the performance is so outstanding that it is sure to be cut out of the picture after the star complains to the producer. Desiring to stay in the picture rather than end up in the "out takes," the actor usually conforms.

Once when I was directing a young woman of some prominence in Rod Serling's *Twilight Zone*, I experienced, not too happily I might add, a situation that almost developed into a full-fledged brouhaha. The actress apparently had been persuaded to do a rather bland role and had accepted, knowing she would bring an interpretation to the character far and away beyond anything that was on mere paper. The character, as written by Serling, was a drab, unsophisticated waitress working in a remote roadside café in Nevada. The character was not supposed to be

William Keighley, who directed many important pictures for Warner Bros., believed in preserving an actor's ego and used many psychological tricks to obtain the perfect performance. Here he sits on a couch with Rosalind Russell and James Stewart who starred in *No Time for Comedy*. The cameraman crouched below the camera is Ernest Haller, himself an Academy Award winner. (Warner Bros.)

anything but that, else why would she stay year in and year out in such dull and unexciting surroundings?

But the young actress, who had a considerable amount of ability, thought she could make the part stand out in the minds of the audience. She proceeded to interpolate, to improvise sophisticated mannerisms of speech and action, and generally to "brighten" the character she was playing. She had no conception of the relationship of her part to that of the others in the story. All she was concerned with was doing an attention-getting job of acting that would boost her stock in the industry. Actually, all she succeeded in doing was to inject a false note in what otherwise would have been a much better film.

With no rehearsal time available prior to shooting, I was hard-pressed to maintain the shooting schedule and still cope with the situation. As the shooting progressed, the actress's hatred for me mounted with every take. I was holding her down, she claimed, making her give a listless and dull performance. Trying to explain my reasoning to her was of no avail.

The scene that brought the shooting to a standstill was one in which she was to walk simply and mechanically, if you will, to the window and look out.

"What motivates me to go to the window?" she challenged.

"The same motivation that's clearly indicated in the script," I retorted. "Now let's see you do it."

The by-now surly leading lady sat down in a chair. "What am I thinking? How do I feel?"

"You're thinking it would be nice to walk to the window and look out. That's what you're thinking!"

She stood up, in a snit. "You're a *result director!*" she snapped.

"Right. And that's what I want out of you—results!"

Needless to say, the results obtained were something short of perfect, since nothing I could say regarding her interpretation would change this woman's mind. If she was going to do a minor role, she was going to make something of it. The unfortunate part was that the director and actress didn't have the time to iron out their differences before going into production—a condition that still exists in most television filming today.

. . . .

Director Don Siegel explains a setup to the camera crew during filming of *Two Mules for Sister Sarah*. Siegel is one Hollywood director who has been "discovered" as an auteur, although his pictures all had different producers and writers.

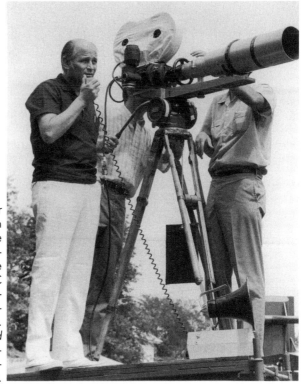

Director Norman Lear gives orders through an electric megaphone to his actors who, judging by the length of the lens on the Mitchell NC Camera, are some distance away. The lens, incidentally, is a 500-mm. The picture is *Cold Turkey.* Lear is best remembered as the creator of *All in the Family.*

THE VALUE OF PATIENCE

Although the foregoing incident perhaps represents an extreme in my relationship with actors, I have always firmly believed in the moderate approach, calmly and quietly working with the players, suggesting rather than giving orders.

The director who screams in anger and impatience does a great disservice to both himself and the cast. It is difficult for a player to act emotionally one way when those same emotions are stirred up by someone yelling, even if that person is the director. How much better it is to quietly communicate with one's actors, giving guidance where necessary and encouragement where deserved. Patience and understanding are two virtues that are not to be misunderstood in dealing with people, whether they are actors or other members of the crew.

A certain director I know is one of the most charming people I have ever met—off the set. But when he has a stage full of people at his beck and call, he becomes a different man. He will harp and pick at an actor until the poor person's nerves are frayed. He will embarrass a bit player

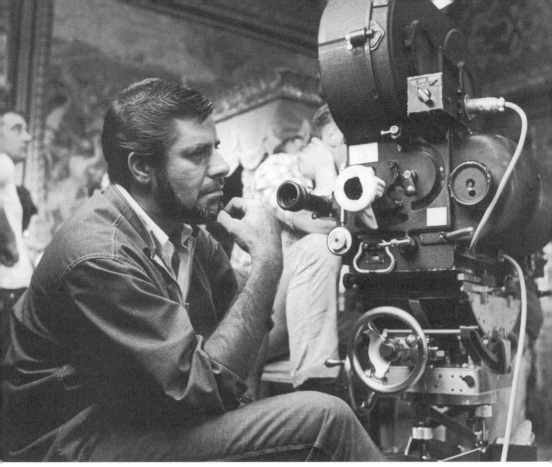

Although a congenial clown before the camera, when Jerry Lewis took on the responsibility of direction, he became a thoughtful and craftsmanlike filmmaker. Lewis was one of the first directors to rig a closed-circuit television camera to his motion picture camera, enabling him to see an instant playback on tape of the scene.

by shouting his dissatisfaction so all can hear, and then he will lapse into melancholic periods of self-persecution wailing, "Why are you all against me?" Yet, despite all his agonizing, he manages to turn out first-rate films along with his ulcers.

I was directing *House Across the Street* for Warner Bros. some years ago, and the studio had flown out a Broadway actor especially to play an important part. Unfortunately, the actor had page upon page of dialogue to learn but not enough time in which to learn it. Besides this, he had never before faced a motion picture camera. He was nearly frightened to death, and his face perspired profusely, keeping the makeup man busy with tissues. The assistant director hovered close by, annoyingly looking at his watch, because we were behind schedule.

After a lengthy career as a child actor, Ron Howard started directing grown-up films as soon as he was, well, grown up. His initial foray as a director was the low-budget *Grand Theft Auto* and soon the studios were entrusting him with high-budget, high-tech films like *Back Draft* and *Apollo 13*.

After sixteen or seventeen takes, it looked like we weren't going to get anything on film worth using. Then, I introduced an approach that I have had occasion to use many times since. I told him two things: we had lots of time and plenty of film. It was only after I took the pressure off him that we began to print usable takes.

Of all the attributes a director should have in dealing with actors, patience is near the top of the list in importance. The word finally revealed its true meaning to me one day when I was directing a leading man in a feature film.

A highly skilled player, this man was also an excitable and restless individual whose boundless energy had a wearing effect on all who worked with him.

We had spent six weeks on the picture and were trying to finish on schedule. Every suggestion I made to the actor caused a discussion. Not an argument—a discussion. If it were simple mechanics, like "Come in the door, light up a cigarette, then think about the call you want to make and pick up the phone," he would nod agreement. Halfway through the rehearsal of the scene, he would stop and say, "How about this? I come in the door and pick up the phone first, then light up the cigarette."

Knowing that if I disagreed a 30-minute discussion would ensue, I shrugged my shoulders and said fine, it didn't make that much difference.

But instead of going on with the change of business, this man would explain at great length *why* he thought it was better, as if he felt that his viewpoint needed some intensive selling before it was completely acceptable to me.

"Okay," I said. "Let's do it your way. I think it's a good way."

And so it would go all the rest of the shooting. He never understood when to quit while he was ahead but continued to take up valuable time in discussion that couldn't have been less important. It is during such times, when the director is fighting the clock to finish, that there is a need for as much patience and understanding as possible.

Needless to say, this actor and I never had any important disagreements. Otherwise, the whole picture would have stopped dead still. But it is typical of a wearing experience that the director can always do without.

One of the most important of the director's psychological tools is the ability to demonstrate that he has confidence in himself. One of the traps that new directors sometimes fall into is allowing the impression to get around that they aren't quite sure what they want, whether it is an interpretation from an actor or a camera setup.

Some actors are like little children. They respect authority yet will behave outrageously when they think they can get away with it. They most certainly will take advantage of the director who frankly asks them what to do in a scene. It is well enough to lead the players into a situation in which you are in a position to extract their ideas, but never let them suspect that you are depending on them. Similarly, to maintain the proper relationship between director and crew, never ask an assistant or the cameraman what to do next. If you don't know, you somehow reached the position of director without being ready for it.

The director can be compared to the captain of a ship. Having been commissioned to guide the vessel safely through rough waters, the captain must keep the ship and all aboard safely in hand. Any incompetence can lead to mutiny.

DIRECTING THE NOVICE ACTOR

Once in a while (especially in very low-budget films), a director may cast inexperienced actors because they *look* like the character as described in the script. Here are ten tips that can help to prepare the nonactor for his or her role. The director should:

1. Make sure that the actor understands the role he or she is to play and what makeup and costumes will be worn.
2. Correct any mistakes on the first reading.
3. Make sure that the actor understands his or her relationship with the other characters.
4. Remind the actor that the role, however small, is important to the story.
5. Make sure the actor studies what the other characters say about his or her role so as to develop a complete characterization.
6. Emphasize the importance of *listening* to the other actors and *reacting* accordingly.
7. Advise the actor to be natural and not attempt to "act"; explain that the actor should read the lines as he or she would in real life.
8. Explain the reason for the entrances and exits and what the character is thinking while crossing.
9. See that the actor doesn't *upstage* the leading characters by utilizing a piece of business or gesture at an inopportune time.
10. Make sure that the actor *stays in character* for the entire picture even though on some days he or she won't be shooting.

And a final tip, but this one is for the director: Above all, make the novice actor feel comfortable. Nothing can affect the performance of a nervous actor more than a nervous director. When mistakes occur, the director shouldn't shout for all to hear. Walk up to the actor and patiently explain how the scene should be played.

DIRECTING STARS IS DIFFERENT

Just as George Stevens, the famous director of such classics as *Giant*, *Shane*, and *The Diary of Anne Frank*, would rather have directed actors than stars (particularly those stars who are "bosses"), most directors feel that they can contribute most creatively when they, rather than the stars, control all elements that go into making a motion picture.

The larger studios seem to agree, since many companies are bypassing the producer in favor of the producer-director. This new modus operandi came about after the studios abandoned the mass production methods that were in vogue before television became a national institution in the

One of the great directors of all time, John Ford (*Long Voyage Home, Stagecoach*) developed a style of shooting all his own. During a period in which he discovered the camera's mobility, Ford, instead of dollying in on the actors, had them move to the camera for a closer look. Here he is shown in a typical pose, comfortably seated next to a rigidly anchored camera. (Republic)

1950s. In the old days, each studio had dozens of stars under contract. They were *assigned* to pictures, not coddled into them. They were told who was to direct them, more than likely a director from the studio's own contract list. Today the important stars pick the stories and choose the studios and directors who they feel will allow a certain amount of collaboration.

In this regard, it is the wise director who refrains from trying to change actors' personalities or, in other words, to make them *act*. The greatest stars Hollywood has ever known were never really considered *actors*, as one would consider a star of the theater an actor. Gary Cooper, Clark Gable and Cary Grant were *personalities*. Harrison Ford and Tom Cruise are much the same in every role they play, and woe be to the director who tries to change that. It has been the great star-personalities who have helped to make the motion picture business the giant that it is, not the handful of actors who, as competent as they are, have portrayed different characters from picture to picture.

A notable exception in today's films is Johnny Depp, whose range as a versatile actor has been demonstrated in films as disparate as *Edward Scissorhands, Benny and Joon* and the swashbuckler *Don Juan de Marco*.

There are those who gauge the quality of acting by the level of re-acting. Gary Cooper was a consummate actor because the audience was never conscious that he *was* acting. With his country boy looks and hesitant speech, Cooper created a unique screen presence. His most memorable roles were as strong, silent heroes as in *High Noon*, but he was an adept comedian as well. (Wombat Prods.)

Once I had the occasion to direct Gary Cooper. It was a patriotic short subject, and Cooper was donating his time and talents. We discussed the brief scene he was to do, and I was impressed by his forthright manner and articulate speech. Even his rehearsals were direct, precise and not at all the Gary Cooper I had seen on the screen. But when I said "action" and Cooper stepped onto the set, there he was in all his characteristic shyness and faltering speech. I learned then that his screen personality was all an act and that he had obviously learned years ago that this was what was expected of him. Changing it could lead only to destroying the image he had built up. In this respect, Cooper has been totally underestimated by those who maintained that he couldn't really act.

In the opinion of those of us who remember with unabashed fondness the "Golden Years" of Hollywood, today's new crop of stars lacks the magic of the stars of the 1930s and the 1940s. Perhaps it is because the major studios no longer make 500 or so pictures a year and accordingly do not develop and guide new stars along the road to prominence. (Today, among the major and independent studios, the yearly total of pictures released is between 80 and 90.) Or perhaps it is due to the changing tastes of today's audiences who support the glorification of an anti-hero and reject the gloss and artificiality of the majority of yesterday's films. Dustin Hoffman, Richard Dreyfus and Meryl Streep, as splendid as they are at what they do, would never have made it to the top were they born into the world of Gable, Grant and Garbo.

At any rate, opportunities are few today to direct the superstar who has a one-dimensional approach to characterization, and more pictures are being turned out today with unknown actors than at any time in screen history. This should make many young directors happy, as the absence of demanding stars can only ease the strain of filming. This is not meant to imply that all stars are a hindrance to the director.

Many times the director will have difficulty finding the right words to tell an actor that a performance was not good, especially if that actor is a star. William Keighley had a method that worked well and that illustrates the effectiveness of psychology. When a particular take was flat or slowly paced, or dramatically uneven, Keighley would let the scene play out, then walk to the actor and in a confidential tone suggest that he or she do it again, this time the way it had been done in rehearsal. The actor's ego was not damaged, since the implication was that the correct performance had been given in rehearsal and all that was expected was a repeat of this achievement.

J. Lee Thompson, who directed *Guns of Navarone*, says in this respect: "I like to listen to actors attentively and with sympathy, making them think they can do no wrong. The actor may be right; if he is, I'm delighted. But he is often wrong, so you employ tact and diplomacy and avoid saying let's do it your way or let's do it my way. I never make one version for the actor and another for me. If I know he's absolutely wrong, I stick it out; but first I talk it over and by the time he walks away he thinks he has really won his point, that my way was really his way."

Surprisingly, the venerable Charlton Heston has this to say on the subject: "One thing I don't think a director has to do—and there are a lot of actors who get a lot of money who don't agree with me on this—is to create an atmosphere or a mood particularly comfortable for me. I get a lot of money for acting, and I think part of what they pay me for is to be able to work any way the director wants. If he wants to work in a kind of drum-tight atmosphere of watch-building tension like William Wyler, scratching and niggling at one little point and then another—that's fine. All I care about is the work.

"I think all the hand holding and the making happy with the work is a waste of time . . . . The director doesn't have to hold my hand; he doesn't have to make me happy; he doesn't have to begin by saying: 'Chuck, that was marvelous, that was simply great, but look, baby, let's do just one more good old take, huh, and if you could just give us a little teensy bit of this . . . .' I don't need any of that. And I think that an actor who does need that is a child."

While we're on the subject of reshooting scenes, there is one rule of paramount importance: Never ask an actor to do a second take unless you can offer a constructive criticism of the performance. Nor should the director show the actor by acting out the part, particularly if the actor is a competent one. Discuss with the actor the concept of the character, what the motivation is, and the overall result that should be accomplished. Then let the actor bring a personal interpretation to the part. Chances are it will be at least as effective as your own anyway.

The established director invariably "suggests" to an actor, never commands. The English poet Alexander Pope said, "Men must be taught as if you taught them not; and things unknown proposed as things forgot." No one likes to be ordered about, and a director can go far toward winning the instant respect of coworkers if he or she adopts a confident but casual manner in giving the cast and crew instructions. If an actor knows anything about psychology, it will be apparent that the director's "suggestions" are really orders to be followed.

Occasionally a director is faced with what seems to be an insurmountable problem in his relationship with a star, and a breach develops so wide that reparation of the damage seems all but impossible.

I was signed to direct a Technicolor feature for Columbia. The day before the picture was to start I had yet to meet the lead actress, who was confined to her bed with a touch of virus. The producer suggested I drive out to the woman's house in Santa Monica and discuss the part she was going to play. She was a fast-rising actress of the day and had just won an Academy Award for her work in an important picture.

As I stood on her doorstep waiting to be admitted, I didn't realize the trap I was about to walk into. Sitting by her bedside, with her mother not once leaving the room, I went over the entire script, scene by scene, almost line by line, with the actress. She would ask me from time to time how I would interpret the various scenes, and I confidently expressed my opinions since I had also worked on the story for many weeks. I knew it cold, or so I thought.

When the discussion was over and I stood up to leave, she made the announcement that was to almost blow me over. "I'm glad we had this meeting because I have no intention of playing the role the way you described it."

I was dumbfounded. I muttered something about working things out and found my way out the door. I thought of all the things I could have said on the way back to Hollywood. I could have been resolute, telling her that she'd play it my way or else she could quit the picture before it even started. I could have double-talked, saying that perhaps I had explained the interpretation badly and that I was sure that we would see eye to eye once we started shooting. But, of course, I said none of these things.

The next morning, when the opening call for rehearsal was made, the actress made the first move. "Mr. Bare, I've been thinking over what you said yesterday. I think I see what you mean—and I want to apologize for saying what I did."

I was almost as dumbfounded as I had been the day before, but I shook her hand and inwardly sighed with relief. I knew then what had happened. Her mother, not one to see her daughter's career go down the drain, had set her straight on the obvious pitfalls of starting a picture by declaring war on the director.

The lesson in this, to me at least, was that sometimes things have a way of ironing themselves out. Had I taken any tack except the one that I did, I am positive that the picture would have been a complete disaster for the both of us.

WINNING FRIENDS AND INFLUENCING ACTORS

Since directing deals with the emotions as well as the mechanics of staging and photography, the director must have a thorough knowledge of human nature and the psychology of dealing with others. He or she must be a born diplomat and a father (or mother) figure as well. There is only one good way to get people to do what you want them to. And that is to make the other person *want* to do it. One of the best ways to accomplish this is to follow the advice of William James, who said, "Everybody likes a compliment. The deepest principle in human nature is the craving to be appreciated." And, since actors are no different in this respect, they respond amazingly well to the director who shows appreciation, and directors have many ways to express their pleasure.

One contemporary of mine carried a bag full of chocolates wrapped in foil to give the appearance of gold coins. Whenever an actor did a scene well, he or she was handed a chocolate coin, the value of which equaled the director's estimation of how well the scene was played. A gesture of small importance perhaps, yet this director gained the reputation of being an "actor's director"—one way of saying that people enjoyed working with him and enjoyed being rewarded. What is of greater importance is that his pictures are noted for the high level of the performances they contain.

CHAPTER THREE
THE DIRECTOR PREPARES
FOR SHOOTING

WORKING WITH THE WRITER

The director's first duty upon being assigned to a feature motion picture is to spend some time with the writer who developed the script in conjunction with the producer. It is here that the director's interpretation first becomes a force, and usually certain portions of the script are rewritten or polished according to the director's viewpoints. This, of course, varies directly with the stature of the director and the importance of the picture.

There was a time during the old contract days of the major studios when a producer would assign a story to a writer and then turn it over to another for "polishing." The story might go through five or six writers, each adding his or her touch, and then be assigned to the director for whatever directorial changes he thought were necessary. The picture could be written, photographed, and edited without the director and the writer ever making contact. Today's feature films are mostly made with the writer and the director working in close concert.

By working closely together, the director and the writer become almost one; the director becomes a cowriter and the writer takes a hand in the direction, although he or she may never visit the set while the film is shooting.

Because more writers are becoming directors, the distinction between the two functions is beginning to disappear. John Huston, one of the first writers to take up the megaphone, made a fine art out of combining his talents. His classic *Treasure of the Sierra Madre*, for which he received two Oscars, remains to this day one of the best all-around examples of cinematic storytelling ever made. The fusion of director and writer makes for a unity of form that does much to dissuade the detractors of the *auteur* theory.

Director Robert Mulligan (*To Kill a Mockingbird*) has a different approach to the writer-director subject. "Not every director should write, anymore than every writer should direct. I don't write in the sense of putting words on paper, but I collaborate with the writer effectively every step of the way. When the film is shot, I show it to him. If he has objections or suggestions, I listen very seriously. But the writer knows that the decision will be mine."

Since the director may be spending days, weeks, or even months with the writer on the final phase of the script, it becomes essential that the director know something of the evolution of the screen story from its origin to the form in which the picture will be shot. If the story was a novel or play, the beginning is obvious. If it was an original for screen, it first became an *outline*, or synopsis, in which the characters were delineated and the plot explained generally.

When a story is in this form, there follows what is known as the "cutoff" point; either the idea is abandoned by the studios or further development proceeds. The original writer may or may not be engaged by the producer to continue the project.

In any event, the next phase of story development is usually the *treatment*. This is an amplification of the outline that details the action and characterizations and divides the story into scenes and sequences. Some writers even furnish relevant bits of dialogue at this stage, but dialogue and camera directions are usually absent from the treatment.

If the story now satisfies all concerned, the writer goes into *screenplay*, which brings the story into a *continuity* that the actors and director use to interpret the author's words. The screenplay is what a blueprint is to a builder: the architect's aesthetic ideas set forth in technical terms.

Some pictures have been marred by poor direction. On the other hand, I know of no case where a picture became a hit without having a story that was basically good, even though it had been brilliantly directed. No one who aspires to direct will deny Shakespeare's words, "The play's the thing."

Roman Polanski, four years after his wife was murdered by the infamous Manson Family, was summoned by producer Robert Evans to direct *Chinatown*. It starred Jack Nicholson as an L.A. detective hired to solve a murder. Instead, he uncovers a shocking scandal of water diversion for private gain. Although the film received ten Oscar nominations, it won only for Best Screenplay. The writer, Robert Towne, appeared to have an inner glow as he approached the podium at the 1974 Academy Awards ceremonies to collect his Oscar. The irony of the moment was that Polanski, with whom he had fought bitterly over the shape of the screenplay (and apparently won) did not win for Best Director.

During an eight-week-long session held before shooting began, the writer and the director tore apart Towne's original script and reshaped it into the final draft that Polanski shot, but not without a feud that resulted in years of acrimony.

Polanski would roll up his sleeves and encapsulate each scene onto a card, tacking them in a row on the wall. Then he would begin to shift the cards, rearranging the sequence of the events until he felt he had a shootable story line. Polanski and Towne would spend eight to ten hours a day writing, rewriting and haggling. At night they would go out and party as if they were the best of friends.

During the shooting, Towne never visited the set, which was all right with Polanski. Neither had the slightest inkling that their creation would become a classic of *film noir*. The biggest fight that the writer and the director had, seemed to be over the ending. Towne wanted a happier one, while Polanski insisted on a tragic conclusion. Polanski won out, with Evans in his corner. No one at Paramount was betting that the picture would earn its cost back. Despite this, in 1999, the film was reissued, much to the delight of fans and film students alike.

Today, Towne admits he was wrong about the ending and adds that he would gladly work with Roman Polanski again.

Director William Keighley worked on a script by going through it and completely eliminating all camera angles, such as close shots, long shots, pan shots and dolly shots, leaving only the dialogue and directions that pertained to the locale of the scene and the actor's business. He maintained that a screenwriter (who did not intend to direct the film) could not properly visualize in advance how and where a pan shot or a dolly shot would be effective. Keighley freely admitted that he usually didn't know himself until he started to stage the action on the set. Dramatic action can be much different on the sound stage or on location than the writer's conception of it as he or she pounded out the script.

By delaying imposing the camera treatment until the action, dialogue and business are worked out, the director is able to photograph action as he or she sees fit, according to the situation at hand. This does not imply that a director does not have preconceived ideas on how scenes will be shot, only that the director will not be bound by the writer's conceptions. Fortunately, today's writers turn in their scripts without reference to camera directions, since they, too, have come to recognize that a director will in most cases disregard them.

Stanley Kubrick, who directed *Dr. Strangelove* and *Eyes Wide Shut*, speaking to would-be screenwriters, has this to say about the subject: "All it takes to write a movie script is to record what people say and do. Don't bother with the camera information. The director will change it all, anyway."

Where most writers and directors are in agreement is in the division of units of a screenplay. These units are the *shot*, the *scene*, and the *sequence*. Although Keighley always believed that the shot should not be indicated in the script, it sometimes appears in order to emphasize an insert such as a gun or an important prop.

A shot indicates a separate component of a scene, and a scene is a succession of shots, although sometimes a scene can be composed of only a single shot. Today's new directors make their "shot lists" prior to production, although I never did, always preferring to stage the action before deciding how I would shoot it.

A sequence is a unit of action in which there is no lapse of time and can be made up of several scenes. For instance, a ten-page sequence in an apartment, with continuous action, may be composed of individual scenes. Let's presume that our script *sequence* has to do with the preparations for a dinner party, the arrival of the guests, and the comic events connected with preparing the food.

The first *scene* takes place in the kitchen with the newlywed wife fixing a shrimp soufflé, the husband arriving at the last moment with the news that his boss is unexpectedly coming to dinner. Conflict ensues when it is brought out that the boss is allergic to seafood. The second *scene* begins when the husband greets the arriving guests and shows them to the living room. He shakes up some cocktails and makes excuses for the wife who has gone out the back way to buy a cooked turkey for the dinner. The husband behind the bar is covered in a *medium shot*, while the boss moves about the room looking at the husband's old football trophies in a *panning shot*. The third *scene* has the wife telling the husband that the delicatessen is closed and the husband concocting a meal out of canned goods. The fourth and final *scene* covers the social disaster at the

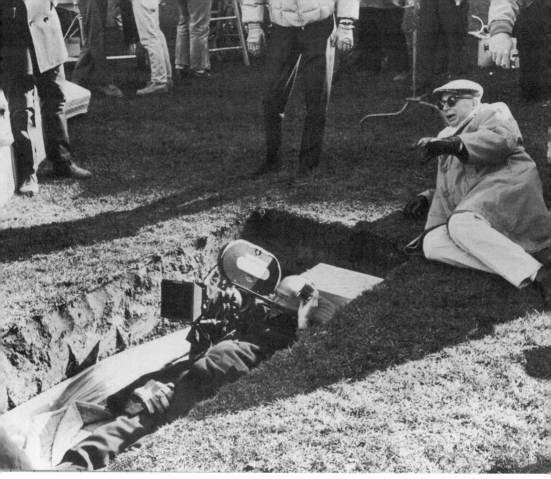

Cameramen will do almost anything to get the shot the director wants; and if that director happens to be Billy Wilder and the camera is an Arriflex, he will even lie down in a grave. Wilder, shown behind the camera, has been nominated twenty times and has won six Oscars.

dinner table resulting in the boss and his wife storming out. The complete *sequence*, including its *scenes* and *shots*, has come to a close, either with a *fade out*, a *lap-dissolve*, or as in most pictures today, the *quick cut*, which is no more than an abrupt transition to the next sequence.

Most scripts indicate *parallel action* at least someplace in the story, and this means interplaying two scenes through the use of *cutbacks*. The granddaddy of them all had Little Nell tied to the railroad tracks with cutbacks between the approaching train and Harold Trueheart riding to the rescue. Parallel action can take many forms, and it can be slow and suspenseful as well as frantic.

Another term that had its origin in early film scenarios is *flashback*. This often-used device labels scenes that portray events happening backward in time.

Imitation Is the Insincerest Form of Flattery

Hollywood is a town chock full of well-paid copycats. Whatever kind of picture is filling the theaters is the one to be imitated. Notice how *The Mummy* resembles the *Indiana Jones* movies? And how *Indiana Jones* reminds us of the old Saturday serials? (Maybe you're too young.) George Lucas's father, with whom I went to high school, told me that his kid was a nut about comic books and showed no early interest in making movies. Yet these early influences turned up later in the scripts of Lucas's films.

The original *King Kong* back in 1933 was a huge success. The producing team of Cooper and Schoedsack decided in 1976 to make it again. The second time, the box office was even better. Not satisfied to rest on their laurels, they made it once more in 1986. When they decided the time was ripe, they turned out *Mighty Joe Young*, another big ape picture, but everyone knew they were merely ripping themselves off yet again.

Copying copyrights is not new to major studios. For over sixty years, studios have been robbing their own literary archives, searching for stories that can be retold. These stories are at least switched around, so that audiences are not too clearly reminded that what they are viewing is really old hat.

Switching is the lazy way to concoct a screenplay and to make it seem fresh. If a man, who is presumed dead on a desert island, comes home to find his wife married to another man, the situation is the basis for an intriguing, though not original, story. But if the roles are reversed by "switching" the story and making the wife the long lost spouse, the studio has what will be seen as a fresh story.

It should be pointed out, however, that the new director should not try to make an impression on the studios by attempting to imitate Hollywood films. The work will attract attention only if it's original, intelligently conceived and, above all, "in focus."

While on the subject of writing, it's pertinent to mention that the director has an opportunity to become the first line of defense against the curse of all evils, the *cliché*.

From the earliest silent movies, cinematic clichés have proliferated, increasing in number and compounding excessively. Let an original line or bit of action evoke a smile, a laugh or merely an appreciative stir by the audience, and Hollywood's bevy of writers will rush to their word processors to be the first to steal it. That pioneer writer who first wrote the lines, "Which way did they go?" followed by "They went thataway," had no idea how many times he would be plagiarized. Hundreds of horse operas that followed have copied those two lines (or slight variations thereof) until they became the hackneyed stereotypes we know them to be.

Lazy writing, the root of the problem, has allowed some screenwriters to put on paper the first idea that comes to mind, regardless of how many times it has been used before. If the situation calls for a character to be humiliated, why not have him slip on a banana peel? The writer could care less who first created that sight gag; it's in the public domain, so why not use it? But isn't there an original, more ingenious way to accomplish the same end without Harold Lloyd, Buster Keaton or Charlie Chaplin *turning over in their graves*? Take what I just said, for example. If I had written that Lloyd, Keaton or Chaplin would *rise* from their graves in protest, I might escape the stigma of cliché, but somehow rising from a grave suggests the macabre while *turning over* is kind of funny when you think about it.

Recently, I've noticed a visual cliché that reappears too many times in both new theatrical films and old movies on TV. When a telephone call is depicted between two actors and the off-camera actor hangs up in anger, as soon as the "click" is heard, the on-camera actor will invariably look at the telephone as if the poor instrument had something to do with it. No one knows who started this time-worn cliché. Perhaps it was an actor, since I can't imagine any worthwhile writer describing the scene's business as "John reacts by looking at the telephone." Nevertheless, the continued use of this bit of action can be blamed on only one member of the creative team, the director. It is up to the director to guard against such moth-eaten clichés.

While we are on the subject of visual clichés, here is another. A director may fall into the trap of letting the movie signal "The End" by having the camera slowly pull back and rise into the sky while the actors either embrace or walk off into the sunset. When I was writing and directing short subjects at Warner Bros. in the fifties, my mentor was an ex-vaudevillian by the name of Gordon Hollingshead, who at the time possessed more Oscars than Walt Disney. He always reminded me never to telegraph the ending. "They'll be reachin' for their hats before the show is over," he would say.

To his credit, director Simon West, in his work *The General's Daughter*, foregoes the clichéd pullback shot and ends his film with a studied close-up of hero John Travolta.

One line of dialogue has been overused more than most in recent film history. It is the all-too-familiar, "What are you doing here?", always spoken when a previously introduced character shows up unexpectedly in a subsequent scene. He or she (it's usually a she) may read the line with the accent on "doing" if her role calls for a touch of disdain. Or she may read it with the accent on "you," as if to belittle the sudden arrivee.

To document my rather harsh opinion concerning lazy writing, I list herewith the overuse of the line "What are you doing here?" during a fifty-six-day period of watching theatrical features, new sitcoms and old movies on television—and even reading a popular novel.

In the theatrical megahit, *The Mummy*, the very first line the viewer hears is, "What are you doing here?" If that isn't enough, I heard it *again* approximately an hour and five minutes later.

After the success of my first log, I was thoroughly obsessed with my research and I listened attentively for more repetitions of the all-too-familiar line. I continued to log in my notebook.

In a period of three months, I spotted the now infamous cliché "What are you doing here?" thirty-three times in nine theatrical features and twenty television shows (plus one novel). I can only conclude that

"What Are You Doing Here?"

Ten Things I Hate About You, Touchstone Pictures

Early Edition, CBS, Channel 4

Total Control, novel by David Baldacci, page 675

Man of a Thousand Faces, AMC-Universal

Seinfeld, Paramount Pictures KTLA Channel 5

Just Shoot Me, NBC, Channel 4

Caroline in the City, NBC, Channel 4

3rd Rock From the Sun, NBC, Channel 4

Friends, NBC, Channel 4

Mayberry, KTTV Channel 11

Entrapment, 20th Century–Fox (Used twice in this movie)

Suddenly Susan, NBC, Channel 4

News Radio, NBC, Channel 4

The Mummy, Universal, Edwards Theatre

Suddenly Susan, NBC, Channel 4

"What Are You Doing Here?" (The Sequel)

Friends, NBC, Channel 4

Seinfeld, NBC, Channel 4

Frazier, NBC, Channel 4

Laverne & Shirley, Nick at Nite

Ice Palace, 20th Century–Fox, AMC, Channel 35 (movie)

Laura, 20th Century–Fox, AMC, Channel 35 (movie)

The Girl Can't Help It, AMC, Channel 35 (movie)

Just Shoot Me, NBC, Channel 4 (Used twice)

Seinfeld, NBC, Channel 4

Frazier, NBC, Channel 4

Die Hard II, KTLA Channel 5 (movie)

Seinfeld, NBC, Channel 4

Just Shoot Me (final episode), NBC, Channel 4 (Used twice)

Indiscreet, with Cary Grant and Ingrid Bergman, AMC, Channel 35 (Used three times!)

this is merely the tip of the iceberg (another cliché) and that the banal line must have shown up in dozens of other film programs that I didn't see. But the all-time record was the TV sitcom *Suddenly Susan*, when I heard the now sickening line *four* times in the scant twenty-two minutes allotted for the story!

Isn't there a writer out there who can devise an original line to convey a character's surprise at suddenly seeing another person? And if this ingenious writer does come up with a fresh line of dialogue, will that not also become a cliché?

The mark of a good director is his or her ability to be original and not to imitate the style of other directors. The director should concentrate on the story, the acting and the "look" of the film, and should not unduly emphasize the camera and its movement. Many new directors have brought unwarranted attention to their craft by ignoring this precept. They are, in effect, shouting to one and all, "Look, man, I'm directing!"

Ten Clichés to Avoid

1. The surprising telephone hangup.
2. The handy file cabinet. Why is the folder always in the top drawer?
3. No mixers and ice for the drinks. Do people really like their drinks room temperature?
4. Selective focus—very annoying two-shot. As the lens is racked back and forth, the audience is thinking more about out-of-focus photography than the story.
5. The police arrive at the crime scene with sirens blaring, giving the crooks ample time to get away (police authorities laugh at this one).
6. The reaction shot where two actors listen to the off-stage dialogue. At a certain point, they both look at each another, knowingly.
7. The camera sails dizzily around the actors for no reason except to call attention to the director.
8. The office scene where the boss rises and comes around to sit on the edge of the desk just to make a cozier two-shot.
9. The music swells just as the actors start to whisper in intimacy.
10. Moving the camera for no reason. The best camera movement is the one that the audience doesn't notice.

Sam Raimi, who directed *For the Love of the Game*, was apparently comfortable enough with the emotional dynamics of the story and its blend of sports and romance to direct the actors while not drawing attention to the camera. The film has very little camera movement, no shaky handheld shots, no wide-angle distortions and not a single one-second shock cut. He even used the almost forgotten lap dissolve for several transitions. The audience was able to become involved with the movie rather than being conscious of technique. Unfortunately, "What are you doing here?" was heard twice, to my dismay.

HOW THE CAST IS ASSEMBLED

If a director has been assigned well in advance of the shooting date, he or she will be concerned with the casting of the leading players. In all cases where a star is not involved, the director will usually have a complete veto over casting. The director may not get every actor that he or she desires for the picture, but seldom does a producer saddle the director with an unwanted performer.

The studio casting department, whose usefulness is unquestioned, merely acts as a procurement agency. The role of the casting director is that of a suggestor and collaborator with the producer and director in the matter of casting the various roles.

If the director is not familiar with a performer, the actor will be asked to read, just as actors audition for parts in legitimate theater. Many actors protest this method of selection. In fact, some refuse under any condition to read for a part, yet it remains the best way (short of making a screen test) for a director to become acquainted with an actor's talent and personality before arbitrarily casting him or her for the role. The most often-used expression connected with a reading occurs when an actor maintains, "I'm a terrible cold reader." Still, the director will make allowances; and many times after such an audition, I've commented most enthusiastically: "That's the hottest cold reading I've ever heard."

When a reading is not feasible, the director can either believe the superlatives of the actor's agent or study some recent film showing the actor in a role that may have similar qualities.

The Academy of Motion Picture Arts and Sciences publishes a voluminous work known as the *Player's Directory* that contains the pictures of several thousand thespians. An obvious aid to the director in casting, it has always been a "must" for an actor. Nevertheless, some actors in Hollywood foolishly refuse to pay the low yearly fee to be included.

The first television film that Warner Bros. produced was the initial episode of *Cheyenne*, which I had been assigned to direct. After spending some time with the writer, I turned my attention toward finding not only the cast for the episode, but a new star as well.

I tested half a dozen potential western leading men. Among them was Norman Walker, a 6-foot, 5^1/$_2$-inch giant of a man, with a velvetlike voice, who had been a bouncer at one of the clubs in Las Vegas. His discovery was due to a Hollywood agent spotting him in the gaming room and then asking him the time-worn question, "Do you want to be in pictures?"

"Nope," said Walker.

"Well, if you ever change your mind, here's my card. Come and see me," said the agent as he walked over to the craps table.

Six months later, Walker lost his job and remembered the agent and the movie proposition. He jumped into his battered car and drove to Los Angeles. The agent took him to see William T. Orr, a studio executive who

Director Paul Newman takes the Arriflex into his own hands to line up a shot of Joanne Woodward during the filming of *Rachel, Rachel*. Many actors have taken up the megaphone, confident that they can direct as well as the directors with whom they've worked.

was overseeing the brand new television activities. That's how Walker came to be tested that day.

Later, when we sat in the projection room with Jack Warner, I noticed that he viewed the various tests with little enthusiasm until Walker's test came on. Although the neophyte actor was rough in technique and a little nervous, there was something—some vague quality, call it personality—that Warner recognized.

"Put the big fellow's test on again," he ordered through the speaker to the projectionist.

When Walker's test was shown again, he was sure of it. "That's the guy. What's his name?"

"Norman Walker," I said.

J.L. cast an upward glance to the ceiling. "Can't call him Norman. Too mild. We'll call him Clint. That's it—Clint Walker."

Walker, while never nominated for an Academy Award, went on to a fulfilling career in feature films. He is best remembered for his roles in *Yellowstone Kelly*, *None But the Brave* and *The Dirty Dozen*, where he played a supporting role to Lee Marvin, whom he beat out for the part of Cheyenne ten years earlier.

CONFERRING WITH THE STAFF

While the director is interviewing actors for the many parts in a feature picture, he or she must determine, along with the art director, the style, size and arrangement of the sets that will shortly be constructed. The budget on the picture, whether for a theatrical or a television production, will determine the degree to which the director may influence the design and construction of the sets. Most art directors will confer with the director on the design of important sets where the placement of doors, windows or other physical elements will have a bearing on the staging of action.

The director who has the ability to draw—even the most elementary sketches—has a decided advantage when it comes to discussions involving sets. This method of communication between director and art director not only provides a positive shortcut to understanding, but saves many disappointments on the stage later when it is too late and too costly to make set changes.

Sets are designed with careful attention given to the aspect ratio with which they are to be photographed. This topic will be discussed in chapter 7, but generally the wider the screen, the wider the sets seem to be.

Sets are sometimes designed especially for the stars who are to work in them. For a western film starring Alan Ladd, all the sets were scaled down to create the illusion that Ladd was larger than he really was. As soon as the feature was finished, I inherited these sets for an episode of *Cheyenne*. Six-foot-five Clint Walker looked slightly ridiculous having to stoop as he came through every door in the set.

During the preparation period for a motion picture, the director confers with the property man and the wardrobe people, and exchanges concepts of photography with the cinematographer. The production department is kept advised of any unusual effect the director plans to use in the picture, and matters such as the number of shooting days, the scheduling of sequences, and the like all are discussed in detail. It is at this time, and this time only, that the director will have the opportunity to influence the production department to shoot the picture in a sequence as near to the correct order as possible. Unless the director speaks up now, he or she may be shooting the tender and dramatic denouement on the very first day.

While we're on this subject, production managers don't deliberately try to shoot pictures backward; but sometimes due to the exigencies of budget, or the availabilities of stage space or actors, a director is required to make many concessions to aesthetic preferences, especially in television. The experienced director understands the need for a proper balance between the pragmatic and the artistic.

THE SHOOTING SCHEDULE

When the assistant director first lays out a shooting schedule, one of the things the assistant takes into consideration is the number of script pages the director will be able to shoot in a day and whether or not the schedule is realistic. The schedule might be six months for Steven Spielberg and one month for Joseph Sargent, who mostly makes TV movies. The director whose background was in editing might be expected to turn in the picture faster than the individual who came from the theater or who had been a screenwriter.

When the schedule has been approved by the production manager (PM) and the producer, the below-line costs are calculated by a *budgeter*. Based on the number of shooting days and the complexity of locations and special effects, the budget is turned in to the producer. The above-line costs depend on which director and which stars have been assigned. Below-line costs signify production staff and crew.

When the budget is complete, the director may be asked to make certain concessions, especially if the picture is a modest feature or made for television. These concessions may range from eliminating a costly location jaunt to obtaining less expensive actors. The experienced director knows in which areas he or she can afford to be cooperative and, conversely, knows when the budget slashing is apt to hurt the quality of the picture.

When Alan J. Pakula was preparing the paranoiac and stylish *The Parallax View*, he took his production manager to a downtown banquet hall that was to be used in the film. After the PM counted the number of extras it would take to fill the hall and shook his head, Pakula had a bright idea. "Don't budget any extras," he said.

The production manager wondered if he had heard the director correctly. "You're kidding."

"No, I'm not kidding. This huge empty space will give a nightmarish quality to the scene. It'll work." The director confessed that the studio thought he'd done it deliberately to save money, so he didn't bother to disillusion them.

Selecting Locations

The director will next want to scout the locations—that is, the exterior locales away from the studio. In a major studio, this is done in collaboration with the location department. On a smaller picture, it may become the director's responsibility to cruise around the countryside—usually in his or her own car. Few directors complain about this when they have genuine enthusiasm for the script they are about to direct.

The modern feature film utilizes natural backgrounds to an extent never realized by the studios in the days when they did assembly line production. Today's more critically aware audiences demand realism in sets and locations as much as in story content and performances. I shot the entire production of *Girl on the Run* in and around Burbank, California, using both exterior and interior locations. Not a single set was constructed, nor was a single scene shot in a studio. The money saved on set construction went for transportation costs, and this sometimes evens out. Only the sound recording budget goes up disproportionately, since most of the sound must be done over, or *dubbed*, back at the studio to eliminate annoying background noise. In a special ADR (Automatic Dialog Replacement) room, the actors lip-sync their lines to the scene that is on a loop, screening it over and over until perfect sync is achieved. It's tedious but important, as there is nothing worse than a clatter of extraneous noises to interfere with the dialogue. Many of the lower-budget films released today are hindered by sound that is simply amateurish.

If the locations selected by the director are within a municipality, police protection must be obtained to control traffic and interested onlookers. If they are in the open countryside, other factors must be analyzed: weather conditions, isolation from highways and airways (which will contribute to the quality of the sound recording), and accessibility of the site for trucks and equipment, for instance. Many a director has enthusiastically walked to the highest ridge only to find that the selected

My first camera was the 35-mm Devry designed for newsreel work. It holds 100-foot rolls of negative and is daylight loading. And you don't need batteries to operate the Devry—it's spring wound.

The Arriflex 435ES is a favorite among cameramen and directors when saving money on camera rentals is a factor. It is also one of the better handheld cameras, especially when used in connection with the Steadicam mount that makes the operator the dolly.

spot is almost completely inaccessible to camera and sound equipment. With today's lightweight, handheld cameras, such as the Arriflex 435ES, the Moviecam Compact and the BL Evolution, however, there is virtually no place a director selects that's impossible for a shot to be made, even if the director must take the camera and do the shot himself.

I own an old spring-wound 35-mm DeVry that I've used in dozens of situations where I needed a silent shot of something. Once, in the final stages of editing a TV show with an air-date looming, the producer needed a shot of a particular drugstore on Sunset Boulevard in Hollywood. I went out, shot it that day and took it to the lab. Not only did my shot save time, it also saved the money of dispatching a crew to make the shot. The DeVry is not more unwieldy than a TV camera, but of course it cannot be used to pick up sound and it holds only 100-foot rolls of film.

THE DIRECTOR PLOTS THE ACTION

Preparing for filming can be an extremely important phase of the director's contribution to the picture, for it is only with careful planning that a smooth production will result.

Directors have widely diverging opinions regarding the working out in advance of camera angles, *coverage* (the number of angles from which a scene is shot) and the positioning and movement of actors. The methods of handling this phase range from the director who works out on paper each movement of the actor and each corresponding movement and angle of the camera to the director who gives no advance thought whatsoever. Frankly, I have had occasion to use both methods, and each can be a valid system of working. There is little sense in intricately mapping out in advance each movement of camera and actors in a short scene involving a small set and only two performers. But when under the pressure of a tight schedule and varied sets to shoot in one day, each with a large number of actors, the wise director gives some considered attention to how each setup will be staged for maximum advantage.

As an example, let's consider a grand ballroom scene that covers twenty script pages. There is an archway at the far end of the set. During the course of the action, nine different actors will make their entrances, and a close shot must be made of each as they come through the arch. The experienced director will take advantage of the camera and lights having been set up for the first actor's entrance, and will then bring all the actors through one after another, thus saving many hours of repositioning the camera and sound equipment, as well as relighting the shot. Of course, James Cameron and George Lucas might find this an annoyance, but then with the budget they are accustomed to they can afford the luxury of shooting everything in sequence.

There is much to be said for the director who prefers to work out all the mechanics of a scene with the actors before shooting. Moving people around the set like chessmen enables the director to obtain many values that are not apparent on paper. Seeing people in three dimensions, in the depth and breadth of the set, and being able to watch the action through the camera will provide opportunities for a freshness and vitality not otherwise obtainable.

I have seen directors who, because they had worked the action out on paper the night before, failed to take advantage of sudden inspirations and proceeded to stage the scene in a static and unimaginative way. Don't overlook the actors as possible sources of excellent ideas for staging. Having an already prepared guide is prudent, and perhaps most of the time the guide will work, but it is the wise director who will deviate from his or her own preconceptions when either an actor or the cinematographer has an obviously better idea. Incidentally, the taking of ideas from others will not in itself lower a director's prestige, and the director who announces to the crew that suggestions are not welcome shuts off many valuable sources for touches in direction. It is much better to encourage these suggestions, taking what one likes and discarding the rest.

A last word on preparation: A director can find himself or herself in a situation where there is practically no preparation whatsoever. Such a thing happened to me once as I was driving out of the studio for the day. I had been under contract to Warners' for some time and had done several features since being elevated to the status of feature director from the short subject department. At the moment, though, I was unassigned.

As I reached the gate, the gateman hailed me down and told me that a certain producer wanted to see me right away. I turned the car around and headed back to the main administration building.

When I reached the producer's office, he told me that I had been assigned to direct a picture that was to start the next day and that he hoped I would like the script. Naturally, I was confused, having known for weeks that another director had been assigned to do the picture and that he had worked hard in all phases of preparation.

This producer, never one to mince words, quickly set me straight. "We had a slight difference of opinion," he ventured, "one that centered around the way a certain scene was to be shot."

Intrigued, but still confused, I told him that since I was going to start shooting the next morning a script I had never seen before, he had better fill me in.

He went on to explain that the other director had refused to stage a scene in which the leading man was to extricate himself from a 30-foot well the way the producer wanted him to, and that the director had even taken his case to Mr. Warner. The producer parenthetically indicated that if I, too, wanted to be removed from the picture, all I need do was similarly bother Jack Warner.

When I asked what the producer's method of having the actor gain his freedom from the well was, and how this differed from the previous director's intentions, I found out what the difficulty was. The producer thought the actor would climb out of the well by extending both arms and both legs and working his way up inch by inch over the cobblestones in a horizontal position. The director differed, maintaining steadfastly that a superhuman achievement such as this could have believability only if the actor remained in an upright position, pulling himself up inch by inch with his hands.

When I had been properly indoctrinated with all the facts and who had said what to whom, the producer, who incidentally doesn't produce pictures anymore, sat back in his big leather chair and said rather testily, "Now, how do you see it?"

"Well," I said, "It doesn't make much difference to me, because with a stunt like this I'm going to have to use a double and pull him out with a wire."

With that, I took the script, went home, boned up all night, and started shooting *This Side of the Law* the next morning.

CHAPTER FOUR
chapter four
THE ART OF
REHEARSAL

And a fine art it is.

A perfect rehearsal is a wasted take.
Insufficient rehearsal causes imperfect takes.
Unused takes waste valuable time and money.

Knowing at what point a cast and camera crew are sufficiently rehearsed is something that cannot be learned by reading a book. Only experience teaches a director the fine art of rehearsing the players up to the point where they are ready for filming. If they are overrehearsed, chances are that take 1 will not be printed; something is apt to go wrong, or the scene will lack spark or vitality. If the players are not rehearsed enough, some error in movement or a fluff in dialogue will surely occur. The knack is to run through the scene so that all the players know their own mechanics and dialogue but are not emotionally exhausted to the point that they have "given their all" before the camera even starts grinding.

Personally, I strive to rehearse and shoot a scene so that take 1 or 2 will be a print. I may go on to make another take for protection, but I usually count on the first one for the spontaneity and energy that the scene demands. Too many run-throughs and eight or nine takes can have only an enervating effect on actors and a resultant letdown in their performances.

A famous director at Metro-Goldwyn-Mayer, after shooting a long and important scene, said: "Print takes 36, 27, 25, and 2." The producer on the picture, in an attempt to discourage the director from wasting so much film and time, had the cutter rearrange the slate numbers on the head of each take. When the director ran the dailies in the projection room with the producer, he defended his position by insisting that "take 27 is the best—anybody can see that." No one in the room dared tell him that he had actually selected take 2, except the producer, who did so with considerable relish.

THE CAST IS ASSEMBLED

When the cast for a picture has been selected, it is important for the director to meet them in an informal reading. At this time, the story, dialogue, and roles may be discussed by each player both individually and in relationship to the other characters in the story.

This get-together is important in other ways as well. It serves to "break the ice," to become acquainted and stay acquainted. It allows the director to become familiar with the players. It allows the actors to become acquainted with the personality of the individual who will guide them through the picture, and who will be responsible for exposing their personalities to the audience through his staging and use of the camera. At this first meeting, the director should plainly state what he wants and also his intention of getting it. This first meeting must firmly establish the director's leadership. Respect must be won, and all misunderstandings or disagreements should be settled now, for it will be disastrous to carry any divergence of opinion regarding characterization to the shooting stage.

During one of these early readings, a well-known television player once stomped off in high dudgeon as a result of a director refusing to make changes in the dialogue of a script. To say the least, the player was summarily replaced by another actor, and shooting started as scheduled. For the director to have acquiesced in favor of the actor would have had a cancerous effect when shooting, since this particular actor had a reputation for undermining directors and took every advantage that occurred to him. In this case, he and the director had it out before the shooting started, and in that way each knew exactly where the other stood. The fact that he chose to give up the assignment rather than acquiesce to the director only points to his own immaturity and unprofessional behavior; but these are the kinds of temperaments directors often come in contact with, and one should prepare for the eventuality.

Richard Donner on the set of *Lethal Weapon 4*. Getting his start in television *(Twilight Zone)*, Donner has done such divergent films as *The Omen*, *Superman*, and *Maverick*, based on the TV series. Leonard Maltin describes him: "A competent mainstream director with an uncanny middlebrow empathy. Donner would no doubt have been a favorite with the moguls in the studio system." (Andrew Cooper, Warner Bros.)

When the first reading is finished, if practicable, a run-through of some of the more important scenes should be given on the actual set if it is available. Even though the entire picture or television film cannot be completely rehearsed, singling out one or two important scenes can do much to establish a rapport between director and actors. Doing this will serve to illustrate the tone and shape of the direction that will follow during the course of filming. The reading is the place for a mutual meeting of the minds about the way each character is to be portrayed. Every misunderstanding that can be cleared up before cameras start to turn is money in the bank for the director, and the production company as well, since many hours and even days can be added to the schedule when actors hold up production with unnecessary discussions about their character or motivation.

THE IMPORTANCE OF BEING ARTICULATE

It is appropriate, at this point, to dwell on the value of the director's ability to communicate. Nothing will serve the director more than a well-organized, articulate approach in dealing with others, both cast and crew. The ability to speak clearly with the proper vocabulary will save hours each day and will elevate the director in the eyes of all who must try to understand his or her instructions. Some directors have good ideas and know what they want, yet can't express themselves in a clear manner.

Originality, leadership, persistence, patience and a true sense of the drama are all requisites of the successful director, but nothing is more important than the power of communication.

For a director, showing an actor how to play a scene is not the best way to direct. Nevertheless, in certain situations this may be the only expedient method of getting the scene right. Perhaps you have an hour to go on a three-day television schedule, and you have run into an incompetent or miscast actor. That training you had in the little theater, or as the lead in your high school play, will hold you in good stead now. Sometimes the finest vocabulary in the world fails, and the director must use other methods to indicate what is wanted. I once lost my voice, because of a severe attack of laryngitis, while directing *Maverick*. I never realized how much I depended on the transmission of an idea by using my full vocabulary until I was forced to whisper certain instructions to the script supervisor, who in turn relayed the information to the cast. Unable to speak personally to the actors, I had to convey the mechanics and business, as well as indicate the way more humor could be derived from the scene—and all this through another person.

CORRECTING ACTORS' MISTAKES EARLY

One of the most serious errors a director can make is to allow misreadings or other false interpretations to go uncorrected in early rehearsals. Things

Director Amy Heckerling (*Fast Times at Ridgemont High*) about to make a running shot for *Johnny Dangerously*, a 1930s gangster spoof. Her later films, *Look Who's Talking* (*1* and *2*) were bigger grossers. (20th Century–Fox)

have a way of becoming implanted in an actor's subconscious mind through repetition; and if the mistake is to be eliminated or changed in time for the take, then it should be corrected the first time the director hears it. Actors sometimes criticize this method as being picayune, especially if they have not yet learned their lines; but I find that it is better than wasting takes to correct some slight but important part of a performance.

Robert Aldrich, former assistant director and director of *Whatever Happened to Baby Jane?*, had his own methods of correcting early mistakes: "One thing I've discovered about actors is that they don't like surprises. A sudden change in the way a scene should be filmed or a role altered throws them off-balance. My own formula for working with actors is to have at least a two-week rehearsal on a sound stage without interruptions. Sitting around a long table, I impart to them my idea of the story, the characters and the problems we face. They, in turn, contribute their ideas. We discuss costume, character backgrounds, and motivations and relationships to each of the other characters in the story. When the scenes are actually shot, the actors will know what is expected of them so that none can say, just as we are set to roll the camera, he doesn't understand the scene or that the dialogue doesn't fit. They will have had plenty of time to have ironed that out during the rehearsals."

Aldrich believed that actors respect a director when they know the director is firmly in charge. Actors who have complete confidence in the director can go about their own preparations and performances with confidence, knowing that the director will protect them.

Clint Eastwood, on the other hand, who has directed many films and won an Oscar for *The Unforgiven*, has this to say about rehearsing: "I don't rehearse in advance. I prefer to run through a scene just before making a take. It works especially well with a fast, startup actor like Gene Hackman."

GOOD REHEARSING IS GOOD DIRECTING

The late George Bernard Shaw had many thoughts on the art of rehearsing and, although he was a man of the theater, many of his ideas are applicable to motion pictures. He believed strongly in the kind and character of criticism. If a scene is wrong and the director doesn't know exactly how to set it right, it is much better to remain silent until someone, either the director or the actor, comes up with an idea. It discourages and angers the actor when the director expresses dissatisfaction with the performance but cannot criticize constructively.

Shaw had thoughts on the director's disposition, too. He deplored directors who lost their tempers or displayed bad manners in any way. This, he felt, destroyed the dignity of the director—and, in his words, "makes a scene which is not in the play."

During the rehearsal of *Pygmalion* in London, Shaw saw to it that his actors did not stop the forward movement of the play at any time. They were told to sit on a line and rise on a line, and that the last word of an exit speech must get them off the stage. When the actors had to cross the stage, they must move as they spoke and not before or after.

Morton DaCosta, who directed *Auntie Mame* and *The Music Man*, made a speech to his cast on the opening day of rehearsal for a Broadway show a few years ago. The following excerpts are set down, as they are appropriate in the motion picture field: "Welcome to the cast. You have all been selected with great care. You use different methods of approach to acting. You have studied at different dramatic schools with different teachers. Please continue to use whatever method is comfortable—I endorse any method that makes you a better actor. However, it would be impossible for me to accommodate myself to your various terminologies and systems, so I suggest it would be much easier for you to accommodate yourselves to mine.

"I will welcome suggestions for authenticity but will not be a slave to realism. The stage is fundamentally a place for selective realism. The phrase 'The character wouldn't do so-and-so' is most often suspect to me, just as is 'The character would positively *do* so-and-so.' Many things can be justified depending on the completeness of the understanding of the character, and the will or the desire to justify them.

"I beg you to impress the idea 'The play's the thing.' If you serve this play well, I promise you, you will serve yourselves well. Let us set aside the usual preoccupation with our so-called position-protocol and other inhibiting factors in favor of being a group of dedicated craftsmen, to try to put aside the insecurities common to most sensitive, creative people and become a family, a happy one, I hope."

Steven Spielberg, who has directed more box office hits than any other director, has his own special way of working. He says, "I don't like to rehearse because I've learned that you can't capture lightning in a bottle twice. I think actors need to know you believe in them. It's amazing what they can do if they believe this."

One of the inequities in modern television filming is the lack of rehearsal time extended toward the director. Certain shows like Rod Serling's *Twilight Zone* always included several days' rehearsal just prior to shooting; too often, however, a director must not only start filming on the first morning of the schedule, but also meet the actors for the first time. If the director is lucky, unimportant scenes will be scheduled for the first day, and the dramatic moments of the film will be saved until the director and cast have properly become acquainted.

In all the 168 episodes of *Green Acres* that I directed, never once did we rehearse in advance. There was no need to; all the actors knew their characters cold. Besides, there was no budget allowed for anything other than a reading where the writers could polish the dialogue after hearing their words delivered by the actors. It seemed to work, as the show lasted six years.

CHAPTER FIVE
chapter five
STAGING AND PLOTTING
ACTION

LEFT TO RIGHT AND VICE VERSA

Every director leans to a certain extent on the script supervisor, whose job it is to keep the records of the shooting, as well as to remind the director of the first rule in the book, "Keep 'em going left to right."

Or right to left—but keep the direction of actors, trains, stage-coaches, rollerbladers, and almost everything else that moves across the screen and progresses from shot to shot going only one way.

Directors who observe this rule provide an even flow to the action. The action is easier to comprehend by an audience, whose point of reference shouldn't unnecessarily change anymore than if they were seated in a legitimate theater watching a play.

Motion pictures are capable of sustaining the continuous action of actors over a multitude of backgrounds. Even in the early days of movie making, standards of consistent movement were set up as a less confusing arrangement than having the audience, in effect, change positions from shot to shot.

This technique, in addition, has always been used to denote actors who were going against actors who were coming. Planes that flew from San Francisco to New York invariably were seen in flight going left to right, as one would view a map. East to west flights were always depicted going right to left.

Bringing an Actor Through a Door

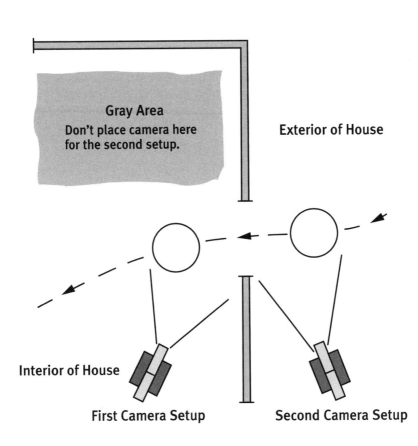

Gray Area
Don't place camera here for the second setup.

Exterior of House

Interior of House

First Camera Setup

Second Camera Setup

If camera positions on either side of a doorway are such that the actor's movement maintains the same direction, then the two shots, when cut together, will not draw attention to themselves. If a second camera setup inside the house is made from the gray area, the actor will reverse his direction midway through the door.

Showing an Actor at a Window

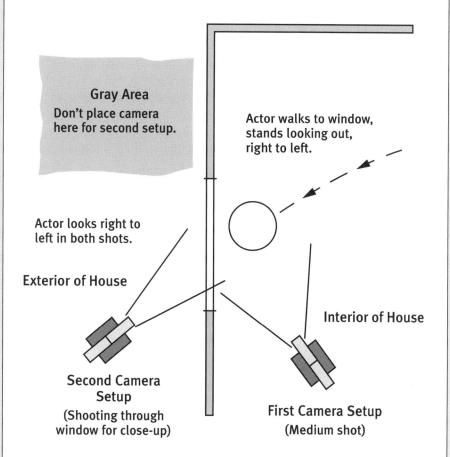

Gray Area
Don't place camera here for second setup.

Actor walks to window, stands looking out, right to left.

Actor looks right to left in both shots.

Exterior of House

Interior of House

Second Camera Setup
(Shooting through window for close-up)

First Camera Setup
(Medium shot)

To maintain a consistent direction of looks, both camera setups should be from the same side of the actor. Placing a camera for a second setup in the gray area will cause an uncomfortable cut when the two pieces of film are spliced together.

For example, an actor moves across the screen from *right* to *left*, walks up the steps to a house and knocks on the door. The door is opened and the actor enters the house—Cut. Now the crew moves inside the house and prepares to continue the scene. At this point, the actor should still be entering into the house from *right* to *left*. If the director insists on reversing this position (that is, crossing the proscenium—discussed later), the actor will be seen entering the door from *left* to *right*.

When the two shots are cut together, a disturbing element (to most viewers) will be introduced. The technique of cutting will not call attention to itself, however, if the progress of movement is consistent on both sides of the door.

Now, as I have pointed out, this is a rule—and rules are sometimes effectively broken. John Ford was perhaps the first of the directors to ignore the rule of maintaining a constant direction. The new directors break rules to provide shock effect, to purposely make an audience uneasy, even restless. The first director who threw away the tripod in favor of the handheld camera was breaking an ironclad rule.

Tom Logan, a very low-budget director (*Escape from Cuba, Dream Trap*), makes an appropriate comment: "For a long time, starting back in

Tom Logan (left, *Dream Trap, Escape from Cuba*), who specializes in efficient, budget-conscious shooting, takes a rare break to pose for a still on *Smooth Operator*.

the thirties, I guess, the motion picture industry became very stylized. The product itself was stylized, and so was the way it was made. Now it's a whole new ball game and we're moving ahead, exploring to see just what you really can do with film. It's more exciting now and it's more creative. Will we keep anything of the old? Sure. There's something rewarding in familiarity. And in quality. You don't hear Beethoven's Fifth Symphony and say 'I don't like that because I've heard it before.'"

However, even Logan, a modern filmmaker, usually does not break the rule of maintaining consistent directions.

If you're inclined to chart new cinematic territory and break all the rules, stop by your local video store and pick up the sexy, irreverent, sometimes psychedelic *All That Jazz*, written and directed by talented Broadway choreographer Bob Fosse. It probably bombed in Peoria, but it's worth seeing as an example of wildly imaginative filmmaking. It was nominated for best picture by the Academy, and *Variety* said, "Egomaniacal, wonderfully choreographed—more an art item than a broad commercial prospect."

THE CONSISTENT DIRECTION OF LOOKS

As long as film editing has existed, one rule has been rigidly observed, and that is the rule of *opposite looks*. Even the most rebellious of the young directors seem to obey this technical mandate, holding it sacrosanct while breaking all other cinematic rules willy-nilly.

Actors who face one another in their opening shot are established with each looking in a certain direction. When the individual close-ups are made of these actors, it is mandatory that the direction in which they are looking be kept consistent with reference to the position of the audience. If two actors are speaking to one another, one has to look left-to-right, the other right-to-left. Yet strangely enough, this fundamental rule acknowledged by professionals all over the world is still one of the hardest to grasp by most of the people who work in the business. I have witnessed near knock-down-drag-out arguments between directors and their script clerks, or their cameramen, over the simplest matter of which way an actor looks—camera left or camera right. The corresponding scene may have been made days previously, with the script supervisor making notes about the exact way it was shot. The cinematographer speaks up and confuses the issue by saying that he or she looked through the lens and remembers vividly that it was not a left look but a right look.

A Basic Rule in Directing

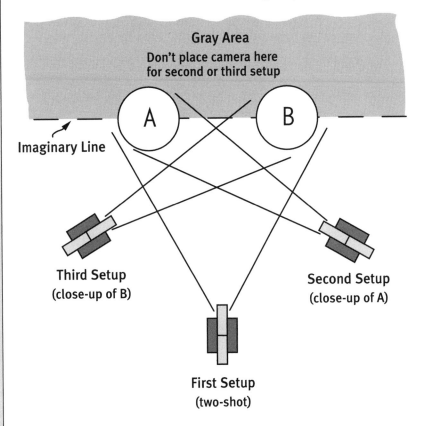

Don't let camera cross imaginary line

Gray Area
Don't place camera here
for second or third setup

A

B

Imaginary Line

Third Setup
(close-up of B)

Second Setup
(close-up of A)

First Setup
(two-shot)

The imaginary line always intersects the actors, shown above as A and B. Facing each other in the first setup, A looks camera right, and B looks camera left. Care must be taken that close-ups maintain the original direction of looks. The second and third setups should stay on the same side of the imaginary line as the first setup. If the director makes a mistake and shoots either close-up from the gray area, the edited sequence will not create the illusion that the actors are looking at one another.

When these disagreements occur, all I can say is that the director had better be sure he or she either calls the shot correctly or shoots the scene both ways to save embarrassment later in the projection room.

Transgressions by directors in this respect are referred to as *crossing the proscenium*, or *crossing the imaginary line*, and it is the director's ultimate responsibility to see that the directions of looks and movements by the actors are consistent.

The imaginary line can be visualized by plotting on paper the positions of actors and camera. Draw two circles to indicate the actors, and a small square for the camera. Project two lines in a V from the camera to encompass the actors; the lines represent the camera's view or angle. Now, draw a dotted line through the circles indicating the actors, and you have the imaginary line. At no time during the filming of a scene that will be broken up with one or more shots, should the camera cross this line. For doing so will take the audience across the line, too, just as if during a play the audience walked up on the stage and viewed the action from the other side of the actors.

This does not mean that in a scene staged with multiple actors and camera movements the camera cannot cross the imaginary line; it means only that for the purposes of cutting together the various component shots of the scene, the audience's viewpoint should remain consistent. A scene that begins with a given set of left and right looks can reverse itself midway and then return again to the original audience viewpoint, since the consistency of looks need be respected only in relation to the cutting in of other shots. What will work at one point in a moving camera scene will not work at another point.

Imagine an apartment living room with a window on the left, a door on the right, a small bar upstage center and a couch downstage center facing the camera. The director decides to make a master shot of a five-page scene. In the scene, a girl rejects her boyfriend.

The boy enters the room through the door and walks to the girl, who is seated on the couch talking on the telephone. The girl looks up at him, camera left. She tells him to fix himself a drink. He walks to the deep end of the set and goes behind the bar, with the camera moving *beyond* the imaginary line that has been drawn through the first positions of the boy and the girl, that is, at the couch.

Now, the intercutting between the two becomes mandatory, since the master shot includes only the boy, with the girl being off camera. The complementary shots at this point have the boy looking camera right and the girl looking camera left, over her shoulder, while still talking on the

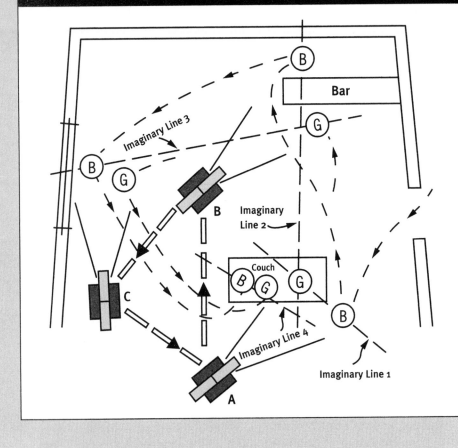

phone. When the phone conversation is finished (filmed separately), the girl enters the master shot while the boy is still at the bar. Surmising by the tone of the telephone conversation that he is being brushed off, the boy moves to the window, with the camera following him alone.

At this point, close-ups would be cut in and the direction of looks must again be consistent—the boy looks right, the girl left. She again steps into the shot, and then the two walk downstage to the couch, she sitting on the right, he on the left. Close-ups are made here, too, and her look will be left and his right.

The camera has now moved all over the set, crossing the imaginary line and then returning to its original viewpoint, but it did this deliberately,

The Action   Boy enters the room and walks to girl seated on the couch talking on the phone. She tells him to fix himself a drink at the bar. When the phone call is over, girl goes to the bar, but boy walks away from her to look out the window. Girl then follows him to the window and takes him downstage to sit on the couch.

Camera Movement   The camera (on crab dolly) starts at A with a two-shot of girl on the couch and boy coming through the door. Camera follows boy to bar, to position B. Girl then walks into this shot, but boy goes to the window, the camera follows and moves to C. Again girl enters the shot and takes boy to the couch, and the camera moves back to A.

Pitfalls   The moving camera has established four imaginary lines: (1) at the couch following boy's entrance; (2) when the camera has moved to B and the line intersects boy behind the bar and girl on the couch; (3) when the camera is at C with boy at the window and girl at the bar; and (4) at A again with boy and girl seated on the couch. One danger lurks in the fact that while seated on the couch, girl gets three separate close-ups: (1) at the beginning when boy stood beside her at the couch; (2) when she speaks over her shoulder to boy at the bar; and (3) when she is seated next to boy on the couch for the end of the scene. Each close-up is from a different angle and will have a different look to match the master shot.

Rule   The camera may cross the imaginary line in a dolly shot, but in so doing a new line is established for subsequent close-ups.

causing no bewilderment on the part of the audience. All that is necessary to make the scene editorially perfect is to have the looks of the close-ups correspond to the looks in the master shot. And this is where the danger lurks, where the confusion occurs.

The girl receives three separate close-ups while she is seated on the couch. One was when the boy stood alongside her after making his entrance. The second was when she spoke to him while she was still on the phone and he was at the bar. The third was after she had brought him back to the couch. No doubt the close-ups will be made all at the same time, and the supervisor must note that two of these shots require a camera-left look and one a camera-right. It is a relatively simple matter

The Importance of Looks

Right: After the direction of looks has been established in the first setup, which is a two-shot, both actors in their close-ups look in opposite directions and appear to be looking at one another.

Wrong: This is what happens when the camera is placed over the imaginary line for one of the close-ups. Although in the two-shot, Eva Gabor is carrying on a conversation with Eddie Albert, she appears to be looking away from him in her close-up.

Vertical looks are important, too: To keep the close-up looks consistent with the master two-shot, Eva Gabor looks below the lens in her close-up and Eddie Albert looks above the lens in his—regardless of the height of the camera. This simple rule can plague the director who isn't concerned with camera height.

Covering a Three-Shot

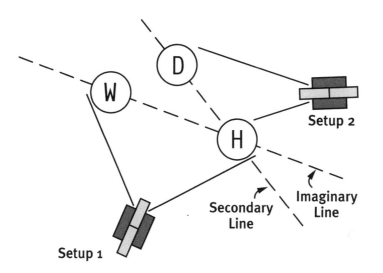

Husband discusses fees with doctor as wife stands by. Master three-shot has been photographed from setup 1, and typically all close-ups or two-shots should be made with the camera respecting the imaginary line. However, when the wife has considerable dialog with both men, first speaking to one and then the other, it is permissible to move the camera across the line and shoot the wife, framing the shot with the doctor on one side and the husband on the other. Shifting the angle this way establishes a secondary line, and all succeeding close-ups should, in turn, respect the new line.

Shooting Troublesome Table Scenes

Sometimes the camera must move beyond the imaginary line.

The direction of actors' looks in close-ups made around a table can be confusing as well as annoying to the director. Actor E has several lines to B. E looks left in his close-up, and B looks right. But then E turns to A and looks right. A's close-up must have him looking left, which when related to the master group shot would seem to be all wrong. Match each exchange between actors with opposing looks rather than matching with the master.

to match looks when the camera remains stationary; it is quite another matter to match looks when it roams freely about the set.

When shooting telephone conversations, care should be taken that the two corresponding shots of the persons talking are made with opposite looks. Although this is not as fixed a rule as if the actors were standing facing one another, it does help to create the illusion that they are talking to one another.

Another common pitfall for the director has to do with the vertical matching of looks from one shot to the next. The establishing two-shot, let us suppose, was made with a man standing and a woman sitting. He was looking down at her; she, up at him. But, when the camera is moved in for a close-up position of the woman, the director and cameraman must be extremely diligent lest a mistake occur. Since women are more flatteringly photographed with the camera looking slightly down on them, our subject must still look higher than the lens to give the illusion that she is looking at the man. Actually, she may be looking too high in relationship to the other actor, who will stand beside the camera to play the scene with her, and a box may even have to be provided for him to stand on so that he can properly meet her correct look. Care must be taken with the man's close-up also; for unless he looks below the imaginary line of sight between the two actors, as established in the master two-shot, the scene when cut will result in both actors looking up.

Certain latitude may be taken with the height of the camera to accomplish a better composition or perspective as long as the fundamental rule is observed: The high actor looks below the lens; the low actor looks above the lens.

WHAT IT MEANS TO CHEAT BACKGROUNDS

William Keighley, who was as efficient a director as he was a teacher, always at the end of a shooting day would walk through the sets to be used in the next day's filming. He and Bill Kuehl, his prop man for many years, would move a chair grouping or place the couch downstage center instead of the spot where the set decorator had put it. He would mentally move his actors about the set and generally line up the next morning's first shot for the camera and electrical crew.

Keighley never photographed anybody sitting on a couch that had been shoved deep into the set or up against a wall. It was always moved downstage so that the entire set was shown in the background, much to

A Simple Rule for Maintaining the Consistent Direction of Looks in Scenes Involving More Than Two Actors

Match to the master: Stage the master scene, or group shot, in the most natural or appropriate manner; then film the coverage shots to match the original looks.

Close-up husband:
The husband looks at all others, one direction only—left to right.

Two-shot wife and mother:
The mother looks left to the husband—right to the soldiers. The wife looks right and up to the soldiers.

Two-shot soldiers:
The soldiers look at all the others, one direction only—right to left.

the pleasure of the cameraman. He also, wherever possible, had the actors make entrances through doors that were downstage or nearest the camera. He kept the action down front, taking advantage of the depth of the set behind the primary action.

Michael Curtiz (*Casablanca, Mildred Pierce*) once shot for a week in a living room set that contained a large grand piano. When the time came to make a reverse shot and show the other wall, which had been behind the camera, the problem of what to do with the piano came up.

"Take it out!" ordered Mike to his bewildered set decorator.

It was forthwith removed, and I am sure no one ever missed it in the theater, except the set decorator.

One of the most glaring mistakes that inexperienced directors can make is to insist on moving in a *wild*, or unseen, wall as background just to make an individual shot of an actor who, in the master shot, was standing with his or her back to the camera. To be technically correct, if the director moves the camera around to get what amounts to a *reverse shot*, the unseen wall, which actually is the open side of the set, would be behind the actor in question. But, the audience has never seen it, so they will accept anything the director provides, as long as it isn't exactly like something they've become used to in the scene. To save time (which is money), directors who know their way around will "cheat," shooting the close-ups against another background, instead of waiting for the grips to move in the wild wall. Any one of the existing three walls will do, and usually all that is needed is to rearrange furniture and pictures on the wall to create the proper background.

Cheating is an accepted part of movie making, but sometimes even the experts can go too far, as Alfred Hitchcock did once in *North by Northwest*. Several times we saw the dignified columns adorning the facade of the stately manor house, but once, when Cary Grant drove up to what was supposed to be the same housefront, the columns had disappeared. This, I am sure, was because certain sequences had been filmed on location in the East, and then a Hollywood home had to be substituted later. In this case, I am not so sure that the audience overlooked the discrepancy.

An integral part of preparing a movie is the *storyboard*, wherein each scene, and sometimes each shot, is meticulously and artistically designated in a series of cartoons, all contained in the frame according to the aspect ratio of the picture. (Aspect ratios are discussed in chapter 7.) There is much disagreement among directors about the use of storyboards. Some feel that storyboards are restrictive and prevent the director from taking advantage of a sudden improvisation that might come up on the set.

Steven Spielberg didn't storyboard *Amistad* or *Schindler's List*, but he did do so on *Jurassic Park* and *Lost World*, since the latter two had many complicated special effects.

James Cameron didn't storyboard *Titanic* because he preferred to feel his way through the intricate maze of sets on the ship.

Oscar nominee Curtis Hanson disdained the daily use of storyboards in *L.A. Confidential*, although he did use them on scenes that required elaborate special effects.

James L. Brooks (*Terms of Endearment*) uses the sketches as a guide. He hands them to the crew so that he can concentrate on the actors.

A director who has the interests of the studio's production department at heart will plan the day's shooting so that the large, physical problems come either the first thing in the morning or the first thing after lunch. This will give the electrical crew more time to light a large area, and the grips time to move out wild walls to better position the camera for shooting. Almost all walls are wild, to be easily removed. Since the crew usually takes a shorter lunch break than do the actors and director, all this comes under the heading of an efficient operation.

THE ILLUSION OF REALITY

For an adult filmmaker, making movies is comparable to a child making barns or helicopters out of Legos. Although film is really make-believe, we don't want it to seem so—all directors strive to bring an *illusion of reality* to their work. There are many tricks a director can use to enhance the realism of a scene.

Suppose the script calls for a certain kind of house to be situated on the shore of a picturesque mountain lake. The director finds the right lake and house, but they are miles apart. How to create the illusion that actors can step out of the house, walk a few feet and dip their toes in the water? The shot could be troublesome and expensive unless the director has learned an elementary rule involving a *point of reference*. In this case, the solution is to order a small section of fence with a distinctive gate or lamppost, and have it erected in front of the house. The director will film exits and entrances, in and out of the house, with the actors going through the gate, apparently heading toward the lake.

Then, the company moves to the lakefront location, taking the same section of fence and gate and setting them up a few feet from the water's edge. The actors who went through the gate previously will do so again, this time continuing on to the lake. When the two pieces are spliced together, the illusion of reality is perfect. No one in the audience will believe for a moment that the fence and the gate don't divide the house from the lake.

A point of reference that brings together two diverse landscapes or backgrounds can be utilized in a wide number of ways. A horseman can gallop down a hill toward the camera, pause to survey the landscape near a wooden shrine and then proceed on away from the camera toward the village in the valley below; only, in this case, the shrine is moved three miles to create the illusion that hill and village are contiguous.

Almost any object that can be transported can be used as a point of reference; the only requirement is that the actor must come into some relationship with the object.

I was once faced with a problem that occurred late in the day. Had I not come up with a shortcut to create the illusion of reality, the studio would have been burdened with the considerable expense of an extra day's shooting.

I was filming on the back lot of MGM, where I had been working with a railroad locomotive of ancient vintage. All day we had shot scenes on the near side of the engine; then came a scene that called for actors to be on the far side. Our sunlight was failing, and we were within twenty minutes of finishing the sequence. It was impossible to get the cameras on the other side, and turning the locomotive around would take a crew of technicians the better part of the night. The delay would require the company to return the following day to complete the scenes instead of doing interiors at the studio, as scheduled.

My assistant director and I were pondering the situation rather hopelessly when the solution struck me. We would turn the film over! We would shoot the scene with action on the near side; but, when viewed in the projection room, it would appear that the action was on the far side and we wouldn't have to move the heavy locomotive as much as an inch.

Quickly, the set decorators reversed the positions of the dressing on the station platform while I set about supervising the re-parting of an actor's hair to the other side. A female star (fortunately with no part in her hair) cooperated by switching a large brooch from one side of her dress to the other. I placed the camera so that no signs or other printing were in view, and started shooting. The script clerk made a notation to have the print optically reversed, or flopped over, before being screened by the producer. No one who viewed these scenes ever questioned that they were not made on the other side of the locomotive.

Creating the Illusion of Reality

Using a Point of Reference
to Combine Two Distant Locations into One

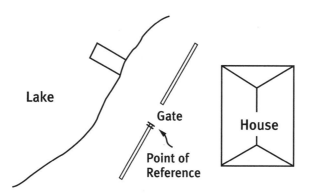

Lake

Gate

Point of
Reference

House

The Story Calls for This Reality

A cottage is situated on a lakefront. However, no such relationship of house and water can be found for shooting.

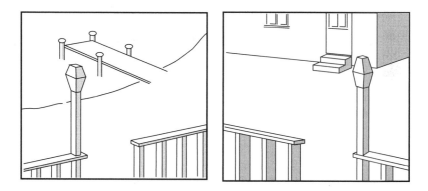

The Director Creates the Illusion

Duplicate fences and lampposts are found, one in front of a lake on location, the other in front of a cottage on the studio back lot. Actor steps out of the cottage and heads toward the gate. Just as he is about to pass through, change camera angle allowing actor to go through the gate and walk to the lake. By using the fence and lamppost as a *point of reference*, common to both shots, you can lead the audience to believe that the cottage and lake are contiguous.

How to Turn a Locomotive Around

The Situation: The sun is setting; the movie company is working without lights. One more scene has to be shot, but it is on the other (shady) side of the locomotive.

The Solution: Shoot the scene on the sunny side of the engine; then turn the film over in the laboratory on the optical printer. Don't forget to change the part in the leading man's hair, or the brooch on the leading lady's dress. Also be sure to avoid the lettering on the engine's tender.

A director can be called upon to cooperate with the budget department. This is especially true of television filming. The director may be denied the use of a stunt double or may be expected to use imagination in filming a hazardous piece of business. One such occasion occurred while I was directing a television film starring Alan Young. The script called for Young's wife to walk down the street, slip on a banana peel and come crashing down while her preoccupied husband was trying to snap candid camera pictures.

As was to be expected, there was no stunt woman, so again my ingenuity was taxed and I was faced with maintaining the illusion of reality while overcoming a major obstacle. My solution was to rely on the proper piecing together of the shots I was to make. The first had the actress walking toward the reposing banana peel. Just as she was about to step on the peel, I made a close-up of her right foot as it came to rest on the peel and started to slip forward. Then, I made a medium close-up of her startled face as she lost her balance and fell over backward onto a prop man's mattress (just out of view). Following this, I made a shot of the husband looking up from his camera to see his wife's predicament; then a shot of the wife sprawled out on the sidewalk rubbing her hip painfully.

When edited properly, the illusion was perfect; and I am sure the audience actually believed it saw a woman slip on a banana peel.

Maintaining the illusion of reality is one of the director's prime responsibilities. Limitless tools and techniques are available to accomplish this. The director has the camera with its own bag of tricks; plus the traditional techniques of the *optical printer, matte shots, glass shots* and variable camera speeds; as well as *CGI* (computer animation), which seems to have no limits to its possibilities.

When George Lucas needed thousands of robotic soldiers in *Star Wars Episode I: The Phantom Menace*, he turned to the Industrial Light and Magic Company. They created the illusion from only one robot. The fact that Lucas owns the special effects company made it even easier, since he had direct control over the final composited shots.

The new director who doesn't have the budget for expensive computer animation may have to resort to some traditional tricks that hark back to the silent days. I was directing a scene on a TV show that depicted a runaway train. To properly create the illusion that the train was coasting downhill, I angled the camera to one side and then had the prop man place a signpost that exactly paralleled the angle of the side of the camera frame. As the train barreled through the shot, the illusion was perfect—it was helplessly running downhill.

COVERAGE

When the director plots the action, whether on the spur of the moment or at home on paper the night before, he ponders the questions: How will I shoot it? How will I break it up? Which scenes can be made in only one shot, and which ones must be *covered,* in other words, photographed from a variety of angles? These and other problems, including movement, business, and the emotion of the actors are prime concerns of the motion picture director.

The *long shot* or *wide-angle shot* has its special dramatic use. It can serve to orient the audience to the scene's locale or to keep the audience detached from the character shown; or it can represent another character's point of view. In script parlance, this latter shot is referred to as a P.O.V. When long shots are used to introduce the locale, they are known as *establishing shots.*

A *full shot* usually denotes a full figure, and the term is more apt to be affixed to an interior scene. A *medium shot* generally is one that takes in the subject or subjects from the waist up. A *close-up* is a character's face only. A *medium close-up* is halfway between a medium shot and a close-up; the word *extreme* can be applied to both ends of the scale to denote an increase in size either way.

The *over-the-shoulder* shot is about the size of a medium close-up, except that the head and shoulders of one actor are included as he or she stands facing the principal subject.

Sometimes a director will mark the script with such shot designations as *dolly shot* (or *truck shot*), *pan shot, up shot, two-shot, down shot, moving shot,* and *insert*—each with its special meaning. An *insert* is usually a close-up of some inanimate object such as a letter, watch or gun.

How the director combines the above-mentioned shots is called *coverage.* Alfred Hitchcock had this to say about it: "If I have to shoot a long scene continuously, I always feel I am losing grip on it, from a cinematic point of view. The camera is simply standing there, hoping to catch something with a visual point to it. What I like to do is photograph just the little bits of a scene that I really need for building up a visual sequence. I want to put my film together on the screen, not simply record something that has been put together already in the form of a piece of stage action. This is what gives an effect of life in a picture— the feeling that when you see it on the screen you are watching something that has been conceived and brought to birth directly in visual terms."

Feeling as strongly as he did about the above, it was a tribute to Hitchcock's pioneering spirit that he directed *Rope*, a picture in which there were no cuts, save for a few that hooked together the thousand-foot rolls of film. Each ten-minute take was rehearsed over and over on a trick set composed of walls that were raised up to the catwalks as the camera glided through the multiroomed sets, never once losing contact with the performers. Of course, this technique can be utilized only where the action of the script covers a short, continuous period of time.

Normally, scenes are shot first in a *master shot*, which usually covers the entire scene (if not too long) in a continuous take. Some directors will even make more than one master shot, each having a different camera approach. Then the over-the-shoulders and close-ups are made. However, the prudent director will consider another method, particularly if the lead actor is getting along in years. That is to shoot the close-ups first when the actor is fresh. Many times people look fine in medium shots but tired and wan when the close-ups are made late in the day.

Close-ups have another important function, one that serves to facilitate editing, especially in the television field. Films for television differ from films for theaters in that they must be edited to a precise length regardless of the dictates of the story or the director's ideas on pace. Therefore, a half-hour film that is first edited in *rough cut* form to, say, twenty-nine minutes must be pared down to twenty-two minutes, leaving the balance for the insertion of commercials. Something has to come out, and if the director has covered the scenes with plenty of close-ups, the job will be easier and the film will not suffer.

Without close-ups, the only way to get the film down to the proper footage would be to eliminate whole sequences. The danger is that the story may become disjointed or confusing. However, if more than one camera angle has been made, preferably the close-up, with the complementary reaction shot, the editor can remove footage by employing *line cutting*—that is, by deftly removing parts of actors' speeches—creating the illusion that nothing is missing.

Even in feature-length films, where there is not a mandatory length limitation, cutting out lines has its merits. Rarely will directors, under the pressure of time, shoot a sequence from only one point of view. Rather, they will give as much coverage as the budget and schedule will allow, for they know what a skillful editor can do when provided with enough film. The editor can even make bad actors sometimes look good, and in many cases can patch up a mistake of the director, as well.

Many directors insist on perfect master scenes. In other words, if there is a *fluff* of a line, or if an actor misses a mark on the floor, or if the microphone boom fails to get a clear pickup on a line of dialogue, the director will insist on starting all the way back at the beginning of the scene. Some scenes are intricately laid out with complicated actor movement and a corresponding amount of camera positions. Now, what

When Alfred Hitchcock made *Rope*, starring James Stewart, he did something no other director had ever done. Every "take" ran a full 1,000 feet, with actors and camera moving about the multiroomed set in complicated patterns. Here, one can see how the walls were constructed to swing aside, making room for the large Technicolor camera and then closing again as the camera passed through the doorways. (Warner Bros.)

these directors don't put into proper perspective is that this almost perfect master scene is going to be hacked to pieces by the cutter when the close-ups and other angles are inserted.

What the director who fully understands the complexities of editing will do is order a print of the master-take that took so long to film. If a line has been fluffed, the director will correct it in the actor's close-up. If the sound mixer claims that one or two words aren't clear, because of the inability of the boom man to swing the mike through a part of the shot, the director will make a *wild track* by having the actor record the line without the camera turning. Almost any variety of inadequacy can be eliminated if the director will think in terms of the combined coverage. Of course, if the scene will have only one angle, and it plays well in this angle, then the master shot *must* be perfect in all respects.

CHAPTER SIX
chapter six
MOVEMENT AND PACE

MOVEMENT, THE PRIMARY MUST

The motion picture as an institution has reached lofty heights because of *movement*; one has only to view the early silent slapsticks and serials to realize that action was the foundation of the movie business. The pioneer filmmakers knew the value of keeping an audience alert by creating a tempo of action across the screen that stirred and excited. Not all pictures of the silent era raced, though; some were ponderously slow, despite the way they appear on television today. While we are on the subject, it might be well to explain that the modern projector runs film at 24 frames per second; silent pictures, however, had a standard speed of 16 frames per second. This mismatch accounts for the jerkiness and comical pace that seem to characterize all silent films. If it were possible to see them projected at the same speed at which they were photographed, the truly immortal quality of many silent films would be evident.

With the advent of talking pictures, the motion picture literally found its voice. But it was so aware, almost self-conscious, of this newly acquired talent that it almost forgot to *move*. Early talking cameras were completely immobile, stuck away in soundproof "bungalows"; and actors and writers became more obsessed by the spoken word than by pantomime or movement. Several years went by before technical advancements produced cameras with soundproof *blimps* that could once again be mounted on dollies and booms.

Today, the element of movement still remains a primary "must" in the making of entertaining films, and the foremost directors accomplish this in many different ways. The four basic methods are *subject movement, background movement, camera movement* and *editorial movement.*

In the case of subject movement, the actors move about the set, roaming freely from chairs to couches to windows, each character moving under the director's supervision and in strict accordance with his or her part in the story. An actor may move upstage or downstage, from a full shot in the background to a large close-up in the foreground. Or the actor may move laterally in front of the camera, the image in the lens maintaining the same relative size.

The second way to get movement in a scene is to move the background, for instance, playing the scenes in moving automobiles or trains. The very fact that the actors, though sitting, are going someplace gives the scene a forward movement and thereby becomes more interesting than if the same dialogue were played in a living room or on a doorstep.

Sometimes in television the economics of the industry forces the director to pull some ancient tricks out of the bag. On the show *Green Acres*, which I directed for six years, I had many occasions to use my ingenuity. If you ever saw the train pull out of the station on that series, it was always done by dollying the camera and the scenic backing behind the train in a synchronized movement. In other words, the train stayed still; but, with both camera and backing moving parallel to the tracks, the train seemed to pull out of the station. Sometimes, I would add a lamppost affixed to the camera dolly and placed in front of the lens to add the illusion.

I solved the problem of how to bring the train *into* the station in another way. Again I moved the camera instead of the train, which was virtually immovable. I had the grips take a short 4-foot-wide window section of the train's interior and mount it on outriggers on the camera dolly. By moving the dolly along the tracks and shooting through the window, we brought the train to a gradual stop in front of our leading characters, who were waiting on the platform. This not only accomplished what the script demanded but gave the scene more style than an otherwise normal setup would have provided were the shot made at a real railroad station. And at only a fraction of the cost.

To bring movement to a shot by moving the camera is most effective when it does not call attention to itself. For instance, the actor who walks

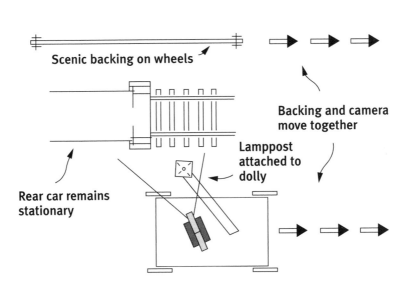

Scenic backing on wheels

Backing and camera move together

Lamppost attached to dolly

Rear car remains stationary

ILLUSION: Train Pulls Out of Station Moving Right to Left

When heavy, virtually immovable objects such as trains or ships must appear to be moving, the camera and the backing can be moved instead. A lamppost, positioned in front of the camera and attached to the dolly, helps the illusion. The relationship of the background to the lamppost and camera makes the camera appear to be stationary while the train appear to be moving. Caution: Don't show the ground or the wheels of the train.

laterally across a set must be followed in a *pan shot,* unless the camera is shooting from a stationary full shot. If the actor moves longitudinally toward the camera, chances are the director will order a dolly shot, to maintain the same size figure during the actor's movement.

A typical shot that combines camera as well as subject movement might be one in which a woman pleads desperately with a man, attempting to persuade him to change his mind about something or other. In a two-shot, the woman approaches the man pleadingly. The man, troubled, moves away, with the camera following him in a medium close-up. Then the woman moves into this shot, which widens to a two-shot, and she continues her arguments; but the man evasively moves out of the shot, leaving the woman alone in a close-up. As she moves after the man, now at the window, the camera dollies back, widening the angle to a medium shot. When the climax of the scene comes, the man moves to the door, with the camera panning but widening its angle to a full shot. The woman enters this angle and follows the man to the door, where the scene ends. It is a complex series of actor and camera moves, requiring perfect timing on the part of the performers, camera operator and the *grips* who operate the dolly, but it goes unnoticed by the audience.

In the pioneering days of pictures, cameras never moved, only actors. The camera was placed on a tripod, and every scene was introduced by a long shot. Actors scurried in and out of doors in camera angles that took in all of the set. Medium shots and close-ups were made but always after the actors reached center stage, never while they were in movement. But, by the time the silent picture reached its highest form, near the end of the twenties, cameras had begun to free themselves from tripods. Perambulators, as they were called, began to move with the actors; and gear heads allowed the camera operator to pan and tilt with the actors wherever they went. The old-fashioned hand crank was replaced with the motor drive, and the operator's right hand was freed, which enabled the operator to give the camera mobility.

Today, the fluid camera is as much an accepted part of filmmaking as a standard close-up, which was originated by D. W. Griffith, the first really imaginative director. Although the use of the fluid camera is almost mandatory in modern filmmaking, there can be no rules set down as to its use. Camera movement is dictated by the dramatic content of the scene, and nothing more.

Modern *zoom lenses* provide a form of apparent camera movement. Apparent because while the size of the picture changes, the camera itself remains stationary.

The final method of providing movement to otherwise static scenes involves the use of a variety of camera angles and the editing thereof. A slow and tearful scene played in an empty cathedral can be heightened in interest by a constantly changing point of view. First, the camera is on the girl who kneels silently in prayer. Then, her point of view: the altar and the Virgin Mary. Next, a long shot taken from a point high in the rear of the church. Then, a medium shot, shooting over the girl as she prays, with the altar in the background. Now, an extreme close-up as a tear falls from her cheek. And so on.

The about-to-be director should study the dynamically directed *La Dolce Vita*, made by Federico Fellini, which, more than any other classic film, demonstrates the full powers of movement on the screen. From the opening scene in which a statue of Christ is, perhaps irreverently, flown over Rome dangling from a helicopter until the last ironic shot of a gaily dressed crowd examining the carcass of a whale, the picture is one splash of movement and cacophony. One may not agree with what *La Dolce Vita* has to say, but the picture is a director's triumph; and Fellini has made an indelible impression on his audience notwithstanding.

My mentor, William Keighley, placed strong emphasis on getting a story, any story, started with a punch, and he always approached every script he directed with this in mind. He felt that if exposition or character delineation could be postponed until the audience was properly hooked, he had money in the bank. One such picture he directed opened up with a train speeding down the main line and a car on the highway alongside, obviously racing the train. By introducing his main characters, one on the train and the other in the car, he got the immediate attention of the audience; and when the train narrowly misses hitting the car at the crossing, the sequence had already paid off.

Low-budget director Tom Logan has his own opposing view: "For some reason in America they think you can't begin a picture slowly. They want to hook the audience before they get bored." Charlie Brackett, winner of Academy Awards for the classic *Lost Weekend*, *Sunset Boulevard* and the 1953 version of *Titanic*, summed it up beautifully when he said that in Europe you could open a picture with clouds, dissolve slowly to clouds and dissolve again to clouds. In America, he said, you open with clouds, a plane comes out of the clouds and then explodes.

The long-running CBS show *Petticoat Junction* was having trouble with directors. It seemed that no one could figure out how to keep such a large cast in a master shot without lining them up in a row before a stationary camera. I was hired for one episode, and after the first day's shooting, the producer came down to the set and asked me if I'd like to do them all. When I asked how he made such an important decision after seeing only one day's dailies, he said, "You're the only director we've had that keeps the whole cast in one shot without standing them up against a wall."

What I had done was start a scene with a two-shot. Then, as each actress had a line, she would step into the shot; when her line was finished, she walked over to somebody else and they read their lines with the camera following. There wasn't a full shot. The entire scene was made with a fluid camera making a series of waist shots between two people. It also eliminated a number of close-ups.

Directors who stand the actors against a wall, then tie the camera down and proceed to shoot a lengthy scene are denying themselves (and the audience) one of a motion picture's most cherished endowments. Nothing gains and holds attention like a well-designed flow of movement across the screen.

THE DIRECTOR SETS THE PACE

Bryan Foy, who produced many action pictures on modest budgets, once told me: "Keep it moving. You can't see the teeth on a buzz saw." What he was really referring to was that if a show is well paced, the flaws in writing or directing will not be apparent. Not that he condoned flaws, but discrepancies have been known to creep into the best of well-regulated movies. A fast-moving picture was insurance according to Foy.

No one is more responsible for the pace of a picture than the director. The director's pace is somewhat akin to his or her personal pace as a human being. The director who thinks, speaks and moves around slowly can hardly be expected to bring great tempo and vitality to the picture he directs. Nevertheless, bustling around the set like a jumping jack is not the key to directing well-paced movies; there are many screenplays whose mood calls for a slow overall tempo. But since the majority of screen entertainment benefits from a crisp forward progression of dramatic action, I will confine the discussion of pace to mean the opposite of lagging action.

What is pace? It can be defined as the tempo with which all things at the command of the director move in telling the story. This can mean the tempo with which the actors move about and speak their lines. It can mean the tempo of the cutting from one camera angle to another and the variety of those angles. The script itself can contribute immeasurably to the overall pace of a picture by utilizing short, action-filled scenes as opposed to long-winded and talky ones.

King Vidor, always a director who appreciated the value of pace, devised a technique that he called "silent music." This involved the creating and putting together of action and shots in time to a metronome, the result of which was a perfectly rhythmical series of movements on the screen.

Vidor had first used this technique in the silent days during the filming of *The Big Parade*. With musicians doubling as assistant directors, he created a visual symphony of moving trucks, marching soldiers and flying airplanes.

When he made one of his first sound films, *Our Daily Bread*, he planned an 800-foot sequence about the digging of a ditch for a community irrigation project. He dispensed with the sound equipment and used a metronome and a bass drum. The workers drove their picks into the ground on the counts of one and three, while the shovels scooped dirt on the counts of two and four. Each shot was enacted in strict four-four time, with the metronome gradually increasing its speed on each succeeding cut.

The finished sequence is one of the most memorable scenes ever devised, and Alfred Newman's musical score complemented the visual action skillfully.

Nothing can kill a comedy more quickly than a director who lacks pace or doesn't understand the mainstay of all comedy, *timing*, or who fails to appreciate the value of reaction.

Hollywood has an often repeated axiom: "Screen actors don't act— they react." Although this is perhaps not an accurate appraisal of the movie actor's functions, it does serve to illustrate the importance of reaction; and the director who fails to make reaction shots extracts only part of the scene's value.

George Bernard Shaw maintained that the secret of pace was found in the actors' deftness in picking up their cues, and he cautioned them never to have a single moment's silence on stage except as an intentional effect.

An interesting sidelight to Shaw's theory is that in some cases actors have to be conditioned to *avoid* picking up cues. The first six months of directing Eddie Albert and Eva Gabor in *Green Acres* found me continually retaking scenes because these two talented performers instinctively picked up their cues when they should have paused and waited for laughter that they could not hear. (The show was shot with a single camera without an audience.) With the four-camera technique, which is shot before an audience, this does not become a problem. With the one-camera process, in which canned laughter is added to the sound tracks of television comedies, actors must *imagine* an audience's reaction and stall, yes, literally stall, until the unheard laughter subsides.

Pace is an instinctive thing, as varied with each director as are his other tastes and desires. It is perhaps the most difficult thing to teach, and little was said about it in the cinema courses at the University of Southern California. I can add only that the interjection of pace into a motion picture is more often than not directly related to the director's own enthusiasm and personal energy. One of the true pitfalls in directing motion pictures is the tendency to be lulled into a state of lethargy due to a long and tiresome shooting schedule. A director who lets down or becomes bored not only will lack pace but will end up with a dull and listless product. Never has a great film been made without the enthusiasm of

Veteran director King Vidor, whose career began in the silent days, is shown here, megaphone in hand, shooting *Duel in the Sun* from a high camera platform. Vidor was the first director to use a metronome to establish rhythm for the movement within the scenes. He is one of the few directors who have received the D. W. Griffith Award of the Directors Guild of America. (Selznick International)

all who contributed, and this is especially important in the case of the director, who, of course, sets the pace for all.

One important device that is under the director's command, and one that is sometimes overlooked in modern filmmaking, is the advantage of *manufacturing* pace by varying the speed of the film as it receives its exposure in the camera. The silent directors, especially of the Keystone Comedy variety, often slowed down the cranking of their cameras, or *under-cranked*, which made the screen movement appear faster. Although 16 frames per second was their norm, a comedy scene would be shot anywhere from 8 to 12 frames per second; and certain dramatic scenes would be slowed down to 18 or 20. Today, varying the frames-per-second is almost a lost art, but in a western it is most helpful in speeding up actors (who can't ride) as they gallop down the road, or to inject more danger or excitement into any situation that involves threatening moving objects, such as a locomotive.

Conversely, slowing down the speed of screen movement (by increasing the speed from the sound norm of 24 frames per second) can have interesting results. I once directed a comedy with a scene that called for an actor to receive a dose of ether by mistake. By slowing down the screen action, his every mannerism and movement as he incongruously floated through the halls of the hospital became extremely funny. His movements, seen in direct contrast to the normal actions of the other actors in the same scene, were photographed at 48 frames per second; consequently, all the other actors were required to speed up their own action exactly double, so that when the film was projected they would appear to be moving normally. This is the most difficult part of this kind of filming, having your leading character act normally while all the others walk and move twice as fast, with your only problem being the proper visualization of the end result!

No one who fully contributes to the success of a complex and entertaining motion picture can do so without using maximum energy. Energy is the mother of enthusiasm; enthusiasm fosters pace. One seldom appears without the other.

THE RIGORS OF DIRECTING

The one requirement of all directors I have failed to mention is physical stamina. If ever a want ad were placed for a film director, it would surely carry the line, "Only the strong need apply." Earlier I mentioned that the director is usually one of the first on the set, and the last to leave. The director stands on his or her feet practically the whole ten-hour day and then goes to the projection room to see the rushes before leaving at night. Nerves are unduly strained after hours of concentration on detail, and the burden and responsibility of the job cause a high degree of stress.

Since the early days, the public has heard of the derring-do of the cameraman, up in high rafters, down in mines, perched precariously on the bowsprit of a ship, operating dangerously close to explosives, grinding the camera atop a speeding train—all these deeds and more. But what has received less publicity is the fact that the director is usually right beside the cameraman, taking all manners of chances, even risking life sometimes, all for the sake of the picture. When someone in the theater said, "The show must go on," little did that person know what a doctrine he had created. Hardly a day goes by in Hollywood, or anyplace else where films are made, that someone doesn't place life and limbs in peril for the sake of the show.

At one point during filming, director J. P. McGowan donned the actor's wardrobe and took a leap from the top of a fast-moving boxcar. He ended up in the hospital with a broken back. There have been other instances where directors have fallen from high camera parallels and speeding camera cars, each case in the call of duty.

Metro-Goldwyn-Mayer once dispatched me to the Caribbean to film scenes for *The Islanders*, a television series for which I had just produced and directed the pilot film. The completed first episode had been in New York for seven days, and it was still too early to know whether or not it had been picked up by the network. Therefore, to save money, I decided to be my own second-unit director.

I found myself in Miami, preparing for the trip and doing the jobs of producer, director, production manager and assistant director. In fact, I was all alone, another illustration of the amount of endurance and stamina a director sometimes is called upon to show. I had to hire the camera crew from the Chicago local, make arrangements for camera equipment out of Miami, interview and hire photographic doubles for certain players unable to come from Hollywood, and charter a seaplane.

The next day, I took off ahead of the crew, who would fly to Jamaica in the seaplane, a somewhat antiquated Grumman Goose that had been recently purchased from the government of Honduras. Upon my arrival in Kingston, I rented a small car and toured the perimeter of the island, searching for and spotting bays and lagoons in which the Goose could make a safe and picturesque landing.

The stars of *The Islanders*, Bill Reynolds and Jim Philbrook, flew in directly from Hollywood, and we all made a rendezvous at Montego Bay, a popular resort on Jamaica's north shore.

For five days we toured up and down the coast, photographing landings and takeoffs against the lush tropical backgrounds. The weather was, as expected, hot. Reynolds and Philbrook ran over half of the island while I filmed a chase sequence against natural backgrounds. On the sixth day, I had shot over 10,000 feet of negative, and I started making arrangements to proceed homeward.

We were at Port Antonio, staying in the hotel that Errol Flynn once owned, the Jamaica Reef. Howard Smith, the pilot, had rowed out to the plane, which was anchored in the bay opposite the hotel, only to find the bilge half full of water. When George Schmidt, the first cameraman, and his assistant, Glen Kirkpatrick, came out in the second boat, they helped bail out the water, which apparently was leaking in through the metal seams in the plane's hull.

Jim Philbrook and the doubles had already started back to Montego Bay in the limousine we had rented, and now the question of how the precious negative would be transported came up. I wanted Bill Reynolds to take it in the other car we had, since I didn't want it to be the sole responsibility of the Jamaican driver. But, Bill didn't want to make the hot ride in the car to the airport at the other end of the island along the narrow, winding road, and he begged to go in the airplane with the cameramen and myself, who were going to make a few more aerial shots en route. Bill Reynolds later wished I had been more adamant, but, as it happened, I agreed that he could come along with us. That settled the question about the negative; it, too, would go along in the plane.

With the plane's bilge dry once again, Howard Smith revved up the engines; and with Schmidt, Reynolds, Kirkpatrick and myself aboard, the seaplane took off with the usual roar. Smith, without any previous movie flying experience, had demonstrated a daredevil style of piloting, and the ten cans at my feet were filled with some exciting footage of his landings and takeoffs. But now we were on our way home, and George Schmidt occupied himself with making aerial shots from the plane's windows.

Suddenly, and without warning, both engines quit. I was standing at the moment directly behind the pilot, with my hands on the bulkhead. Instantly, Smith put the plane into a dive to avoid stalling. The 300 feet of altitude we had at the moment of losing power was fast diminishing, and Smith frantically hit switches, turned knobs and activated the wobble pump in an attempt to find the trouble and restart the engines. For approximately six seconds, I stood frozen in the aisle; then when it was apparent that we were going to crash, I hurried to my seat and started to fasten the seat belt. It never got fastened.

My next recollection was a return to consciousness, a cooling plunge in the darkness of the water and the knowledge that I was floating free and not entangled in seat belts or other wreckage. But, where was I? In the plane, or out of it? Instinctively, I swam to the surface and then saw what was left of the Grumman Goose. The left wing and engine nacelle were completely ripped away from the main section and were sinking. My first exclamation was, "Save the film!" I heard a voice from the other side of the wreckage, "To hell with the film!" and that is when I discovered that I had been injured.

The first thing I did when I rose above the surface of the water was to feel my head and upper portion of my body. Although there were a few abrasions, I was not bleeding too much and my mind was clear. I quickly stripped down, getting my shirt off preparatory to swimming, if necessary, to shore. I reached down to pull off my shoes, when I discovered a frightening fact considering we had crashed more than four miles offshore. I had two broken legs.

The pilot, Howard Smith, was floating 30 feet away from the main section of the plane, which was sinking fast. He was in a state of semiconsciousness, and when I first saw him he had his face under water. I managed to get him to raise his head by calling his name, and presently he caught hold of a piece of the plane's nose section that had completely broken off and was floating in the water like a giant eggshell.

On the other side of the plane, I saw Kirkpatrick treading water, his head a mass of blood. Bill Reynolds and George Schmidt were floundering near the fuselage, which had a gaping wound in one side, obviously where we had made our escape at the moment of impact. In a matter of seconds, the wreckage sank, all except Smith's nose section, a piece of pontoon that was for the moment holding up Kirkpatrick, and the four cabin seats, which had broken away and were floating. I had always carried the impression that the reason passengers in planes fastened their seat belts was to stay with the frame in case of a crash. In this vintage Goose, the seats broke away like so much papier-mâché. However, they did float, having been packed with kapok by some thoughtful Honduran aide-de-camp, since this had once been the private plane of the Latin country's president.

George Schmidt reported that something was wrong with his legs but minimized the trouble as he climbed aboard one of the chairs. Reynolds had pushed a chair to Kirkpatrick, and as I pulled myself onto another, I began giving orders. Since I had for five days been in charge of the troupe, no one questioned my commands at this decisive moment. Reynolds, who had one broken leg, and I, with two, were still in the best shape, so we would head to shore to get help. By lying on our backs, with the chairs supporting us, we were able to do a backstroke and to maintain our injured legs in a neutral and, fortunately, painless position. Reynolds, a former collegiate swimming champ, took his strokes rhythmically and efficiently. I, perhaps, splashed the water too fast, but all I could think about was, where were the sharks? Weren't all Caribbean waters shark infested?

Soon the swells obstructed our vision, and Reynolds and I could see no one but each other as we headed for the Jamaican shore. I had estimated that at our rate of speed, with no sharks, we would make shore by nightfall. But what then? How do two fellows with only one good leg between them get off the beach of a lonely stretch of coastline and get to a doctor? These, and other thoughts plagued me; I couldn't help thinking of my wife, my children and what would happen to *The Islanders*, on which we had all worked so hard. There is one scene I now feel eminently qualified to direct, and that is the one where a character, anticipating sure death in a plane crash, reacts to his or her impending fate. In the case of Schmidt, Reynolds and Kirkpatrick, there wasn't a sound. Pilot Smith was only cursing as he frantically worked to avert disaster. Myself? I was feeling but one emotion, anger. I was damned mad to have to die in such a stupid fashion. My whole life did not flash in front of my eyes, and I only briefly thought of my wife and family, but I *was* mad.

Two and one-half hours later, Reynolds and I heard the putt-putt of an outboard motor, and two young native fishermen hauled us, broken legs and all, into the thing they called their boat—a carved-out cottonwood tree with a freeboard of no more than an inch and a half.

We were taken ashore at Annotto Bay, transferred into a jeep, and then to a country hospital. The fishermen put to sea again in their crude dugout in search of the others.

Later, awaiting the Jamaican doctor's return from a Friday afternoon cricket match in Kingston, I counted the survivors as they came into the hospital one by one. I heard planes roaring overhead, searching the area of the crash, but hours passed and George Schmidt did not arrive. Three days later they found his body, washed ashore, apparently dead from loss of blood.

Eight days after that, I said good-bye to Reynolds and Kirkpatrick, as they prepared to take a plane back to the States. A few days later, I was transferred to a hotel at Ocho Rios, leaving only Howard Smith in the Annotto Bay hospital, still speculating the cause of engine failure—a thing that to this day remains a mystery.

This move to the hotel was, of course, arranged by MGM, never an organization to miss an exploitable opportunity. They had invited Ollie Treyz, president of the American Broadcasting Company, and Terry Clyne, account executive at McCann-Erickson advertising agency in New York, to join George Shupert, Metro's head of television, on a trip to Jamaica. The point, of course, was to meet the creator of *The Islanders*, who had so spectacularly crashed in the Caribbean.

So, while basking in the tropical warmth of Jamaica's infectious climate, Treyz and Clyne considered the purchase of the series. Before they left, Clyne promised to sponsor, Treyz had cleared air time, and I had sold my first television show—the hard way.

The infamous Grumman Goose that almost killed us while shooting *The Islanders* for Metro-Goldwyn-Mayer. Depicted are stars James Philbrook and William Reynolds in the rowboats. (MGM)

chapter seven

CHAPTER SEVEN

THE CAMERA AS THE DIRECTOR'S TOOL

WHY THE DIRECTOR SHOULD KNOW CAMERA BASICS

When I was sixteen years old, I graduated from the New York Institute of Photography and was well on my way to becoming a Hollywood cameraman, or so I thought.

This feat is not quite so amazing when you understand I was still in high school and all the lessons were through correspondence. Still, it did give me a basic education in photography, which has been invaluable in my work as a film director. Later, I taught Cinematography at the University of Southern California and photographed the short that was the turning point in my life.

One of my first jobs in Hollywood was as assistant cameraman, and later I was on George Pal's photographic staff making his series of Puppetoon shorts for Paramount. As I said in an earlier chapter, everybody wants to be a director—even the cameraman—but in my case I wanted to be a cinematographer. And, I feel I could have been, except for one thing. The cameraman's union, Local 659, I.A.T.S.E., was closed to newcomers unless the applicant happened to have a father or a friend who was a cinematographer. The union allowed me to work around in the independent field, or for Pal's Puppetoons, but as far as being invited into their inner circle of major studio cinematographers, it was out of the question.

So, I decided to be a director, since the opportunities for succeeding were not dampened by a union that invaded the sacred domain of the right to work. The Directors Guild has from its inception held that any individual who could get a job and who could pay the initiation fee was duly qualified for membership, an encouraging attitude for any young person attempting to get a start as a director.

Second only to the ability to communicate with and inspire actors into giving creditable performances is the ability to use the camera in telling a story. From the earliest silent films, the camera played a dominant part in the director's interpretation of the author's words, and today the individual who fully understands the camera's power is a step ahead of fellow directors who do not have that understanding.

Occasionally, the director will work with a cinematographer who, for one reason or another, either fails to comprehend what the director wants or is not inclined to try for it anyway; and it is here that the knowledge of the camera's limitations is important. The director who freely admits that the camera is a mystery is at a decided disadvantage, but the director who can communicate with the cameraman *on his own terms* will usually end up getting almost any known or experimental effect that he desires.

LENSES AND WHAT THEY DO

Knowing the characteristics of lenses is a valuable and timesaving talent on the part of the director, and anyone who understands the capabilities and limitations of the "glass," as the cameramen call them, is far ahead of the game.

The standard lens on a motion picture camera, one that photographs a scene as near to the way the eye sees it possible, is the 50-mm, or 2-inch, lens. The lens that has come to be used as a standard lens under most conditions is the 40-mm lens. Lenses that have smaller numerical designations than either the 40 mm or the 50 mm are known as *short focal-length lenses*. Lenses that have larger numerical designations are called *long focal-length lenses*.

The short focal-length lenses, also known as *wide- angle lenses*, are the commonly used 35 mm, 30 mm, 25 mm and the occasionally used 17.5 mm, which has an extremely wide angle of view.

The usual long focal-length lenses are the 75 mm, 100 mm and a 300 mm, or 6-inch, sometimes called a telephoto lens.

The long lenses tend to bring objects closer. The short lenses make objects appear farther away and sometimes tend to distort their shape and size. The shorter the lens, the more distortion, especially when photographing objects close up.

When the director understands what these lenses can do, he or she can properly stage the action and camera movement to complement the camera's point of view, and thus obtain the proper screen effect.

Since the 40 mm and 50 mm are the normal lenses with little or no distortion, let's consider what the lenses that are longer than the 50 mm do for the director. In the first place, since there is an absence of distortion in these lenses, they are ideal for glamorous close-ups. In this respect, the 75 mm and 100 mm are most often used. These long lenses will tend to blur the background, and they will be called upon by the director when he or she wishes to place all attention on the foreground action.

Obviously, when a universal focus effect is desired, one in which all things in the scene are crisp and sharp, the director does not ask for a long focal-length lens but rather a wide-angle lens.

Another point to know about long and short lenses: the size of the picture is determined by the selection of the lens. With the camera placed well back, a long lens will photograph only a portion of a given set, whereas a short (or wide-angle) lens will take in practically the whole room.

Sometimes the director wishes to photograph the action from a particular point of view but realizes that to do so would require removing a wall to accommodate the camera with a 40 mm. The director's solution is to call for a 30 or a 35 mm instead; this gives the same size picture, and no valuable time has been wasted in removing the wall from the set. Conversely, when the camera and the subject are separated by non-transversible objects, such as a river, a canyon or a city street, the director calls upon the long focal-length lens to bring the action closer, therefore making the image the desired size.

Remember the shot you've seen of an actor or a car coming directly toward the camera? The actor or the vehicle continues to approach but never seems to get any closer. That shot was made with an extremely long lens.

You've seen shots where one actor's face looms large in the foreground, slightly three-quarter angled, while another stands squarely facing the camera, slightly farther away? Chances are the shot was made with a lens at least as wide as a 30 mm, with the overall intensity of

Lenses and What They Do

30 mm: This lens takes in virtually the whole set, reproducing it sharply in focus. It establishes where the actors are in relationship to one another and to the room itself. The 30 mm tends to make the set look larger than it really is.

40 mm: The normal lens, used under most circumstances. The scene as now photographed makes the room look its normal size, and there is an absence of floor and ceiling. In other words, the center of attention is directed toward the people, with a minimum of accent on the set.

50 mm: Now we have eliminated three of the actors on the right. This lens is used when it is impractical to move the camera closer or when camera shadows from the key light show up.

75 mm: All other actors have been eliminated. The use of this lens, which is the standard close-up lens, directs the viewer's attention to the subject and tends to "fuzz up" or hold background in soft focus.

lighting built up to accommodate a short lens t-stop. (For some reason, the t-stop has replaced the venerable f-stop.)

The *t-stop* indicates the amount of light reaching the film; the wider the opening in the lens, the more exposure. "Stopping down," or narrowing this lens opening, increases the sharpness of the image. Shots made with a wide-angle lens have a way of looking around the curve of the face, so to speak, and are dramatically effective. Both faces will be in sharp focus, and the distortion seems to add to the mood created, especially if the face that is closest to the camera is not the one of your glamorous leading lady.

Then there are the shots of your leading man as he walks in close-up along the sidewalk on the far side of a busy city street. When you see fuzzy objects such as automobiles or street signs blur by in the foreground between you and the actor, you will recognize this shot as having been made with a 250-mm lens. When the close-up zooms back into a 25-mm wide-angle view, you may speculate that the lens used is a French-made Angineux, a popular choice of the commercial directors.

Elaborate preparations are made to film a close-up of the driver of a moving automobile. Most of the time the cameraman merely rides in the passenger's seat and makes the close-up of the driver against the moving scenery outside. But director Francis Ford Coppola insisted that the view of the driver be outside the car, hence the specially designed camera mount. (Warner Bros.)

Richard Burton leads Sandy Dennis in a drunken dance in *Who's Afraid of Virginia Woolf?* while the Mitchell Camera records. Judging the distance from camera to subject, the scene was probably filmed with a 30-mm lens. Directed by Mike Nichols. (Warner Bros.)

Orson Welles, together with Gregg Toland, revolutionized the technique of universal focus in their exceptional film *Citizen Kane.* Extreme depth of field was obtained by using short lenses and building up the keylight to reduce the lens aperture that sharpens the image.

The result was dramatic and astounding: an actor standing in the foreground in a huge close shot while another stood full figure in the background. Both were in critically sharp focus.

There are times when extreme motion, or jiggling, of the camera is unavoidable, as when it is tied down on the rear end of a speeding camera car. In this instance, the wider lens will do much to eliminate the effects on film of the jiggling of the camera.

The *zoom lens* places another tool in the director's hands by allowing the camera to, in effect, dolly without ever leaving its stationary position.

The camera can zoom from a long shot into a huge close-up in a much faster time than two grips could push the dolly forward.

USING THE CAMERA FOR MOVEMENT

The proper use of the motion picture camera, of course, takes into account its ability to move about the set in almost any position, vertically or horizontally. All it takes to achieve this maximum mobility is time, for the more the camera changes its basic point of view, the more lights, *scrims* and *gobos* are required. *Scrims* decrease the amount of light; *gobos* block a portion of the light.

To illustrate that there is actually *no* limitation to this camera movement, consider a shot I once made for Rod Serling's *Twilight Zone*. The scene called for a bridge game; and since the results of the game had no story value, and the scene itself was the only one to denote a passing of time, I pondered how to make it interesting. The first angle I set up was from below the glass-topped table, showing the cards and faces of the players as the cat might view them. The second, and the one that demonstrates the complete scope of the camera, was made by placing the camera in the center of the table and panning it from the face of the leading man, across the faces of the other players as they made their bids, and right on around through 360 degrees until the leading man came into a close-up again. Although this shot took a little doing, it was accomplished by first enclosing the open side of the set with wild walls to make a four-wall room, and then removing all the lights and grip equipment from around the camera. All crew members were obliged to leave the set, and the scene was lighted by lamps suspended from above. As the camera was panned from face to face, only the operator and myself walked around behind it, keeping out of its view.

On this same episode, I had occasion to use the camera in other ways for an effective overall result. The idea of the story was to depict a group of persons who were planning to leave for another planet in the face of the threat of a terrible and destructive war. Only at the end, when they were safely aboard a spaceship, did one character ask another the vital question.

"What is the name of this planet we're heading for?"

The pilot of the ship thoughtfully perused his radar scope and replied, "It's the third from the sun—it's a place called Earth."

The sudden twist at the end is what made the film, and the objective in the scenes that led up to the climax was to avoid betraying Serling's secret that we were actually watching members of another planet preparing to come to ours. It was decided to use conventional-looking, -acting and -sounding players, living in conventional Earth-like surroundings; but they would be treated differently with the camera.

I ordered the widest-angle lens that Metro-Goldwyn-Mayer Studios had, a 17.5-mm bug eye. I told the cameraman that I wanted this lens used exclusively, even on close-ups. I explained I wanted the distortion that this lens gave everything and suggested that the cameraman work out unorthodox sources for the lighting, sources that would bring an unusual aura to the film. In addition to this, every camera setup was cocked to one side or the other, which further served to take away the feeling of normalcy. What I was striving to do was protect Serling's surprise ending and yet give the feeling of oddness so that when the picture was over, the audience would understand why the "kooky" camera treatment was used. A cautionary point regarding camera angles: Never make an unusual or self-conscious angle unless there is a reason for it. The director who abuses the privilege of a mobile and versatile camera calls attention to himself or herself as if to say, "I'm the director, and I'm more important than the story and actors!"

In the sixties, filmgoers were bombarded by every conceivable camera trick, old and new, ever thought of by a director or cinematographer. Zooms were used to distraction; selective focus shots to the point of no return (in a *selective focus shot,* only one person in the scene is actually sharp). And such effects as shooting the sun, wildly aiming the camera at the tops of buildings so that they swirl dizzily, and duplicating shots in a pattern of multiple images not only call attention to the fact that the picture is being "directed," but detract from the pure involvement of the audience in the story.

Billy Wilder, director of numerous artistic and successful pictures (*Lost Weekend, The Apartment*) says: "In filmmaking, I like the normal setup, like Wyler uses, like John Ford, like Chaplin. I'm against this fancy stuff. It reminds an audience that artisans have intruded. I don't want them to grab their partner and say, 'My God, look at *that!*' Besides, we tried all those things in the old UFA days," he added, referring to the famous German studio.

Arthur Penn used a variety of camera tricks, including the first of the slow-motion picture deaths, in making *Bonnie and Clyde.* When he got around to making *Little Big Man,* he had changed his directorial approach. "It has no slow motion and no camera tricks. It is an effort in orthodoxy. The fascination with camera techniques is getting a bit ripe. If it contributes to the whole experience, then it is valid. When it becomes something independent of the film, then it's of no use."

The three basic types of conventional movement are: (1) sideways movement of the camera called *panning* and *tilting*, which is used to follow actors about the set when they move on the same lateral plane; (2) movement of the camera on a dolly, which causes the camera's viewpoint to change laterally or longitudinally; and (3) movement of the camera on a crane, which combines the above with a vertical dimension, as well as allows the shifting of viewpoint from any one point in the set to almost any other—in other words, complete mobility.

The use of the panning and tilting feature of the camera is so basic that anyone who has held a camcorder understands its uses and limitations. The same warning that all camera stores give to their video camera customers applies in professional productions: namely, don't pan too fast. This is because the background will blur if scanned too quickly. Of course, if the camera is centered on a moving object and stays with it, there is no limit to the speed of a pan shot. *Whipping*, the fast panning off

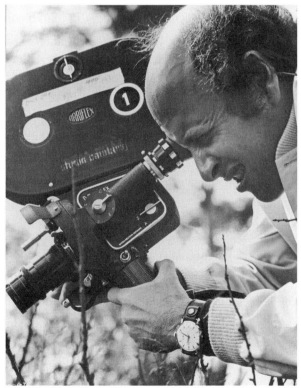

In filmmaking today, the director is likely to pick up the camera and start shooting—too bad if the sun is not in the right place. With realism the key word, the photographic results have accidentally started a new vogue: erratic photography. The handheld Arriflex is to blame for the spate of shaky camera shots, seen in almost all commercials and in features where the director calls for an unsettling effect. (Columbia Broadcasting System)

The Camera As the Director's Tool   121

of one subject and onto another, can be used effectively as a technique to bridge two scenes together when a quick cut or a dissolve is not desired.

A director who becomes involved with the movement of the camera on the dolly had better know the lenses, as well as the other virtues and limitations of the camera. However, the director who gets the reputation of being a "dolly rider" needlessly slows down the cameraman's work, viewing each rehearsal through the viewfinder as the camera makes its moves about the set. I have found that, after lining up the shot with a handheld *wild finder*, it is best to work with the actors away from the camera.

Then, when the cinematographer notifies the director that the set is lighted and is ready for a camera rehearsal, all that is necessary is one "ride," watching the action through the camera. This is merely to confirm that the cinematographer has interpreted the shot as the director had lined it up originally.

There was a day when directors were known by their megaphones, but today they are more apt to be recognized by the small object hanging by a chain around their necks. This is a *director's finder*, a device that approximates all the lenses on the camera. There are two types of finders. The first type has a small inexpensive viewing lens on one end and a slot on the other end into which various matts are slipped, each one corresponding to the scope of the lens it matches. The other is an optical type that works like a zoom lens, allowing the director to rotate the barrel of the finder and select any image size desired. By referring to a scale on the barrel, the user can determine which lens corresponds to the image size selected.

Most experienced directors avoid as much as possible what is known as *unmotivated camera movement*, that is, when the camera pans from one subject to another without any motivation. The most widely used device—in fact, it has become a cliché—for shooting restaurant or nightclub scenes is to use the waiter to cross from one table to the next, thus giving the camera something to concentrate on as it moves its view from one point to another. There are many interesting ways a director can move the subject action about to give proper motivation to the camera movement.

The newly arrived director, if given the chance, usually becomes obsessed with the crane, and stays up nights thinking of ways to confound the cinematographer, whose job it is to light the shot. One such director photographed a long scene on a huge set at Paramount, taking all day to get one take. The scene started with the camera angling through a brandy snifter and then following the brandy drinker over to a piano

It sometimes takes hours to construct a dolly track such as the one shown here. The director normally will lay out such a shot in advance so that the grips won't delay the shooting. But using the Steadicam is much quicker because it eliminates the dolly and the tracks.

that was being played at the edge of the dance floor. The camera dipped under an archway, half of which was swiftly pulled to one side by the grips, then proceeded to shoot the piano player from a point of view under the drinker's arms. Then, when the music was finished, the camera wandered over (motivated by a crossing waiter) to disclose the full figure of the leading lady as she entered the café. After twelve takes, the scene was pronounced a masterpiece of rhythm and motion by the director, who thought he had accomplished enough that day and wanted to go home. When the cameraman asked him which set they were going to shoot the next morning, the director told him that he wasn't through with this set yet—that he still had to make close-ups.

"You mean you're cutting close-ups into that scene we took all day to get?" asked the tired but incredulous cameraman.

"Of course," replied the director.

"Then why did we have to get the whole damn scene in one take?" the cameraman demanded.

"It's for the front office—they love to see that kind of stuff."

Sometimes as many as three cameras are used on the "insert car" to get different angles on action shots. Here William Holden prepares to gallop behind the car while a long shot, medium shot, and close-up are filmed simultaneously. From *Boots Malone*. (Columbia)

Here is an example of selective focus, although not as extreme as would be accomplished by a 6- or 10-inch lens. All the gaiety of a drinking party is depicted, but the eye goes to Dyan Cannon who is the leading player. *This Rebel Breed,* directed by Richard L. Bare. (Warner Bros.)

The next day, the company spent all morning doing several close-ups, which would be cut into the involved master shot, the complexity of which would never be appreciated by the audience.

The longest and most involved moving camera scene, to my knowledge, was done by Robert Siodmak in *The Killers.* Siodmak had the camera alternately moving from interior scenes to exterior scenes involving hundreds of people, and at least that many individual camera moves. The effect was spectacular to those of us in the business, but I doubt if a layperson could recognize the feat.

Stanley Donen in the Cary Grant picture *Indiscreet,* once made a moving camera shot that defied previous limitations. The camera

■ ■

The Arriflex camera proves its worth in the filming of *I Sailed to Tahiti* by obtaining shots the Mitchell camera could never get. The sound man holds an overhead microphone to record dialogue for a "cue track" only. All sound had to be "looped" back in Hollywood, with actors adding new voices to the picture. Wind, waves and camera noise are thus eliminated, with the wind and the waves added again in proper perspective. (United National) followed Grant into a building, moved inside the elevator with him, rode up several flights with him, then followed him out into the corridor and moved down several doors with him until he disappeared through a doorway.

Battery-operated cameras and lights facilitate the making of unusual shots as never before. Today, the reliable Steadicam and its successor, the Glidecam, which are extensions of the traditional handheld camera, can do wonders for the director, as well as for the producer who has an eagle eye on the budget. With the Steadicam strapped to the operator, there are no dollies or dolly tracks to lay, and shooting can start as soon as the actors are ready.

Movement of the camera is not merely confined to broad sweeps from a close-up of a champagne bottle to the waiter's dash to a table in a busy party scene, to a long shot of the floor show. More subtle movements have a definite dramatic value, and their use can give positive illusions. One of these illusions created by camera movement is that which creates the feeling of flight in an airplane, or headway in a boat when you are using mockups of the real thing. The gentle but slight tilting and panning while a scene is in progress provides the unsteadiness an audience always associates with movement of planes and ships.

The pilots in the cockpit of an airplane are usually photographed on the ground with a plane mockup. A painted cloud background (or a blue screen so that clouds can be added later) is visible through the window, with both camera and key light moving up and down to simulate the slight rock of the airplane.

These rules are for studio-made shots. Shooting the real thing poses another problem connected with camera movement: how to minimize it.

I once made a film in its entirety in and around the Hawaiian Islands, most of it aboard a 55-foot sailboat at sea in the Molokai Channel, one of the roughest bodies of water in the world.

The problem here was how to keep camera movement to an absolute minimum, lest the actors bounce all over the screen. This was the first feature picture I had ever made in which there was not one dolly shot. During the land sequences, actors were moved to and from the camera to give impact to their scenes in the best John Ford style. But on board the *Samarang* on the high seas, not only was dollying out of the question, but keeping the subjects in camera range and the camera steady became paramount.

It had been decided that we would take aboard only one camera, an Arriflex with a lens complement of a 75 mm, a 50 mm, a 40 mm and

Acceptance of the handheld camera as the prime photographic instrument has brought a new mobility to feature production. Under such adverse conditions as shooting on the deck of a 55-foot sloop, the cinematographer is able to counter the roll of the boat and keep the horizon level. (United National)

a 25 mm. The camera was, of course, battery operated and tied in a sync-pulse system to a Nagra portable recorder.

The cinematographer, Lenny South, wanted to use a tripod that would have had the horizon rocking around wildly. I said no, the camera should be handheld so that the operator could keep the horizon level. I won.

Audiences can be subject to an inner ear imbalance when the horizon does not remain relatively constant, and one has only to remember the first Cinerama pictures to be convinced. So, the sea shots were made with the handheld camera and with the operator attempting to hold the horizon level—no little chore in light of the heavy seas encountered. I recall that at least three of us steadied him with our bodies, forming a kind of human tripod to keep him from losing his balance and falling overboard. One last word about shooting under these conditions: Only wide-angle lenses can reduce that unsteadiness of shots made on a rocking boat, and in this case almost all were made with a 25-mm lens.

Of all the directors who understood the camera, Josef von Sternberg, perhaps, made the best use of it. It would be nothing for von Sternberg actually to operate the camera himself on a long and intricate crane shot rather than to stand to one side and depend on the camera operator's interpretation of what he wanted.

Once, while shooting a Warner Bros. western, *Shootout at Medicine Bend*, I had occasion to combine what I had learned about the psychology of handling actors with the essential illusion of reality.

We were halfway through the feature, and the script called for James Garner, Randolph Scott and Gordon Jones to be swimming in a river while their clothing was being stolen. Scott had never mentioned to me, or anyone else as far as I knew, that he wouldn't go in the water. When we got around to setting up for the wet work, the assistant director came up to me and told me what Scott had just told him, that he wasn't going in the river.

I knew that talking to him would do little good, so I proceeded to task my imagination. I first asked the assistant if Scott minded stripping down to his underwear. No, that was all right; he didn't mind that. It was just that he had a cold and wasn't going to get in that dirty river. With this hurdle past, I proceeded to stage the scene. I put Scott's double out in the middle of the stream with Garner and Jones, and placed the camera behind a fallen log that was lying on the water's edge. I put Scott behind the log and told him to crouch down out of sight. Just as the camera rolled, the prop man dumped a gallon of warm water over him, and the boys in the river started to swim in a dash to the shore. As they approached the shore and disappeared momentarily behind the log, the double stayed hidden, and Scott popped up alongside Garner and Jones, breathing heavily and looking for all as if he had been swimming right along with them. I was happy; we stayed on schedule; and Randolph Scott, no doubt, picked up a few more fans.

THE CAMERA AND ITS COMPONENTS

The history of motion picture cameras that have been adopted by the film industry is consistent—only one brand of camera at a time has found favor with the Hollywood studios. In the beginning there was the rear-cranked Universal, followed by the boxy DeBrie, and both were shoved aside by the more reliable Bell & Howell. When sound came in, the movie studios abandoned the Bell & Howell for the resolute BNC Mitchell, which introduced a rackover device that allowed the camera to be slid to one side and permitted the operator to view the scene through the lens before shooting.

But around the time of the sixties, the impressive Panavision arrived with its advanced Reflex viewing system that allowed the operator to view the shot as it was happening. That was the death knell for Mitchell, although they retooled their BNC and for a while they were still in the race.

Today, Panavision (who only rents its cameras) has a virtual stranglehold on the industry, its cameras having proved to be superior to anything on the market. The Panavision camera is so heavy that it must be handled by at least two grips, who place it on a *crab dolly*, an innovation that allows a camera to be perambulated around corners rather than on straight metal tracks as previously.

Along the way, the smaller Arriflex, the Eclair and the tiny Minicam were introduced. These cameras are also made in 16-mm versions that many low-budget producers find efficient and economical. For "wild" shooting without sound, the Beaulieu R16b and the Bolex H-16 are favorites for the cost-conscious director. If shooting in 16 mm, be sure you use Super 16 film with its sprocket holes only on one side, since it blows up to 35 mm with better resolution than normal 16 mm, resulting in an aspect ratio of 1.85 to 1, the way most theatrical films are shot.

The primary parts of the camera are the *magazine* (which holds the films), the *matte box* (which acts as a sunshade), the *drive motor* (which turns the camera in synchronization with the sound recorder), the *lens mount* (which serves as a fastening base for the lens), and the *intermittent movement* (which pulls the film through the *gate*, exposing one frame at a time, while the *shutter* is briefly open).

On a shoot, the camera is lined up on its dolly and is *threaded* by the assistant cameraman, with color *negative*. The lens is *focused* for distance by the assistant, and the proper *stop* determined by the director of photography. In a studio production, the camera is then turned over to the whim of the director.

Of course, the director has already rehearsed the action of the actors and has lined up the course that the dolly will travel. The camera operator has been instructed to avoid the palm trees across the street, since the locale of the story is in Philadelphia. The director also has ridden in the operator's seat and watched the scene through the camera during the first rehearsal, giving the grips instructions to move the dolly with the action

As soon as the Bell & Howell came on the market, all other cameras such as the Universal and the DeBrie were doomed. Its precision and optics were vastly superior, and every studio started shooting their pictures with this workhorse. Of course, the movies were silent in those days—a good thing because the B&H made a racket when hand-cranked.

The Panavision camera, engineered to be absolutely silent when only six inches away from the microphone, has become the industry standard. In the process, it doomed the reliable Mitchell, which had been the mainstay of production companies after having pushed the Bell & Howell into the background.

of the scene. When the leading man drives up to the curb in a full shot, the dolly must be on No. 1 mark. When he walks around to open the car door for the leading lady, the dolly must be on No. 2 mark—no sooner and certainly no later.

The makeup man has been called to remove the perspiration from the actors' faces, since the time of the year is supposed to be December, not August, which it really is. There is a last word of advice to the actors and a turn to the assistant. "Let's make it!" the director exclaims. When the camera crew, sound crew, electricians and grips have all indicated their readiness, the assistant calls, "Quiet, and roll it!" and the camera and recorder start to turn. The assistant cameraman slaps the *clap sticks* in front of the lens simultaneously with getting a *slate*, that identifies the scene number. The director calls, "Ready, Action!" and the scene as rehearsed proceeds.

The car then drives up; the actors get out, with the grips pushing the camera to the proper mark. The actors walk toward the house, the camera panning with them so as to avoid the palm tree and then dollying with them to the porch, where the camera then swings around and takes

Sometimes directors "jump right in" with the actors. Director Blake Edwards (in trunks) shoots a scene for *Experiment in Terror*. Stephanie Powers has just received an imaginary blow from her unseen assailant. Here is an ideal place for the handheld camera. (Columbia)

A Typical Fluid-Camera Shot

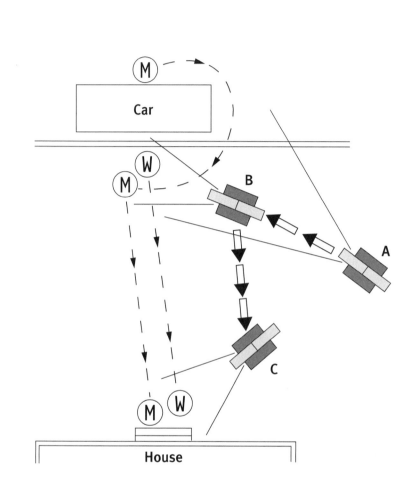

The camera is on a crab dolly or small crane with a 40-mm lens. A car pulls up to the curb as the camera shoots a full shot from position A. As man gets out of the car and moves to assist woman, the camera dollies in to position B. As man and woman start toward the house, the camera dollies slightly ahead to the end of the track at C, where the camera then pans around, taking actors into the house.

them into the house in a full shot. The director calls "Cut!" and everybody takes a breath and starts talking again. The director asks the camera operator and the sound man if they're happy and, if so, prints the action and moves on to the next shot. That's the way it goes, setup after setup, all day long. The director, with little time to sit down, is either rehearsing the actors or lining up the shot with the camera crew, working out the camera movement smoothly so that it will not call attention to itself. On the other hand, the movement of the camera sometimes is designed to shock and startle—the content of each scene dictating the style of such movement.

COMPOSITION

Since the *framing* of a shot by the cinematographer is subject to the director's approval, the art of composition should be part of the director's basic training.

The fact that a landscape is pleasing to the eye does not necessarily mean that it will be pleasing in a picture. The human eye takes in a

An example of foreground objects that "frame," or set off, the main action. The incidental action is kept darker or, in this case, silhouetted to throw the center of attention deeper into the shot. (Warner Bros.)

Some cameramen go to great lengths to control the harsh rays of the sun and to give their scenes photographic "balance." Here is a movie troupe on location at Lake Arrowhead, working under the protective cover of a huge scrim. However, today's style is to shoot it "as is." (Paramount Pictures)

wandering, all-encompassing angle of view, but the camera has an outside boundary and a sharp edge on all four sides. A movie, even though real in its illusion, can represent only a portion of nature. With the landscape captured or framed, the eye can see only what the director wants it to. If the eye strives to go beyond the limits of the picture frame, the result will be a restlessness on the part of the observer. That is why objects that are important, which attract the eye, should not be placed near the margins of the picture.

A photograph has two functions: to represent nature in a realistic manner and to remain decorative and artistic at the same time. The lines and masses contained in the picture must have a balance or rhythm in order to please—hence the importance of composition.

The director uses several methods to achieve a pleasing and well-composed picture. One method is to move the subjects, the actors, to positions either pleasing or displeasing to the eye. Another is to pan or tilt the camera, thus changing its angle of view to include another background against which the actors play their scene. A third method is to shift the height of the camera, either up or down, backward or forward, or move it to a completely different spot to obtain a better overall composition. It is necessary that all parts of the picture contribute to its general effect, and extraneous objects that cause a division of interest from the force of the picture.

The subject of a picture is its most important part, and it is generally placed near the center of the frame, with the subordinate components leading to or balancing it. Unless one portion of the picture is more attractive and interesting than the other, the eye will shift from one side to the other, creating a restless or monotonous effect. This condition exists many times in the two-shot, wherein two actors stand facing one another, showing their profiles to the camera. Each actor is equally important, and the eye has no choice but to flick from one side of the frame to the other. This fact, I'm sure, contributes directly to the tendency of film editors to use a preponderance of over-the-shoulder shots in putting together a lengthy dialogue sequence. This way, there is only one point of interest, the person speaking, with the other person becoming subordinate in the composition.

. . . .

There is no spot where the camera can't go, say some of Hollywood's more cooperative cameramen. "Give the director what he wants" is the mode of the day. Here Lucien Ballard (top) prepares to shoot a somewhat prickly scene. (Warner Bros.)

Composing Individual Shots

Right: The medium close-up is properly composed—proper headroom, sides and bottom.

Wrong: Here there is much too much headroom, and the bottom of the shot gives no base for the judge's arms.

Right: With camera moved slightly back, the picture is still pleasing to the eye.

Wrong: Here there is not enough headroom and too much bench for good composition.

Right: This close-up crops the top of the head in a "Warner Bros. Close-up," as it is known in Hollywood.

Wrong: This close-up is too close and disturbingly cuts off part of the actress's chin.

Right: This medium shot properly depicts the subjects in their relationship to one another, the man impudently lying on the bench as he makes notes on the judge's calendar.

Wrong: The composition of this shot fully shows where the man lies on the bench but has placed the judge too far to the left sideline, diminishing his importance.

Right: This close two-shot gives both subjects equal prominence and, when followed by the longer shot above, leaves no doubt as to the man's continuing impudence.

Wrong: This two-shot is too close. Not only are both heads too close to the sidelines, but the shot doesn't include the man writing on the calendar.

Composing Shots for Both Wide-Screen and TV

Most films for theaters are shot in so-called wide-screen (aspect ratio: 1.85 to 1). It is incumbent on the director and the cameraman to protect the composition of these films when they are shown on television, which uses the aspect ratio of 1.33 to 1.

This scene, composed for standard wide-screen (1.85 to 1) will not compose satisfactorily when shown on television. Both the girl on the left and the man on the right will be cut off.

This scene, although composed for 1.85 to 1, will not suffer in its television showing because ample room was left on sides, top and bottom.

This shot has too much headroom and is not pleasing to the eye, despite the subject. Proper headroom is a matter of individual choice, but most directors and cameramen would agree that the above headroom could be reduced by 50 percent.

Although this shot has the same headroom as the picture on the left, the scenic background gives the top part of the picture additional interest that warrants the breaking of the headroom rule.

Some Shots Are Awkward in Wide-Screen

The near-vertical composition of man and horse does not lend itself to good use of Cinemascope or Panavision.

When composed in the traditional 3-by-4 frame used by television, a more pleasing effect is achieved.

These Shots Lend Themselves to Wide-Screen Processes

SPECTACLES: *Hello, Dolly!* made good use of Todd A-O, a 70-mm process that is higher but not as wide as the anamorphic processes. A 20th Century–Fox production directed by Gene Kelly.

THREE-SHOTS: This scene from *Gaily, Gaily*, directed by Norman Jewison, composes well in 1.85 to 1.

The tendency today is to place the actor off-camera in close-ups instead of squarely in the middle. I'm not sure whether this is a good idea, especially when the movie goes on television, where it will be cut at the top and bottom and on both sides.

Although good composition is something that should come naturally to a director, there are a few basic rules that can serve as a guide in setting up a shot for the motion picture camera.

The idea that the picture should be divided into thirds is one of these rules. Let's take a sea view, for instance. You might position the camera so that the waves lapping the shoreline occupy a position one-third of the frame up from the bottom, while the horizon in the distance coincides with the imaginary line one-third down from the top. On the right side of the frame is a steep cliff, rising from the beach. You angle the camera so that this line is one-third of the way in from the side, while the setting sun disappears below the horizon at a position near the upper horizontal and the left vertical imaginary lines.

Attendant to the rule of positioning the subject near the center comes the question of what to put near the borders of the picture. A colonial mansion with its impressive columns can serve as the focal point of interest, and the sweeping lawn in the foreground forms a restful threshold. The winding driveway that leads to the house serves to further take our eye to the center of attention. To one side of the frame, a huge magnolia tree rises majestically in silhouette, its branches tipping into our picture from the top. So much for background. When our subject, let's say a small boy, comes running down the driveway and stops to see something off-camera, he comes to a position approximately center, and slightly to the left, thus balancing with the tree at the right.

Foreground objects, such as trees, pieces of statuary, table lamps and the like are called framing pieces. Such objects should not be strongly lighted, because a strong light calls too much attention to them.

Since the motion picture camera has the ability to change its viewpoint during a scene, the compositions become a series of flowing, moving canvases, altering their shape and mass as the action progresses from one point to the next.

A well-composed scene may start with a mobile camera framing through the banister of a stairway and shooting down on the foyer of a stately mansion. A woman enters the shot, camera right, and starts down the stairs to the floor below. As the camera moves down with her around the archway to the living room, it makes another composition with a foreground piece, a statuette, dimly lighted so as not to detract from the dramatic action. The lady pauses momentarily and then walks into a close shot (composed slightly off-center so that she is looking toward the empty side of the shot). She hears the doorbell ring. Suspecting the identity of her caller, she reacts fearfully but is drawn to the door.

The camera moves with her; and as her hand falters on the doorknob, the camera lowers to focus on the knob. The doorbell rings again, and the woman's hand turns the knob. As the door swings open, the camera tilts swiftly upward to disclose the looming face of the mysterious caller, composing a scene that gives dramatic emphasis to the sinister nature of the situation. In a continuously changing series of compositions, the camera has provided a variety of dramatic effects.

Composition of close-ups can be as important as the framing of more comprehensive shots. The extreme close-up, which is common to television pictures, can be so unbalanced that it causes a feeling of restlessness within the audience. If the bottom frame line is too high, the subject's chin will disappear as soon as he or she speaks. Too much *headroom,* that is, the distance from the top of the head to the top frame line, is another factor that can contribute to an unpleasant effect. Usually, in these large close-ups, if the subject's eyes are slightly above the imaginary horizontal center line of the frame, the rest of the face will be in balance.

Creating dramatic illusions through composition is just another use that the director can make of his or her knowledge of the camera. A typical example of a dramatic illusion can be found where the illusion of height is to be created. Let's suppose that the script calls for an actor to be perched precariously on a ledge many hundreds of feet high. The studio art department has probably built a portion of this ledge on the stage, which matches an actual mountain location and which was used to film the long shots with the actor's double. You wish to establish this set, called an interior-exterior, taking advantage of everything you can to create a feeling of height. Shooting a point of view from below can help, but the real trick is to compose the shot so the man on the ledge will be toward the top of the picture, with a mass of rock filling the screen below. Normally unorthodox when the only dictate of the scene is pictorial, this composition aids the dramatic telling of the story. The opposite is true when other actors are to be depicted as being at the base of a cliff. Framing up, so that a mass of rock is above the actors, will do much to accomplish this feeling.

The technique of composing camera angles that are shot from below the subject has a tendency to emphasize the powerful, dominating qualities of a character, whereas angles from high looking down create an

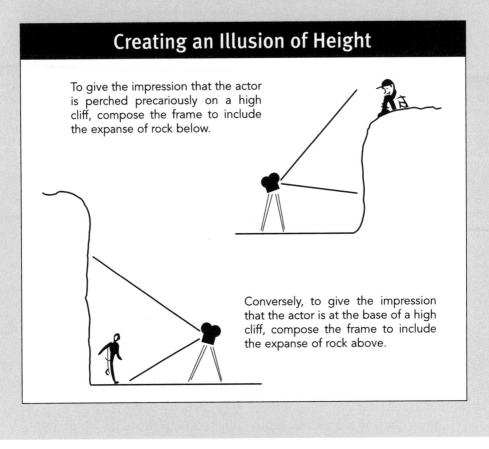

Creating an Illusion of Height

To give the impression that the actor is perched precariously on a high cliff, compose the frame to include the expanse of rock below.

Conversely, to give the impression that the actor is at the base of a high cliff, compose the frame to include the expanse of rock above.

opposite effect of weakness, helplessness and even sympathy for the person.

Even the inanimate can take on another quality when viewed from below. I once had the occasion to shoot a scene in which a piano was being hoisted from the sidewalk to a third-story window. Since this was a comedy and the piano was destined to fall in the picture, I placed a camera directly below and with a very wide-angle lens created a quite frightening shot as it was slowly pulled upward.

ASPECT RATIOS

No chapter on composition would be complete without a discussion of *aspect ratios*, the various frame sizes with which the motion picture business plagued itself some years ago.

For fifty years, the standard proportion for framing movies had been a 3-by-4 ratio, easy to balance frame, which still provides the best compositions under most conditions. The obsession with "wide screen" caused industry leaders to abandon the traditional 1.33 to 1 aspect ratio in the early fifties.

Through the years, there have been other attempts to stray from this 3-by-4 standard, the most notable of which was Fox's Grandeur—a 70-mm film process that was used for only a few pictures. This occurred about 1929, but it failed because exhibitors balked at the expense of equipping their theaters with larger screens and bigger projectors.

After Fox's first experiment with large film, nothing much happened to increase film size for almost twenty-five years. When Fox tried it again, Cinemascope was born. This is an *anamorphic* process, which means that 35-mm film is used but that the image is "squeezed" in the theater by placing another lens onto the projector so that the film can be shown on a large panoramic screen. The ungainly dimensions of this Cinemascope screen, with its slight fuzziness of focus, have kept this process from becoming a standard—a thing that many people agree is necessary in a worldwide industry.

With 20th Century–Fox pioneering and staking all on Cinemascope, other producers followed their lead with processes and aspect ratios of their own. Paramount, for a while, exploited Vista-Vision, a wide-screen process that many agreed was the closest answer to perfect projection. The other companies merely convinced exhibitors worldwide to reduce the tops and bottoms of their projection apertures and latched onto the aspect ratio of 1.85 to 1 as the most desirable screen proportion. This may be the ratio that will stand the test of time, since films that are photographed this way are most easily projected on television, the complexities of which eliminate a portion of the top and bottom, as well as the sides, of theatrically designed films.

Today, more changes have been thrown into the mix. A new aspect ratio has been adopted. It was born out of an acrimonious squabble between the American Society of Cinematographers and the Society of Motion Picture and Television Engineers. The cameramen wanted the TV aspect ratio to be 2 to 1 while the SMPTE lobbied for a ratio of 16 to 9 (16 units wide, 9 high). The reason for the support of 16:9 was the fact that it is a compromise between broadcasting old movies (3 by 4) and anamorphic films. In fact, the new standard will continue to plague filmmakers who wish to see their films shown on television the same way they looked on the theater screen. And they must frame their shots to protect the new TV standard.

Aspect Ratios in Film

Old 3 × 4
The original frame proportion of motion pictures from silent days through twenty-five years of talking pictures.
1.33 to 1

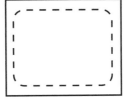

Television
Video projection cuts down on all sides but still conforms to traditional 3 × 4 ratio.
1.33 to 1

Wide-Screen
The present "standard" of theatrical films, arrived at by cropping off the top and bottom and then blowing up to a larger screen.
1.85 to 1

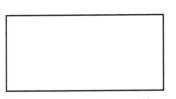

Cinemascope and Panavision
The two most popular anamorphic processes project an extra-wide image from a 35-mm negative that has been "squeezed." Special lenses are required in projection.
2.35 to 1

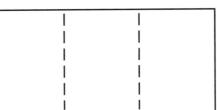

Todd A-O and Super-Panavision
Todd A-O is a 70-mm film process that results in a giant-sized screen image with unusual resolution. Super-Panavision achieves the same results by using a 65-mm negative.
2.21 to 1

Original Cinerama
Although not currently used, the largest screen size ever developed was three-screen Cinerama. It took three cameras hooked together and three synchronized projectors in the theater to achieve this gargantuan picture.
2.33 to 1

Problems of Aspect Ratios

The following two photographs illustrate what sometimes happens when a theatrical feature made in a 2.35 to 1 ratio is released to television. If the director has not considered the future television exhibition problems and placed the actors at the far extreme of the frame, both actors can end up "off camera," only their voices being heard. In these instances, special television prints are prepared by the laboratories that provide optical "pans" from one face to another, hardly satisfactory at best.

Two-shot photographed in anamorphic process.

Same two-shot projected on television: two noses and venetian blind.

Most Directors Protect TV Showings by Properly Placing Actors

Sides of picture are for incidentals only.

Nothing will be lost when shown on television.

Lining up an unusual angle through the rear window of an automobile is director Ralph Nelson, whose credits include television's *Requiem for a Heavyweight*, which earned him an Emmy and brought him offers to direct movies.

Whether a motion picture is photographed on 35-mm or 70-mm film, whether it is composed in a 3-by-4 ratio or a 1.85 to 1, whether it is in Cinemascope, Techniscope, Cinerama or Panavision—the creation of film entertainment remains basically the same. Cameras are tools with which the director transfers the pages of a script onto a screen, large or small, in a theater or a living room. A director could make a picture on 99-mm film, turn it sideways and call it a "tall screen" but still not impress the audience unless the story is one worth telling and has been filmed in style, without calling undue attention to himself.

Mike Nichols let his views on this subject be known: "Frankly, I would hope I live never to see a zoom again, a long lens, any of the things available to the people making Pepsi-Cola commercials. It should all be stripped away. Techniques should serve the thing you're concerned with. The films that I most admire are those in which there is no apparent technique at all."

THE MULTI-IMAGE SCREEN

Although the technique of combining multi-images on a single screen is not new, it has reached ultimate complexity in films such as *The Thomas Crown Affair* (the Norman Jewison version) and *The Boston Strangler*. Like so many other techniques, the multi-image screen had its start with D. W. Griffith in *The Birth of a Nation*. He used several images simultaneously to make a single statement—soldiers rushing up the hill, the sacking and burning in the valley, and a leading character being helped up the hill in the foreground.

Ralph Nelson, in *Charly*, used the technique to enhance a scene between two characters seen just talking with one another. Rather than cut back and forth between the close shots of the two, he combined the shots optically onto one frame. The audience could see both the action and the reaction, in effect, doing its own cutting.

In the original *The Thomas Crown Affair*, Jewison effectively used as many as fifty-four duplicate moving images simultaneously, which enabled the director to cut a twenty-minute sequence down to four and a half minutes. In the film's polo sequence, Jewison intercut his multiscreen images with single images with great effect. From a fifty-odd image shot of a player bearing down on the polo ball, Jewison cut to a huge single close-up of the ball being hit. The impact was much greater than if the sequence had been edited in a conventional way.

The multi-image technique can, of course, be overused, but it has proved itself to be an effective way to combine action and reaction, to show parallel action simultaneously and to bring greater movement to an otherwise static situation.

I once "pitched a story" (as a presentation is called in Hollywood) to Dan Melnick and Jack Haley, Jr., who were then in charge of development at MGM. They read my script and called back the next day to tell me that I had a deal. What intrigued them was the nature of the new technique I was going to use on a horror film I called *Wicked, Wicked*. I had designed the movie to depict two full-sized screens, side by side for the full 105 minutes of the movie that would allow parallel action to be shown as it really happens in real time. The main action with the protagonists (a hotel detective and a nightclub singer) was on the left screen with normal dialogue, while the right screen showed the antagonist silently planning and executing his diabolical killings.

The picture was shot with Panavision cameras on 35-mm film and projected in a 2.65 to 1 aspect ratio that, when divided down the middle, allowed a 3-by-4 ratio for each panel.

The technique not only solved the clumsiness of parallel action that has been depicted since the origin of the movies (as in the old subtitle: "Meanwhile, back at the ranch . . ."), it also presented cause and effect, the truth and the untruth, flashbacks in time, visions of the future and, above all, comedy, without interrupting the main thrust of continuity. *Wicked, Wicked*, admittedly an experimental film, showed with caustic candor the situation the way a character believes it to be and the way it really is. For example, on the left screen an old lady tells of being in the Paris Ballet and performing for the crowned heads of Europe. On the right screen, the audience sees what really happened—she danced nude on a table for a crude bunch of drunken revelers.

I shot the film in thirty-five days at the spooky old Hotel Coronado in San Diego. It was simple and straightforward to shoot but involved twice as much negative. I framed each shot in an aspect ratio of 3 by 4, the same ratio the film would have after the two panels were combined in the optical printer. I held all camera movement to a minimum, knowing that the audience would have enough to do to absorb the two screens.

No filmmaker has attempted to do what I invented, and the so-so business the picture did may have had something to do with it.

The hotel used in *Wicked, Wicked*.

LIGHTING THE SCENE

The director who has to rely on his or her own level of communication with the cinematographer sometimes goes to the projection room and views a scene somewhat differently than the way first imagined. More often than not, this disappointment is due to the cinematographer's lighting approach—one that produced an effect unlike the one the director had in mind.

At least a rudimentary understanding of the techniques of lighting should be understood by all directors; otherwise, they will continue to be surprised from time to time during their careers. The lights and their placements are the greatest single tool of the cameraman, and the great cinematographers of this industry have reached their place in the sun because of their knowledge of the intricacies of lighting. Cinematographers not skilled in lighting are only mechanics concerned with mathematical formulas of exposure, the theories of optics and other scientific data. But when skilled cinematographers move lights about, they truly take on the status of artists, just as if they had picked up a brush and palette.

The glamour queens of old-time Hollywood were perceived as glamorous because cameramen knew where to place the lights that flattered them. Because they needed special photographic handling, Lupe Valez and Merle Oberon even had pieces of lighting equipment named after them: the "Lupe" and the "Obie," especially designed to flatter the stars.

In general, a properly lit scene has three components: the *key light*, or main source; the *fill light*, which opposes and balances the shadows created by the key; and the *back light*, which gives actors a slight halo, or Rembrandt effect, making them stand out from the background. Added to this can be an *eye light* (for certain colors and qualities of eyes) and a miscellaneous assortment of *peanuts, babies, broads, juniors, seniors,* and *10 k's. Arc lights* usually provide illumination for expansive night exterior scenes.

The arrangement and balance of this multitude of equipment is the cinematographer's secret, and it is a knowledge that wasn't acquired overnight. The usual approach to lighting is to first have the electrician light the walls of the background. Then the key light is positioned, and a *meter reading* is taken to bring the intensity of the main source of light either up or down to a proper *foot-candle* measurement. This intensity of the key light has previously been determined by the cinematographer in relation to the *speed* of the film and the lens aperture, or *t-stop* desired. Following this, the fill light is positioned, and this is balanced by eye through the *ground glass* of the lens. Then the back light is directed toward the subjects and balanced for density. After this, the cinematographer gives attention to the electrical set dressing (the floor lamps, wall bracket fixtures and so forth), and each is positioned and brought to its proper balance of illumination; this is generally done by eye.

Directors who appreciate the purpose of each light can determine, through practice and experience, what effect is being made on the film. They, too, can look through the ground glass of the camera and tell whether an object in the foreground is too "hot" and thereby distracting, or whether the moonlight coming through the window is too low in intensity to permit recognition of an actor.

Cecil B. De Mille can be properly credited with introducing what is now referred to as low-key photography. In one of his early silent films, he had experimented with lighting and achieved a result that was startling. Only half of the actors' faces were lighted brightly; the other half were in deep shadows. This added a suspenseful mood to the picture, and De Mille had taken great pains in obtaining it. Many long weeks later, when the final print was ready and shipped to New York, his distributors viewed the picture with some misgivings and wired De Mille in Hollywood that they were at a loss to know how to release the picture, since they couldn't very well charge people full admission when only half of the actors' faces were visible.

This disturbed De Mille, but he finally came up with the argument he needed to ensure the picture's acceptance. He wired the distributors in New York: "What's the matter with you back there? Don't you recognize Rembrandt lighting when you see it?"

Naturally, with this shot in the arm, the picture was released and became a big success. It was the start of mood lighting in motion pictures.

The lighting of subjects for the modern film is not solely an indoor sport. Much thought must go into the lighting of exterior scenes as well; when actors are involved in a scene, the natural rays of the sun must be augmented or in some instances either filtered or completely replaced.

Nothing has a more disastrous effect on a beautiful actress than improperly handled sunlight. It is much better, as a general rule, to let the sunlight act as a back light, and provide by artificial means the key light and fill. Huge *scrims* are often suspended over the foreground action to filter the harsh effects of the sun.

Cinematographers use the word *balance* about as often as any other. The low-budget director who appreciates the full meaning of this word can quickly endear himself or herself to the director of photography by

Here is an example of effective mood lighting that highlights the main character of a scene while subordinating the lesser elements. Having the dominant figure stand apart and slightly above the others adds to the overall effect. *This Rebel Breed,* directed by Richard L. Bare. (Warner Bros.)

not demanding camera setups that place an undue stretch on the range of light and shade. As an example, a director may be shooting a scene just inside a barn on location. The interior scene may be artificially lighted, just as any studio setup would be, but the director wants to pan an actor from some place in the barn to the open front door. This places too much of a strain on the balance of lighting; that is, the exposure for the incandescent portion of the shot is not consistent with the exposure for the glare of the sunlit portion. If the director demands the shot, the cinematographer (with plenty of time) can accomplish it. The desired result can be achieved by either building up the value of the light inside, or reducing the value of outside light through the placement of a large scrim over the barn entrance. The cinematographer may also balance the exposure in the pan shot by changing the shutter setting, which has an effect similar to changing the t-stop.

In the mid-1960s, a disregard for balance in lighting began to come into vogue. When the new young directors took the handheld camera and started using it, their own lack of knowledge created some interesting effects. Knowing little about the rudiments of photographic balance, they

My experimental film, *Wicked Wicked*, had the antagonist on one side of the anamorphic frame and the protagonist on the other, which allowed the parallel action to be shown in real time. Randolph Roberts peers through an air vent grille at singer Tiffany Bolling who is performing in a nightclub. (MGM)

aimed cameras at the sun. Never having heard of the term "depth of field," they started to make long shots with long focus-length lenses. Some interesting results literally came to light, and new styles were introduced, much to the dismay of many old-time cameramen.

The camera is truly the director's prime tool, and through the motion picture's years of evolution it has never been underestimated. Just as no carpenter should attempt to build a house without first learning to saw a board or hammer a nail, the film director should be thoroughly acquainted with the many tools available, so that the most imaginative and entertaining film may result.

chapter eight

CHAPTER EIGHT
TELLING A STORY WITH
THE CAMERA

THE USE OF TRANSITIONS

I have won a few awards in my professional life, but the one that gave me the biggest boost in morale was the Paul Muni Award presented to me after a banquet and screening of *The Oval Portrait*, a 35-mm amateur film I made while a student at the University of Southern California. Since I was writer, director, editor and cameraman, I had the opportunity to proceed in autonomous fashion in working out interesting techniques for telling the story without sound and without subtitles.

The story had been adapted from one of Edgar Allan Poe's works and concerned itself with a painter who, in his intense devotion to his art, painted the very life out of his subject, who happened to be his new bride. I employed the camera with the reckless abandon of a child with a new toy: I used a frog floating on the surface of the water of a rain barrel in a storm to denote the passage of time. I started him at the bottom; after it had rained all night, the barrel overflowed, and he hopped happily away. I used the melting of burning candles to indicate how long the leading man had slept, and even allowed the candles to be snuffed out by a faint breeze from an open window to denote his death. I crammed every device, every cockeyed camera angle, and every bit of inspiration I could muster at the age of nineteen into this picture; for a nonprofessional

A scene from *The Oval Portrait*, adapted from a story by Edgar Allen Poe, the first student film ever made at USC's Department of Cinematography (now the School of Cinema/Television).

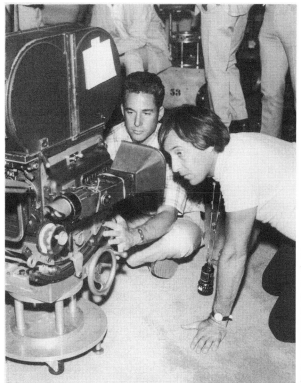

Paul Mazursky, who wears a director's finder around his neck, crouches to check a low-angle shot through the Mitchell BNC camera on a "high hat." Mazursky directed *Bob and Carol and Ted and Alice,* his first try at directing. (Columbia)

attempt, it did much to demonstrate how a story could be told with the camera. It ran at Grauman's Egyptian Theatre on Hollywood Boulevard for a week and was reviewed glowingly by the *Hollywood Reporter* and *Daily Variety.*

Without violating my own personal rule that demands that the director place the emphasis on the story and acting and not on himself, I have used many techniques to create more interesting scenes.

One that I used recently (and as long ago as *The Oval Portrait*) is as follows: to bridge an actor moving from one set to another, simply have him pull out his watch in a medium shot, cut to a close insert of the watch and pull the camera back to disclose that the actor is now going through the same action in another locale and at another time. This can be

· ·

Norman Jewison has solved the problem of the low-angle shot: Put the cameraman down into a manhole. Shown kneeling (left), Jewison is one of the directors who made the successful transition from New York television to Hollywood movies. (United Artists)

Telling a Story with the Camera   155

successfully accomplished by the device of taking out a cigarette, or a woman starting to apply her lipstick. It is simply the starting of an action in a medium shot and the completion of it in a close shot in another setting. In the college film, the transition was accomplished by the leading man proposing to his sweetheart. As he tentatively placed a ring on her finger, I cut directly to a large insert of the girl's hand with the ring continuing its movement on the finger. The camera dollied back, and our two lovers were disclosed kneeling before a priest in a marriage ceremony.

A character can be shown preparing for a big speech at his luncheon club. He starts to memorize his lines in his living room, reading from his prepared speech. Cut into a close-up and then pull back, and we see the man is now speaking to the club members.

Any business or dialogue that, as a matter of story development, must repeat itself can be handled in this manner—starting the action in a medium shot, then finishing the action in another location in a close shot.

Transition shots have been with us for a long time. One of the oldest cinematic clichés is the *wheel-to-wheel dissolve:* the camera pans down to a spinning roulette wheel that dissolves to a spinning automobile wheel.

THE ANGLE OF APPROACH

The *angle of approach* in filming a scene is of great importance, second only to that of the actors' performances. From what point the director allows the audience to view the action becomes vital in the telling of a story. Chaplin seldom took full advantage of the camera's infinite power, but, in one instance, he devised a gag that depended on the angle of approach for its effect. In *The Immigrant*, Charlie was aboard a violently rocking boat, with everyone feeling the effects of *mal de mer*. When Charlie was discovered, he was hanging over the side of the rail with his back to the audience, his body heaving to and fro, apparently in agony. Suddenly, he pulled himself up, turned to face the camera, and the audience saw that he had merely been fishing and had caught a fish by using his cane as a fishing pole.

The director who photographs scenes from imaginative angles forces the spectator to take a keener interest in the work, one that goes beyond mere acceptance. Many times a production with an oft-told story and no stars can be lifted by the director into a reasonably worthwhile film, simply by utilizing *style*. The director's style may be peculiar to his or her talents, or it may be in imitation of others; but this is unimportant if the film avoids the hackneyed. The directorial touches and the skillful manner in which the director handles the camera seldom add any cost to a picture's budget; rather, it is indecision or confusion on the director's part that can contribute to lengthy production schedules.

A German film made many years ago introduced an actor in a close-up, standing in a courtyard and shaking his fists at someone behind the camera. The next angle, a full shot, showed the object of his wrath, a jail guard, but the camera had been placed on the other side of the prison bars. Now, the audience received the full import of the scene, a man being released from prison, not all at once, and not in a conventional manner.

Another film depicted the parting of two lovers as they stood on the deck of a luxury liner, a tender scene that had as its climax the young man leaving as the loudspeakers blared, "All ashore who's going ashore." As he moved away, the audience saw a heretofore hidden life preserver. On it was written the name of the doomed *Titanic.* What better way could there

When the horses gallop, the camera must go along, too. Gregory Peck and Camilla Sparv handle the ponies while the camera crew hangs on for dear life on the "insert car." Director J. Lee Thompson is at extreme right. From *Mackenna's Gold.* (Columbia)

be to show that these young people would never see one another again. A thousand words could not have done it with the same impact.

A glamorous female spy has killed a Russian general in his study. Outside the door, soldiers knock peremptorily. The lady quickly manages to lift the general's body into his high-backed leather chair and turn it so that the back faces the door. Then, she sits on the arm of the chair and calls, "Come in."

The soldiers enter, salute and ask for orders. The lady spy, fondling the dead man's hand, turns to him and apparently asks him what he wishes the soldiers to do. She pretends to converse with the general, then turns to the soldiers and tells them that they are dismissed and that the general does not wish to be disturbed for the rest of the evening. The danger has been averted.

The director, by staging the angle of approach to coincide with the soldier's point of view, placed the audience in a position to receive the full impact of the situation and to understand how the soldiers might misinterpret what they saw.

Joseph von Sternberg, always one to devise unusual approaches, once shot a suicide scene without ever shooting the action from the conventional angle. The camera was set up to shoot the water under a bridge. Nothing was in the shot except quivering water and the reflection of a woman, looking down and about to jump over the railing of a bridge. As she jumps, her reflected image races toward the lens, and then she enters the scene, splashing away her own reflection. The result of the indirect upon the direct can be startling and effective.

Another example of the indirect approach involves depicting the effect of a loud noise, such as a gunshot. Rather than photograph the gun going off, wouldn't it be more interesting to center on a group of birds, watching them take to the air as the shot is fired?

In today's motion pictures and television scripts, the writer usually concentrates on telling the story through the characters, what they do and what they say, with little regard for the visual powers of the camera as an adjunct to telling the story. The great directors of the silent pictures—Eisenstein, von Sternberg, Lubitsch and Griffith—told their stories visually, not only because sound had not yet come into use, but because they understood the dramatic force of the camera's angle of approach. King Vidor, himself a top silent director, continued to use his unique handling of the camera when he moved into talking pictures, and Federico Fellini and Ingmar Bergman display truly great understanding of the articulateness of the director's prime tool.

Modern stage directors are aware that a principal problem is the proper control of the *center of attention*. Taking *center stage* has always implied a position of importance; but because the full stage is usually in view at all times, there can be many things that rob a star of the center of attention. "Scene stealing" is as old as the theater itself, and an actor who scratches his beard at the wrong time can cause the audience's attention to be distracted quickly. Shakespeare solved this problem by having his other actors leave the stage while the important performer delivered a soliloquy.

The motion picture, through its ever-shifting camera, provides the director with complete control over the center of attention. When D. W. Griffith introduced the close-up, he locked in forever a rigid technique that forces an audience to look at what the director wants them to. Unlike the stage director, who must carefully balance all elements, the film director can instantly bring anything to center stage through the techniques of cutting and camera angle.

The great majority of directors consciously attempt to use the camera advantageously, but there is one type of television production prevalent in Hollywood that, although shot on film, completely ignores the basic concepts of the motion picture as an art form. These productions are the three-, sometimes four-, camera shows that are filmed before an audience and that are common to most sitcoms dating back to the original *I Love Lucy* programs. *Friends*, *Seinfeld* and *Cheers* were all rehearsed thoroughly and then shot in one day. *Green Acres*, *Petticoat Junction* and *The Beverly Hillbillies* were all shot in three days with one camera, which I prefer because it still allows the director to use the camera as a tool to tell the story. How could I have directed Arnold the pig in a show shot in front of a live audience?

Effective lighting on a multicamera show is rare, and seldom can a director bring a sense of style to the work. I am inclined to exclude this type of filming from the category of motion pictures; rather, it would seem to me to be merely a visual record of a stage play.

TRICKS OF ILLUSION

Although references to "the magic of the motion picture" seem trite, I continue to be amazed at what can be accomplished through *illusion* in telling a story. Practically any effect the director calls for can be produced on film, one way or another. Not so with the stage director who must come to grips with reality in creating the illusions.

Since the advent of computer animation, the director with a major budget can ask for any effect he or she can dream up. Not so with the director who is making a film on a shoestring. With this in mind, let me cite a few tricks that are not special effects.

The cowboy who took an Indian arrow in his chest right before your eyes did exactly that when the film was made; however, a two-inch board was beneath his shirt, and the arrow sailed down an invisible wire, safely under control. The director picked an angle of approach that would be most effective in heightening the illusion.

Another Indian draws his bow and lets an arrow fly, but this time the camera whips swiftly to the victim who is seen staggering backward, his hands clutching the arrow in his chest. This time no wire, no needless delay in lining up the shot; merely a trick on the audience, whose eyes follow what they think is the arrow. When they see another arrow in the victim's chest, they assume it to be the same arrow that left the Indian's bow. Actually, the Indian shot his arrow some distance upstage of the intended target, but the illusion is perfect.

The screen, being flat and two dimensional, has an inability to reproduce depth in a scene, and many of the director's tricks depend on this photographic limitation. People who watch current television shows, especially the action and adventure variety, must wonder how those leading men take all those socks on the jaw. If the angle is just right, and the aggressive actor swings his fist across the screen, he can miss by two or three inches and still create the illusion of a smashing blow. Of course, the addition later of sound effects helps the final result.

The actor who is mauled by a lion is benefited by a double-barreled illusion. In the long shots, a stunt double, dressed in the same clothes, rolls and tumbles on the ground with the real lion, partially tamed for the movies. In the close shots, the actor duplicates the same action, this time clutching and wrestling with a stuffed lion's head. When the menacing sound of the animal's roaring is added, the audience truly sees its favorite movie star locked in mortal combat with the king of beasts.

The ability to stop and start, to shoot just what is needed, to throw out the bad and keep the good, is the film director's stock in trade. A synthetic tear placed on the cheek of an unemotional leading lady, or a few drops of blood dripping from the villain's jaw, can do much to create the right effect; and only in the medium of film can these be applied just when and where the director wants them.

Many of the illusions created in motion pictures are accomplished through the use of the process known as *rear projection,* and more

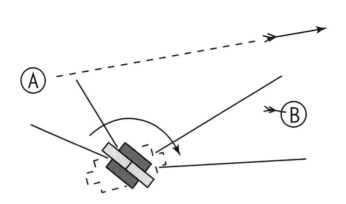

The Indian Arrow Illusion

As actor A shoots an arrow, the camera whip-pans to actor B who already has another arrow lodged in a board concealed under his shirt. As B comes into view, he clutches the arrow and falls to the ground. The real arrow sails harmlessly by on the same level, but the camera's one-dimensional view does not discern the difference.

commonly referred to as *process shots*. In simple terms, a process shot combines the foreground actors with a background that is either impractical to go to, or too costly or impossible to duplicate. For instance, the script calls for the leading man to be standing on the deck of a ship as it enters the Panama Canal. A film of the background, called a *plate*, is projected onto a translucent screen, and is rephotographed with the actor standing in the foreground on a simulated deck.

Process has its limitations, too. The angle of approach is limited to the width of the rear projection screen. Camera movement is limited as well, and of course the movements of the actors are restricted according to the size of the screen in front of which they must work.

There is another process called *front projection*. A special projector shines the moving background onto a screen from the front, even on the actors themselves. But the projector light is so dim that the images on the actors do not photograph. The secret lies in the super-reflective qualities

This Air Force training film crew is shooting what some call the "poor man's process," in which moving clouds are supplied on a background without the use of movie projection. When the scene starts, the camera is slowly moved forward and backward to give the feeling of motion, and an arc light (extreme right and top) is slowly raised and lowered, casting movable shadows inside the plane.

of the background screen, which allows the camera to record the moving background as well as the actors in a much lower photographic key than ever before.

Another method of combining foreground action with backgrounds is the use of *travelling mattes*. The advantage of this technique is that they don't restrict the actors' movements. Two pieces of film, one with the actors and another with a background, are merged in an *optical printer*, a device that photographs all or part of another film.

Most directors, in their desire for realism, prefer to shoot their films in natural locations, avoiding completely the use of process. When the actors are called on to converse in a speeding car, they do just that, much

Process Shots

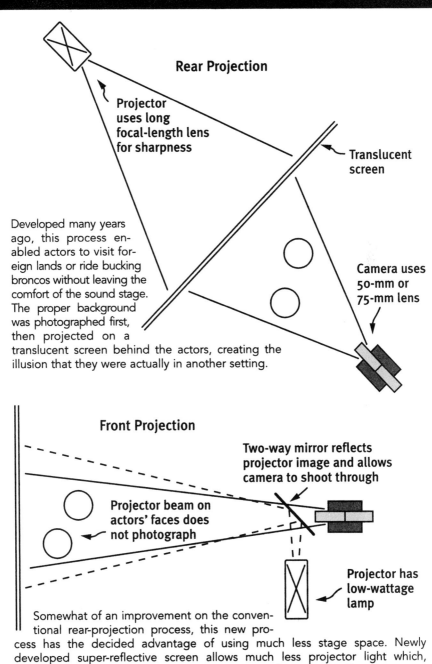

Rear Projection

Projector uses long focal-length lens for sharpness

Translucent screen

Camera uses 50-mm or 75-mm lens

Developed many years ago, this process enabled actors to visit foreign lands or ride bucking broncos without leaving the comfort of the sound stage. The proper background was photographed first, then projected on a translucent screen behind the actors, creating the illusion that they were actually in another setting.

Front Projection

Two-way mirror reflects projector image and allows camera to shoot through

Projector beam on actors' faces does not photograph

Projector has low-wattage lamp

Somewhat of an improvement on the conventional rear-projection process, this new process has the decided advantage of using much less stage space. Newly developed super-reflective screen allows much less projector light which, although shining across actors, does not register photographically.

to the dismay of the cameraman and sound man, who must record both action and voice under more difficult conditions.

Andrew Stone is one director who almost never shot a picture in the studio. His film *The Last Voyage* is a masterpiece of realism with every foot of film shot aboard the *Île-de-France* while it was actually sinking. Stone, a stickler for practical locations, bought the ship from a salvage company that was about to dismantle it for scrap, and used it as his "studio" for many weeks.

Ring of Fire is another example of Stone's penchant for getting realism on the screen without the help of process or other special effects. In this film, he bought a sawmill and then proceeded to burn it down for his movie. Even a locomotive, which was required to push three passenger coaches through a flaming forest, actually moved through the fire, accomplishing an excitingly realistic sequence for the highlight of the picture. The scenes in which a small Oregon lumber town was burning down were the sole ones to be faked by the superimposition of flames. I'm sure that Stone resorted to this trickery only after the city fathers refused to sell him their town.

To achieve the effect of a man running like the wind, have some extras on the sidewalk moving in slow motion, say 50 percent of normal speed. Then have your actor run as fast as possible down the street, and shoot the action at 12 frames per second. When the film is projected, the extras will be walking normally and the actor will streak by.

Some cameras will run in reverse; if yours won't, turn the camera upside down if you want a scene to appear in reverse. Say you want a train to back out of the station. Just shoot it pulling in and coming to a stop—the upside-down camera will do the rest.

Suppose you want an actor to appear to leap from the ground to the top of a shed. He starts at the top of the shed, then jumps backward to the ground and hurries out of the scene, backward. The upside-down camera will make it appear as though the actor were truly Superman.

There are some directors who frown upon the accepted tricks of illusion. They like to "tell it like it is," rejecting the traditional practice of cutting from one shot to another, which allows the director the opportunity to indulge in a form of fakery or illusion. They believe it is only the uninterrupted scene that can result in a total commitment to truth.

Perhaps the outstanding adherent to this philosophy is Mike Nichols who, in his *Catch-22*, conceived some of the most expensively uninterrupted scenes ever filmed, as truthful as they were. As Nichols puts it, "Every time a character says, 'Good morning, sir,' twenty-five planes take off." One scene involves two actors talking against a background of planes taking off. As the scene progresses, the actors enter a building and the same planes are seen through the window, climbing into formation. For every take, the planes had to be called back and made to take off once again, much to the annoyance of the production manager. No need for such extravagance today, what with the availability of CGI and the optical printer.

MONTAGE

No book on filmmaking would be complete without an analysis of the subject of montage, even though it seldom appears in modern films. *Montage,* by way of definition, is a succession of individual, sometimes diverse shots that, when viewed as a whole, create a unified emotional impression.

A typical montage sequence might cover a man's alcoholic downfall, first showing him taking a drink after having been established as a reformed but shaky drinker. A series of different angles would depict the man taking drink after drink, and then the sequence would cut to cocked angles of electric bar signs, with his face superimposed, drinking, drinking, drinking. Finally, his complete downfall would be represented by his figure lying prone in the street on Skid Row. Weeks of imbibing are condensed to a minute or less of screen time.

Filmmakers have long looked on the montage as an expedient in favor of the production budget. Many sequences in screenplays have been condensed to a montage treatment, both to shorten the running time of the picture and to reduce the cost thereof. Yet, on a cost per foot basis, the montage can be the most expensive type of filmmaking, since a variety of sets and camera setups are used without accomplishing the shooting of an appreciable number of pages, a thing that any assistant director will always abhor.

Montages take many forms. Sometimes they are a series of quick cuts, involving erratic camera angles. Other times, shots are blended together, one on top of another, in a succession of long dissolves. But whatever form a montage takes, it is usually designed to cover quickly, in terms of screen running time, a long period in the story in which an actor goes through a decided change of character or circumstances.

The new directors have borrowed many techniques from the masters of the silent days, but montage does not seem to be one of them. An

Director Robert Wise uses his director's finder to line up a shot for the cameraman. The small finder approximates the lenses on the camera and tells the director what he is going to get on film. Wise directed *The Sound of Music* and *West Side Story*, both of which brought him Academy Awards. (United Artists)

exception to this would be, of course, the TV commercial directors who appreciate the value of condensing a succession of ideas into the shortest possible time.

Today's erratic tempo and cutting would seem to make a virtue out of handling our drunken actor's downfall in as abrupt a fashion as possible; one shot of him looking at a bottle, another lifting it in contemplation, while the last shot would have him unshaven and lying in the gutter. Perhaps this is a concession to today's more sophisticated audiences.

chapter nine

CHAPTER NINE
WORKING WITH THE
FILM EDITOR

THE EDITOR AS AN EXTENSION OF THE DIRECTOR

The process of editing should start with the final draft of the shooting script rather than when the shooting is over. In today's high-budget movies, directors think nothing of shooting a 200-page script when 130 pages are enough to make a two-hour film. These A-list directors relish the luxury that allows them to make editorial choices in the cutting room instead of on paper. I have always as a matter of principle objected to this extravagance.

Let's dream a bit and imagine that you wrote a character-driven screenplay that was quickly snapped up by the fictitious Bigtime Productions. You convinced them that you should direct the film, thus maintaining a single point of view, to say nothing of eliminating time-consuming squabbles between the director and the writer.

The company agrees with you and budgets the film at a tight $3,000,000. The schedule is twenty-one days, and the production department has ordained that you must shoot $4^{3}/_{4}$ pages a day. The studio has put a clause in your contract that you will deliver your cut within so many days and that it will run no longer than 100 minutes. But your precious script is as tight as you can make it and still runs 150 pages. Nevertheless, your experienced producer shows you some scenes that can be easily cut. In agony, but realizing the practicality of the moment, you give in and start hacking. The producer assigns a film editor early, and the editor submits his 121-page version. You are ready to commit hara-kiri, but your wife says she'll leave you if you blow the job. With your baseball cap in hand, you tell the producer you want to be cooperative, but why is Bigtime Productions so arbitrary? The producer explains the financial facts of life: The 100-minute maximum length is because the exhibitors will play the picture (they can squeeze in more showings per day). Not only that, long pictures mean higher print costs, and making movies is a business, not an art.

This story has two morals. The first is, you are making a film that must stay on budget and on schedule. The second is, don't be a prima donna. Rock with the punches because you don't know it all—yet.

There are certain variations to be considered about script length. If you are making a wild, slam bang comedy of 100 minutes, the shooting script should have no more than 150 pages, because the camera eats up pages at the rate of 1.5 per minute. If the script is a moody, character-driven one, allow 1 page per minute (100 pages = 100 minutes).

Thriller movies are a little different. They have very little dialogue and lots of action that we call hugger-mugger. The final shooting script may have only 80 pages, since the action may be amplified by the director. One writer came to the final scene in which the hero and the heavy were to lock horns in mortal combat. Knowing the director, he merely wrote: *They fight.*

The bottom line is this: It's a lot cheaper to cut a movie on paper than on film. Make your decisions in the quiet of your office, not on the set when the meter's running at the rate of $142,000 per day.

The director's work is far from finished when the last take of the picture is completed. For now starts the sometimes long and arduous editorial process that includes the selection of the best takes and angles; the forming of the first *rough cut;* the trimming and tightening of the picture to improve the pace and tempo; the addition of sound effects, musical score, and titles; the inclusion of optical effects, such as *fades* and *dissolves;* and the final *dubbing* that transfers as many as ten sound tracks to one. At this point, a temporary print is made, and the picture is ready for the preview—an event in which the director is vitally interested.

The director's store of knowledge pertaining to the many facets of film production should include a thorough background in the techniques of editing. Cutting is just another extension of the director's ability to tell a story well, to derive good performances from the actors, and in general to entertain. Just as the director must know the camera, he or she must also know the secrets of editing, for in the small, cramped cutting room lies an ever-present danger. Good actors can be made to look less than adequate, and a director's painstaking efforts toward style can be obscured, while pace and tempo can completely disappear. It is for these reasons the conscientious director will supervise the editing and make sure that his or her ideas are faithfully transformed into the *final cut* of the picture.

WHY EDITING IS SO IMPORTANT

Although the Directors Guild in concert with all of Hollywood's studios have a firm agreement that, on paper, ensures the director's right to direct the cutting of the first rough cut, nothing prevents the studio, or its representatives (usually the producer), from recutting the entire picture; and in some cases this has been done.

Certain directors practically "cut in the camera"; in other words, they shoot the film so that the cutter has a minimum of editorial freedom. John Ford was a pioneer in this respect. Those who take this course had better be right, for many errors in shooting can be fixed in the cutting room, provided there is sufficient film shot with enough angles to enable some editorial latitude. While on this subject, it might be good to mention that many an ordinary picture has been literally saved by an astute film editor who took an imaginative approach to the film and in a sense created what wasn't there.

The first cut of *High Noon* was a disappointment to both its producer, Stanley Kramer, and its director, Fred Zinnemann. The film editor then started to experiment on his own. He took the final portion of the film, wherein Gary Cooper attempts to enlist the support of the townspeople in his pending confrontation with the killers, and condensed it to exactly one hour of screen running time, making it conform to the fictional time in the script. The afterthought but effective cutting to various clocks in the town as time ran out served to heighten the tension and make the audience become involved with Cooper in his frustration.

In the sometimes hectic pace of television production, the director seldom sees a rough cut, if at all. He or she is usually engaged in filming another show at another studio when the rough cut is shown; so the right of the director to see and approve the first cut is a theoretical one. Only on feature pictures can the director be assured of the opportunity to follow through in the various phases of editing.

The director who picks up a roll of film and its corresponding *sound track*, lines them up in *sync* and runs them in a *Moviola* or the *Kem flatbed*, is well ahead of the game. This process is actually the mainstay of all editing. The various takes are viewed, selected, trimmed and then spliced into the *makeup reel*, one at a time and in proper sequence.

TECHNIQUES OF EDITING SOUNDTRACKS

Sound in motion pictures has evolved through three separate and distinct stages: *sound-on-disc*, which came first; *sound-on-film*, which carried either variable area or variable density optical modulations; and the now universally used *sound-on-tape*, with its invisible magnetic impulses, which reproduce sounds with amazing fidelity.

In editing, there is greater latitude in the cutting of sound tracks than the picture itself.

Francis Ford Coppola (right), an ex-student of cinema at UCLA, supervises the editing in the cutting room with a Moviola. He runs the separate picture and track in synchronization back and forth until he finds the spot to make the cut. Coppola now prefers the Ediflex or Avid, both of which are flatbed editing systems that speed up the process. (American-Zoetrope)

A faulty reading on an actor's part can be fixed by substituting a sound track from another take and synchronizing it carefully over the best visual take. During editing, after shooting has closed down, a retake sometimes can be avoided simply by calling one actor back for a *wild line*, which is then matched to an over-the-shoulder shot that doesn't reveal the actor's lips.

Many times I have completed an intricate moving shot, which took an hour or so to line up and shoot, only to have the sound man come to me and say that one line did not record well. Rather than shoot the entire scene again and risk some other mechanical or human error, I have relied on the skill of the film editor and ordered a wild track of the single line that needed redoing. The actor simply reads the line into the microphone sans camera, and the tape is dispatched to the cutter with the proper notation.

THE EDITOR'S TOOLS

Since editing involves the joining of scenes, the director should know the various methods involved and their time-space implications. Although some of the techniques of cutting have been passed up in recent years, old styles have a way of becoming new again. It is in this respect that the traditional methods are enumerated here. The *straight cut* is the basic manner of bridging one scene with the next and usually denotes consecutive or continuous action. The *fade-out* and *fade-in* (which involve the gradual going to black and vice versa) are used to denote the maximum passage of time or a complete disassociation with the preceding scene.

The *lap dissolve*, where one scene blends into the next, is usually used to eliminate unnecessary action, but it is also substituted for the fade-in and fade-out, simply as a device to maintain the forward movement of the picture. In plainer terms, the fade-out is the director's period mark; the dissolve, the director's comma.

The lap dissolve has found many tricky variations, and each can have its own special significance. The *wipe*, a sharp line moving across the screen to make the transition from one shot to the next, usually brings the feeling of accelerated pace, whereas the *flip-over* blends one scene with the next in much the same manner that a page in a book is turned. The trick wipe has at least fifty variations, each of which causes the audience to be reminded that here is a mechanical trick interloping into their consciousness that would much better be served by being trained on the story. Fortunately, wipes are not frequently used in today's movies.

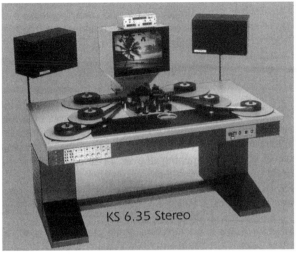

This model of the Kem editing table with its screen large enough for the editor and the director to view the various takes has all but replaced the Moviola. It can play all formats from Cinemascope to Super 35 to 16 mm.

KS 6.35 Stereo

Wipes and dissolves and other similar optical effects to denote the passage of time or the elimination of unnecessary action have all but disappeared in the modern motion picture. Today's filmmakers use the *direct cut* to bridge two sequences, completely disregarding the traditional use of optical effects. The technique, strangely enough, was born out of the advent of color television. Optical effects in color were much too expensive, so producers started releasing their films without any. The crisp, abrupt style caught on, and now major motion pictures (which can well afford dissolves and wipes) use direct cuts between sequences.

REFINING THE EDITORIAL PROCESS

The mark of good editing is to put the many takes and scenes of a motion picture together in such a manner that the smooth flow of the dramatic action is not interrupted and the audience's attention is not diverted to the editing itself.

Perhaps the most basic of the many techniques involved in film editing is what is known as *matching action*, or splicing two pieces of film together in such a manner as to cause the splice to be unnoticed. Let us suppose we wish to join a medium shot of our leading lady with a close-up of the same action. We will view the two pieces of film on the Kem or Moviola, and search for a place in the action that is common to the two takes. For instance, the actress may have reached for her drink just before

Three Editorial Transitions

Straight Cuts

Lap Dissolve

Fade-Out/Fade-In

Straight cuts: The most elemental of the editorial transitions is the straight cut, and yet it is used most in the modern motion picture. When the industry went to color almost exclusively, dissolves and other optical effects became too expensive, and filmmakers found that the straight cut gave films a "new" look.

Lap dissolve: The lap dissolve for years denoted the elimination of unnecessary action. In the above illustration, dissolving eliminates the carousers going home and takes the audience directly to next day's luncheon club meeting. Today's no-nonsense cutting technique would do the same thing in a direct cut.

Fade-out/Fade-In: Up until the mid-forties, the fade-out and fade-in were used to denote the passing of time, but this tended to slow down the action. Fades were replaced by dissolves and now are almost completely confined to the very beginning and end of a film.

she spoke her line in one angle, while in the other angle she spoke the line, then reached for the glass. (A good script supervisor would not have allowed this to happen.) The two pieces of film are closely scrutinized, and finally a place is found on each that will make a smooth cut—in other words, the actor's head, lip, and body movement match between the two scenes.

HOW THE DIRECTOR HELPS THE EDITOR

A director should understand thoroughly the problems that can arise in the editing room. It is important to learn right away the fact that a smooth cut is achieved by *cutting on movement*. This means that, other things being equal, the editor would splice the two takes somewhere during the actor's action of reaching for the glass and drinking. Or, the editor would cut on the actor's movement as the actor rises or turns or in some other way causes movement.

The director who wishes to win the respect of the film editor will always *overlap* the action from one camera angle to the next. For instance, our leading man has sat on the couch in a medium shot and has carried on a long conversation with the leading lady. He has taken a photo out of his pocket, and the editor has chosen this spot to cut to a close-up to smoothly make the transition to the closer angle. The actor, after a page of dialogue, rises and heads for the door, and the editor accordingly *cuts back* to the medium shot at the spot where the actor starts to rise, again choosing a place in movement to join the two scenes. Unless the director has the actor rise out of each shot, both medium and close-up, the overlapping of action will not occur; and the editor will not be able to find a common spot in movement between the two pieces of film so that a smooth cut can be made. The editor may have to resort to a *cut-away* shot, provided the director has made one. A *cutaway* is any shot that can be used to divert the audience's attention and is sometimes used to avoid a direct mismatch of action. A cutaway shot can be a close-up of a cat lounging on a chair, or a close-up of a secondary actor reacting to the dynamics of the scene.

The casual visitor to a movie set sometimes hears the director turn to the script supervisor after a take and say, "All right, print that—and we'll *pick it up*." What the director is saying, in effect, is that the scene was good to a point and that only the balance of the action need be done again. So the actors return to their positions, the director tells them from what point in the dialogue or action they will start, and the camera turns. Although this is a valid solution, herein lies danger, lurking silently, only to show itself later in the cutting room—unless the director remains alert.

There are only two ways in which a scene can be picked up and expected to cut in with a previous take. First, the director must provide a shot that will *bridge* the action, such as a close-up to be inserted between the last part of the preceding take and the first part of the succeeding take. Second, the director must change the angle or picture size on the pickup shot to allow the film editor to splice it to the preceding take in case there is no logical bridge shot. This follows the rule that no two shots made from the same identical point of view should be cut together.

Many times a scene plays perfectly in "one"; in other words, the movement of actors and camera around the set makes unnecessary the insertion of close-ups. The problem arises, then, of how to make a pickup and properly bridge the parts of two different takes. A simple solution is to first determine at what point the two takes should be cut together. If at this point the preceding scene is a medium shot, all that is necessary is to move the camera into a close-up of one of the actors; then as the succeeding scene gets underway, dolly back to the medium shot and resume. If, in the preceding scene, the camera was in a close-up of one of the actors, the succeeding scene should start either in a close-up of the other actor or in a medium shot of both.

Although lenses are covered more thoroughly in chapter 7, their use in relation to editorial techniques should be mentioned here. As already explained, cutting from one shot to another without changing angle or picture size makes for an awkward *jump cut*. The director can vary the angle in two ways: Move the position of the camera itself or change lenses.

Let's say that a scene is being made with a 40-mm lens and the director wishes to pick up without otherwise cutting away from the scene. To increase the size of the subject, that is, bring it closer, shooting must resume with a 75-mm lens. Cutting from a shot made with a 40-mm lens to one made with a 50-mm lens will not sufficiently change the angle to make a smooth cut. Similarly, if using a 35 mm, the following shot must be at least a 50 mm to provide the proper change in screen size.

By fully understanding the film editor's problems, the director can avoid mistakes on the set that cannot be rectified in the cutting room. Many shots are put aside and never reach the screen because the editor finds it difficult to fit them together with their counterparts. An instance of such a shot, which is doomed to end up on the cutting room floor, is

Image Size in Cutting

In editing the various pieces of film in a given sequence, only shots that vary image size sufficiently will cut together smoothly.

Assuming that the camera remains in one place, these lenses will provide enough change in image to make good cuts:

From	To
18 mm	30 mm
30 mm	50 mm
35 mm	50 mm
40 mm	75 mm
50 mm	75 mm
75 mm	100 mm

These shots will cut smoothly:

| 50 mm | 75 mm | 40 mm | 75 mm |

So will these:

| 30 mm | 50 mm | 35 mm | 50 mm |

But these shots will not cut smoothly:

| 30 mm | 35 mm | 35 mm | 40 mm |

the one in which the only logical place to make a cut is in the middle of a dolly movement. Let's say our leading man is about to read a key line to our leading lady, casting suspicion on her for some ignominious deed. For dramatic emphasis, the director decides to dolly in on the leading man just as the accusation is made. The camera dollies in at the proper moment, the corresponding reaction shot of the leading lady is made and the sequence is complete.

The director will discover the mistake soon enough, either as the dailies are viewed in the projection room or when the editor puts together the first rough cut. It will be obvious that the dolly in to the leading man came at an inopportune time, because for the scene to play properly the actress's reaction shot must be cut in immediately after the actor makes his accusation. But, because the camera was in movement at the precise moment that the audience should see the woman's reaction, an awkward cut must be made or the reaction shot dropped altogether.

Sometimes this situation is compounded because the director has ordered the camera to dolly on the reaction shot as well. The director must fully visualize the proper sequencing of all the shots, *as they are made*, particularly in the matter of camera movement. The director should literally "cut in the camera" in relation to camera movement as scenes are built one by one throughout the shooting of a picture, but the director should not fail to *cover*, that is, to provide the editor with more than one take of each scene. This is a protective device that every filmmaker must heed, for many things can go wrong between an okayed take on the set and the assembling of a rough cut. Purely technical matters, such as a scratched negative in the camera or a damaged piece of film in the laboratory, can completely eliminate the use of any given take. If the director shot the scene only once, and from only one angle, a costly retake must be made. Many times, the filmmaker has ordered a print on a scene, has rushed forward to congratulate the actors on their performances, and then has turned to the crew and said, "Now, let's do one for protection."

Directors such as John Sturges, Mark Robson and Robert Wise have one thing in common: Their pictures have a slick craftsmanlike look to them, composed of a succession of perfectly balanced shots, flowing gracefully from one to the other and containing smoothly coordinated camera movement. These three men were top-notch film editors before becoming directors, and they have never forgotten the importance of what they learned years ago in the cutting room.

As a former editor, Martha Coolidge is extremely confident in the cutting room. She has had experience on Moviolas, Kems and the electronic Editroid, CMX and Avid, which she prefers, having made the first film to use this new technology.

On the other hand, Steven Spielberg prefers to edit the old fashioned way and shuns the Avid or Lightworks, which transfer the film to video.

"I don't want to see my movie on TV until it's on network television," Spielberg has said. There is more than his method of editing that harks back to a traditional era. His selection of material and his directorial technique are rooted in more conventional times. And Spielberg is unquestionably the most successful director in the history of motion pictures.

CHAPTER TEN

chapter ten

THE DIRECTOR'S INFLUENCE ON PERFORMANCES

THE DIRECTOR'S MEDIUM

Film has been called the director's medium. The theater has been called both a playwright's and an actor's medium.

Unlike a stage director who, in lengthy rehearsals, guides actors through a series of sustained performances, the film director must do his or her job in bits and pieces, fitting them together like a giant jigsaw puzzle. The director may be required to shoot the end of the picture first or may have to shoot several sequences on the same day that are at opposite ends of the emotional spectrum. In the theater, the director builds drama gradually from beginning to end and watches it emerge as a total creation. But, in motion pictures, the director, as each scene is created, must know how it will fit in with the one it follows and precedes. The director, and the director alone, is held responsible for the correct level of performances, characterization, and mood in each of the hundreds of nonconsecutive bits that he or she fashions one by one. The director does not depend on the actors to give a sustained performance; rather, they depend on the director to *construct* a performance, which will appear sustained.

Charlton Heston is one actor who agrees with this: "I believe that the stage director is less important (than the film director). On a stage, no matter how much the director gives you or how talented he is, on opening night he goes across the street and gets smashed because there is nothing he can do once the curtain goes up. Very few directors can bear to watch the whole thing through because it can be an agonizing experience. On the screen the director is practically the whole picture. When an actor realizes the way film is made and the way an actor's performance is used, it becomes clear that he must depend on the director in a far more complete sense."

Heston firmly believes that in films the actor depends on the director so completely that there must almost be a father relationship. An actor can assess his or her performance on the stage, but in films the actor cannot always tell whether it is working or not. Therefore, declares Heston, an actor must trust the director's taste, intelligence, experience and judgment.

TWO KINDS OF ACTING

To gain proper insight into the profession of acting, especially as it relates to direction, the director should be familiar with the two major styles of acting: the *method* and the *technical*. An actor who is called a technician has as heritage the thousands of years of the theater itself. The actor's main concern is to portray the character the way the author created it; and this technique probably reached its peak during the days of traveling stock companies, when an actor would be called upon to do a variety of roles each week, changing back and forth from character to character, and portraying each one with conviction and skill. Modern television has been compared to the days of stock, since its insatiable appetite provides a variety of roles to Hollywood's more competent performers.

The method actor approaches an assignment from an altogether different viewpoint. The actor doesn't just want to act the part but to *be* the part. A method actor relies on improvisation and the inspiration of the moment. This actor must be *in the mood* before he or she can do a scene, and can't *turn it on and turn it off* the way the technician does.

The great Stanislavsky, director of the Moscow Art Theatre, developed the method style of acting and directing over eighty-five years ago, but it did not become popular in America until sometime in the 1930s. Following it were a rash of "method" plays—all downbeat, each consistently unromantic and realistic. As these plays began to reach the screen, Hollywood became aware that there was another kind of actor besides

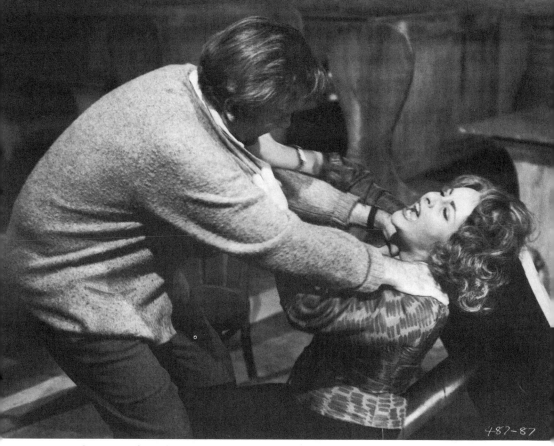

Scenes such as this must be directed and acted with great care to avoid "ham-miness." Here Richard Burton vents his anger on Elizabeth Taylor in a drunken domestic quarrel in *Who's Afraid of Virginia Woolf?* Directed by Mike Nichols. (Warner Bros.)

Clark Gable and Errol Flynn. Marlon Brando and James Dean arrived on the scene and were instant successes. Flynn's romantic flourish and Gable's manly stride were replaced by Brando's slouch and stammering speech. Soon the *method* influenced the direction of pictures, and Elia Kazan turned out the startlingly realistic *On the Waterfront*, which was made on natural locations in New York with method actors and some nonprofessionals. The film was an instant success at the box office and won several Academy Awards for its artistic merit.

With Hollywood rapidly forming sides in the preference of acting styles, it becomes more apparent that certain directors are better at one style than another. The romantic, the escapist, and the fanciful have their proponents, whereas the realistic and downbeat themes attract other directors.

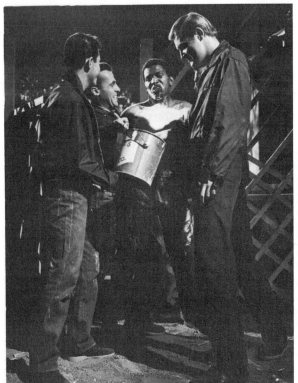

In *This Rebel Breed*, three white gang members capture a rival black gang member and "integrate him" by painting him white. This scene caused one of the white actors to break down from a sense of guilt. The actor had literally "become" the race-hating character he was portraying, an extreme example of method acting. Directed by Richard L. Bare. (Warner Bros.)

When I directed *This Rebel Breed* for Warners', I found myself in a sea of youthful method actors. The film, a hard-hitting realistic exposé of crime in high schools with an overtone of juvenile racial intolerance, had a rather shocking scene as one of its highlights.

Three youthful gang members had captured a black teenager, a member of an opposing gang. The white leader ripped off the actor's shirt and said, "You guys are all talkin' about integration—well, we're goin' to integrate ya." With that, he dipped a large brush into a can of white paint, and while the black actor struggled futilely, he was painted white—body, hair, face and all.

When the scene was over, the actor who had so worked himself up to hate the black actor in order to give a realistic performance dashed off to his dressing room. Ten minutes later, he was still sobbing.

"I feel so ashamed," he said, uncontrollably.

I tried to explain to him that *he* didn't hate black people, that it was only the character he was playing. It took an hour to bring him back to reality. While shooting, he had literally become the character of the race-hating gang leader.

DEALING WITH EMOTION

Someone once said, "If you want me to weep, first you must grieve." The audience will not be *moved* by a picture unless the actors feel strongly the emotions of the screenplay they are performing.

A director who reproduces emotion in a scene and thereby stimulates the emotions of the audience must have the emotional sensitivity to also be *moved* by good dramatic work. The person who has gone to the movies and never shed a tear is certainly not the one to try to make others cry.

The writer may cause an audience to become interested in a character, but the director must make the audience *care* about the character. It is this state of *caring* that causes the emotional reaction known as *empathy*, otherwise described as the complete understanding of another's feelings.

When William Wyler made *Ben-Hur*, he demonstrated his skill as a director. He took a multimillion dollar pageant and, by telling a story of human beings in personal terms, created an empathetic response in the audience. He made galley slaves, leprosy and chariot races seem as familiar to the audience as if they were watching events in the twentieth century. A similar picture, *The Ten Commandments*, reached lavish heights of production and told a similar story, but it lacked the emotional vibrations that helped the audience find identification with the characters on the screen.

In the most absorbing moment in *Titanic*, after the ship disappears into the freezing water, Rose tries desperately to hold on to Jack's hand. When he slips away to his death, the audience chokes with emotion. James Cameron skillfully directed that scene to create an empathetic response not usually experienced in such huge, action-packed productions.

Whether an audience will have an emotional response to a film depends on many things: the general character of the script, the sensitivity of the actors and, of course, how adroitly the film is directed. Unfortunately, a thing as delicate as emotion cannot be measured, since the very stimulus of the emotion may mean different things to different people. A simple expression, "I don't want to die," can vary in emotion from one actor to another. What sounds right for one can be "overboard" for another. How can the director tell when the line is properly read?

A scene may call for one character to scorn another, or there may be a situation where a father grieves over his dead son. Attempting to achieve genuine emotion, the director may extract only "corn." What, then, can guide the director in this delicate and elusive area?

Achieving emotion cannot be learned from reading books on film directing. It cannot be learned from watching others act or direct.

It is akin to the ageless question, What makes one painter better than another? Both may paint the same scene, use the same paints and canvas; but one picture will bring an emotional reaction from the viewer, whereas the other is just a painting. So it is with the art of directing. The mechanical techniques of picture-making, the basics of dramatics and playwrighting can be mastered by the would-be director; yet unless you are born with, or develop a high degree of, taste and sensitivity, you will never become a fine director.

Occasionally, an actor will be cast in a key role, and it will become apparent that he lacks the ability to create emotional values. The director may be a sensitive individual, but the problem remains of how to transfer his own feelings to the actor. Émile Franchel, the well-known teacher of hypnosis, tells of instances in which inadequate actors gave emotionally moving performances while under the spell of a hypnotist. Linda Darnell once used the services of a hypnotist to facilitate the memorization of many lines for a stage performance in Chicago. She had been called on to do the show on short notice, and this method apparently aided her in absorbing the voluminous dialogue. But, short of becoming a Svengali and hypnotizing the actors, what can the director do to stimulate the actor into feeling a scene?

George Stevens once went to a great deal of trouble to bring genuine emotion to a scene while he was directing *The Diary of Anne Frank*. Anne and her family had been hiding for some time in Nazi-occupied Holland when they were to look through their window and see an American plane, a symbol of hope, blasted out of the sky.

Stevens told his players that the pilot was a friend, trying desperately to help them; that when it was shot down by the Germans, they should not feel sorry for themselves, but rather they should think of that flyer as a human being with a wife and children, dying for the cause of freedom. The prop man rigged a cutout silhouette, and when it was projected on a large backing, the outline of a small plane moved across the sky. A flashbulb would explode to indicate the plane being hit by antiaircraft, and the image of the plane would sink toward the ground. None of this, of course, was in view of the camera; it was merely to stimulate the actors. When Stevens was ready to make a take, the actors were well conditioned to the mechanics of the scene and were ready to let their emotions go. But Stevens hadn't told them everything. As the take progressed, and the plane fell, the actors heard something other than George Stevens's voice as he told them the story of the lone Yankee flyer. A carefully hidden record player was filling the sound stage with "The Star-Spangled Banner." The actors were suddenly moved, and the tears flowed copiously. They were playing Dutch Jews, but they reacted as Americans; and Stevens got his scene.

Jackie Coogan told me what his director did to him when he was a five-year-old in early Chaplin pictures like *The Kid*. Just before he was expected to cry, the director walked up to Jackie, holding an opened telegram, and said, "Jackie, I'm afraid I have bad news. Your dog, Spot, just got run over by a car."

Jackie, of course, broke out into tears, and the camera ground out true emotion. Manufactured somewhat cruelly by the director, genuine feeling came across to the audience, and little Jackie Coogan endeared himself to millions.

Establishing emotional values in actors can be easy, difficult or impossible, depending on the person involved. Some respond quickly; others need much help from the director. Stanislavsky maintained that we know only the emotional experiences that we have lived, and the actor may recall these and apply them to the role he or she is doing. He called this method the *memory of emotion*. If the scene calls for the actor to mourn for a relative, the actor may be able to transfer a similar past emotional experience from real life to that of the character being played, and the director can do much to effect that transference.

How many times have you come out of a theater or moved away from your television set saying, "I don't believe it"? You may have been impressed by many things in the production, but there was something about the performances that didn't quite ring true. What probably was at the root of this trouble was a lack of *sincerity* or the presence of *false emotion*.

It is the director's job to inspire truthful performances, to make the actors *really believe* the character and scene they are portraying; for if the actor fails to believe it, the audience certainly won't.

The director must be a sounding board, ever vigilant for the first sign of insincerity. Inexperienced or incompetent actors display insincerity by tending to overact, and the director's only defense against such actors is to somehow manipulate them into underplaying. The most often-used phrases by directors who find themselves in this predicament are, "Try the line again, completely flat," or "Do it once more, simply, ever so simply."

Anthony Quinn (left) and director Stanley Kramer discuss the script during the filming of *The Secret of Santa Victoria*. After an initial setback with his first production, Kramer went on to become one of the Hollywood "greats" with *The Defiant Ones*, *Judgment at Nuremberg*, and *Guess Who's Coming to Dinner*. (United Artists)

WORKING WITH ACTORS

Each director has an individuality just as each actor does. In every walk of life, people meet people they like—and do not like. The matter of *chemistry*, as it is sometimes called, can become a great factor in the relationship between the director and the actors.

The Wild Bunch, which was directed by Sam Peckinpah, was a high point in movie violence. Death scenes were explicit and gruesome, almost to the point of being sickening. Here an actor is about to jump on a bloodsoaked victim for good measure. (Warner Bros.)

Violence in motion pictures is not always faked. Richard Rust does a realistic stunt in *This Rebel Breed*, which points up the hazards of acting. (Warner Bros.)

The Director's Influence on Performances 187

When two people hit it off, great achievements can result. When they do not, the achievements may occur, but they most certainly will involve greater effort.

When first starting to work with the actors, the director must first size them up as human beings. In the theater, this process of analysis may continue for several weeks. But, in pictures and television, the director must appraise the actors' personalities quickly, often within moments of their first meeting. Similarly, actors go through the same procedure, for they too must discover as quickly as possible a common meeting ground with the person who will be directing their performances. Methods that work with one person will not work with another. Some people are outgoing and expansive, and approach the job of acting in a businesslike manner. Others are introverted, childlike and sensitive to small hurts. One person can be talked into a performance; the other must be inspired to give one. Some can be given instructions within the hearing of the whole crew, and others must be taken aside for a more private discussion.

When the preliminaries of getting acquainted are over, the director can devote attention to the problem at hand, the transferring of the author's words into film. First, the director must make sure that the actors thoroughly understand the meaning and purpose of the story, that they understand that each scene and character are there for a reason. With the leading players, this early indoctrination comes with office meetings or preproduction rehearsals, but the exigencies of television filming may find the director and the principals getting acquainted, discussing the roots of the story and rehearsing the first take simultaneously.

The director must see to it that the actors know the interrelationships of the central characters and especially what their roles contribute to the whole. The makeup person must be instructed in the use of any special character makeup, and the wardrobe person cautioned to make certain the wardrobe fits in with the general feeling of the scene.

Above all, when scenes must be shot out of sequence, the director must make sure that the actors understand fully just where the scene they are doing fits into the story.

While we are on this point, one of the pitfalls that can plague the new director concerns the understanding of the juxtaposition of the scenes. Sometimes a director might shoot a scene without bothering to even reread the scene that will play just prior to the one now being filmed. The attitudes and physical condition of the performers must match from the end of one scene to the beginning of the next, and unless care is given to this detail, an unevenness will result.

During the rehearsals just prior to filming, the director will soon become aware whether the players are Hollywood picture actors long used to the microphone or whether New York stage actors have been hired for the job. When too much *projection* or playing to the balcony occurs, the director must caution the actors to use a natural, intimate voice level.

By the time several takes have been made and the best one printed, the director will know whether the actors have been cast correctly. If an actor is right for the part, emotionally and physically, the director will be rewarded. The director may have selected the actor after hearing just a few lines read and instinctively felt that this was the person for the role. Of course, the judgment is not confirmed until the actor has fully entered into character, with makeup and wardrobe completed for the visual impression. Even in character roles that do not demand the addition of makeup or wardrobe, the true actor will *look* the part after starting to *feel* the part. This getting into character by a stage actor is usually done standing in the wings preparatory to making an entrance. In films, a different set of circumstances prevails, too often to the detriment of the player. Attempting to get into character, the film actor searches the floor for the chalk mark and dodges the assistant cameraman's tape measure while bells ring frantically; the assistant director shouts for quiet, and the sound slate claps loudly right under the actor's nose. The director calls "action," and the actor is expected to make you believe that she is truly shaken by the news that her husband has left her for another woman.

Early film directors gave instructions to their actors by using the word *register.* "Register surprise," they would say, and the actors would respond promptly with quivering nostrils, raised eyebrows and popping eyes. Today, the good actor gets to the root of the emotion, imagining the mental and emotional processes that the character would go through. The actor's face and eyes will show a change all right, but not with a superficial expression, rather with something real. The actor doesn't register; the actor creates.

Sometimes a leading role will be filled before the director has been assigned; and if there has been no time for rehearsals or preproduction conferences, a player will walk on the set with a preconceived idea of characterization not in accord with the author's, the producer's or the director's idea.

Roy Huggins, whose success with *Maverick* at Warner Bros. catapulted him into the vice-presidency of 20th Century–Fox television, had fashioned a political satire that I had been assigned to direct. Before starting to shoot *How Does Charlie Feel?*, which starred Cliff Robertson and Diana Lynn, Huggins and I discussed the pitfalls in this kind of comedy; the actors were to play it straight, right from the heart, just as they would in a drama. The situation would provide the humor; the actors should at no time try to be funny.

After the first day's shooting, it became apparent to me that Miss Lynn was not in tune with our philosophy. Although a capable and talented dramatic actress of considerable experience, she was playing it strictly for farce. After each take, I tried different ways to convince her that we were not making a wacky comedy and that a more honest approach to her characterization was in order. Miss Lynn, a beautiful but strong-willed leading lady, seemed to agree, but still when the cameras rolled for each successive take, her performance changed very little.

That night, I pondered over a way to get her to change her concept, since the next day her truly important scenes would be coming up. It has never been my nature to create "scenes," to harangue or to direct in a dictatorial manner. Causing angry exchanges on the set can lead only to production delays—a thing no television show can afford. So, having a showdown was out. I had to find some subtle way to bring her into accord with the dictates of the script. I finally decided on writing myself a note, ostensibly from producer Huggins. The note would point out the trouble with Miss Lynn's performance and order several scenes retaken. I called Huggins at home, and he agreed to this method and even the forging of his name on the letter.

The next day, the assistant director, who also got a copy of the note, showed it to Miss Lynn. It pointed out that if, in comedies of this nature, the actors were having a ball, it was a certainty that the audience would not. The retakes were made, and Diana Lynn gave the performance that she had always been capable of. After that, whenever there occurred a tendency to slip back into her previous style, I merely alluded to the fact that I was sure that when Mr. Huggins saw the dailies another retake would be ordered. It worked fine, and Diana Lynn was both attractive and sympathetic in the part. No actor enjoys having scenes reshot while the other members of the cast and crew stand by watching.

Although standard practice in the legitimate theater has long been to not correct line readings until full memorization takes place and the character begins to take shape, the opposite is true in motion pictures. Perhaps the reason for this is due to the brief rehearsal period, sometimes less than five minutes before an actor must "go on." Whatever the reason, correcting misreadings and mispronunciations in early rehearsals seems to prevent the eventual forming of small mental blocks while filming a

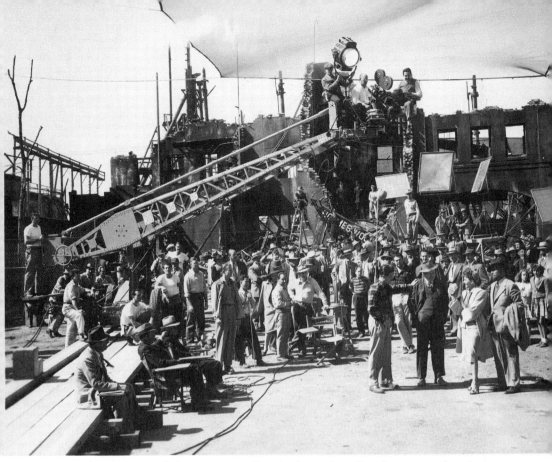

When you see all those names roll up in the end credits, do you wonder why it takes so many people to make a movie? Here are some of those people, and they are only the shooting crew.

take. Many times, the misreadings are due to the actor's lack of understanding of the content of the scene and can be corrected easily. Other times, an actor may continue to misread a line because he or she believes that way to be the right one, or the actor may be *tone deaf* and lack the proper *ear* to hear the line any other way.

I have never seen a script so perfectly written that it justified the producer demanding that "not a line be changed." The fact that an actor transposes, interpolates or otherwise changes a line does not in itself become a violation. Only when the actor changes the meaning behind a line, or disrupts the next actor's cue, is it time to insist on "sticking to the script." Often a better performance will result when the actor puts the thoughts expressed by the line into his or her own particular phrasing. The director who disallows this freedom does a disservice, for restricting the actor in this respect hampers the free flow of creativity so important

Director Blake Edwards poses with his whipped-cream-covered cast after the pie-throwing sequence of *The Great Race*. Almost identifiable are: Tony Curtis, center, in white; and standing on table, left to right, Jack Lemmon, Natalie Wood and Peter Falk. (Warner Bros.)

to obtaining a perfect scene. It will be perfect not because every word is delivered as the author wrote it, but because the idea behind the words is interpreted in a way natural to the character.

I have known actors who, because of their own lack of concentration, couldn't retain even the idea behind the dialogue. The more they would blow a line, the angrier they would get, and the first and logical target to attack was the writer. Invariably, they use the same lines in expressing their vitriol, "How can anybody remember stupid words like these?"

It is true that well-written lines are learned more quickly than cumbersome or *non sequitir* dialogue. However, just as often these attacks on the writer are defensive maneuvers by the actors, designed to cover up their own inadequacy.

Sometimes actors can remember pages of dialogue but have trouble with one small line. I have known actors to write the line on a slip of paper and hide it behind a vase or some other object on the set.

Actors study their lines in many different ways. Some stay up half the night, pacing the floor while being cued by a friend or relative. Others get up early in the morning and, with a fresh and rested mind, absorb dialogue with ease. Many actors never look at their lines until they are seated in the makeup chair before the day's long shooting, and then there are the lazy ones who wait until they can walk the rehearsals with the scripts in their hands.

The quickest study I ever worked with was John Carradine, who read a script just once and remembered every line, word for word. He was blessed with a so-called photographic memory and could digest pages of dialogue with great facility.

Years ago on *Dragnet*, Jack Webb made what he considered a virtue of the problem of memorization. He simply banned it. No actor was permitted to learn lines; rather, Jack preferred the actors to read their lines off a machine called the TeleprompTer, which contained a large roll of paper on which is printed the dialogue. The machine was controlled by an operator, and the lines appeared in front of the actor at whatever speed the actor chose to deliver them.

Webb accomplished one thing with this technique. He was able to lop off many hours of shooting time through the virtual elimination of successive takes. In less skilled hands, this technique can produce stilted performances and many actors cannot adjust at all to the TeleprompTer.

Among people in show business there is an axiom that performing for movies isn't acting, it's *reacting*. Actors who merely stand, frozen faced, waiting for their cues and then speaking their lines, are doing only half the job they are being paid for. *Listening* can be one of the most important single techniques in the actors' repertoires, and they must *listen in character*. During rehearsals, actors have listened for cues and listened to the remarks of the director and cinematographer, but once the camera starts to turn, they must listen to the other actors' words as if *hearing them for the first time*. This is important, for unless they can accomplish this, the scene will not carry with it the illusion that it is being performed in reality. If a player steps out of character while another is speaking and doesn't properly react through listening, the scene will result in a disjointed, one-sided affair. Conversely, if an actor listens as if interested and hearing something for the first time, then thinks over the reply before delivering his or her line, a well-executed scene will result. An axiom of the drama is to "pick up your cues." However, sometimes too much emphasis can be placed on this rapid-fire delivery, and the scene suffers because the actors don't seem to be *listening*.

The alert and sensitive director will be quick to recognize when an actor *anticipates*. Since all drama is based on the premise that what is transpiring is happening for the first time, the actor who turns the head in anticipation of a sudden sound, or opens the door as if knowing who is on the other side, is guilty of anticipation.

A scene that "plays," in other words comes alive with vitality or emotion, is usually a *master shot*. The actors were all in the same shot together and received the benefit of contact with one another. But, the demands of the film business require that the director *break it up*, or *cover* with additional shots, usually closer angles. When this happens, the director comes to grips with a very real problem, that of re-creating the same spark from the actors when perhaps only one of them is on camera at the time with the others reading their lines off camera. In the master, there was no problem with *overlapping*, that is, picking up cues so fast that one actor starts to speak before the other actor finishes. But now the sound recordist cautions the director before each close-up is shot, "No overlaps, please." The director explains to the neophytes that the film editor cannot make clean cuts on the sound track unless there is a separation of the spoken lines. This observance of the recordist's request can change the flow of the scene considerably and can result in shots that lack the vitality of the master. One way to solve this is to design the shooting in such a manner as to film fast- moving and overlapping dialogue with a fluid camera, getting the entire scene in one continuous shot. If the actors are moved about, constantly changing position, with the camera dollying in and out accenting first one and then another in close-up, many times a much better scene will result.

The director may determine that a key line of dialogue is worthy of emphasis, and will suggest that the actor pause just before delivering the line. Or, the director may place emphasis on the line by having the actor rise or sit or walk toward the camera into a close-up. There are many ways to emphasize a line—by repetition, raising volume, lowering volume or making it an exit line—and the director should decide which is appropriate to the scene.

If the locale of the film being directed is a foreign country, the question of accents will arise, usually in conferences with the producer before the start of the picture. Hollywood has always tended to require its actors to "flavor" their speech with the accent indigenous to the country that is being depicted. Yet, how wrong this seems when one reverses the situation and imagines German actors doing *A Streetcar Named Desire* in German with an American accent. A better rule to follow is this: When English-speaking actors portray characters in their native land, let them speak a neutral Standard American diction.

Stanley Kramer, who produced and directed *Judgment at Nuremberg*, solved a touchy translation problem in an imaginative way. As each witness was called to the stand and started speaking in German, the camera traveled inside the translation booth where the witness's words were heard in English as spoken by the translators. As the camera moved back to the witness, he or she continued to speak, but this time in English. Audiences accepted the device, grateful not to have to read the translation in subtitles.

Although all players should be well trained in the rudiments of acting, they may not be experienced in the mechanics of film acting, especially if they are from the theater.

An *on-camera* turn means that the actors turn with their face nearest the camera. An *off-camera* turn means turning in front of the camera with the face upstage or away from the camera.

In crossing, actors maintain strength by crossing in front of the other actors or making a downstage cross. If the director wishes an actor to be dominated by the other players, the actor makes an upstage cross. When two characters cross during dialogue, the upstage (and more important) actor walks slightly ahead of the other player.

In vaudeville, there was a stage area known as *in one*. It was as far downstage as the actors could get without stepping into the footlights. When two actors stand almost shoulder to shoulder in a two-shot facing the camera instead of each other, the *in one* feeling is reproduced. Comedy scenes are often filmed with this camera treatment. When one of the characters in this shot decides to make an exit, he or she should make a *long* side exit, with the camera slowly centering on the actor who is left behind. The actor who pops out of a scene on the short side of the frame actually gets away too fast, unless the camera pans with the exit.

Opening and closing doors sometimes can be awkward even for experienced stage actors. The ability to glide gracefully through a door is still one of the hardest for actors to master. If the door is on one side of the set, an actor making an entrance should grasp the knob with one hand, swing the door open, then pass through and, without breaking the rhythm, grasp the knob with the other hand and close it from behind.

The staging of a love scene, especially if photographed in full figure, should seem easy and natural, and skillful players usually have no difficulty. But with less skilled players, the director should strive for a graceful and believable scene. The two actors embracing should stand close to one another; any other position would appear awkward. The position of the feet must be predetermined to avoid sudden collisions upon embracing. When the director shoots the same embrace in close-up, he or she must decide whose face is to be featured at the moment of the kiss or full embrace. The scene should be unhurried, with the accent placed on anticipation of the actual kiss, longing in the eyes, hands moving slowly upward to touch the shoulders or neck. And when the kiss is finished, it should not end too abruptly, but the players should linger again with their eyes, hands withdrawing slowly.

Let's consider the ingredients that make any kiss romantic. A soft June night, a full moon, a quiet country lane—and solitude. In pictures, you have the full moon and the country lane, even though they may be made of plaster of Paris and plywood. But solitude? If you don't count the director, the camera crew, six grips and twelve electricians, you might say the actors are alone.

In the staging and direction of death and murder scenes, great care must be given to avoid the overemotional and the "hammy." Although expert direction and performances coupled with a convincing story can lull an audience into a sense that they are watching reality, no one for a moment believes it when a player dies or gets killed, and, therefore, the director should strive for truth. If an actor has been shot and the script calls for him to be in great pain, his vitality should be at a low ebb, for nothing mars a death scene as much as an actor speaking his last words in full voice or gesticulating with energy.

If an actress dies in bed, for example, she should be immobile, her voice barely audible, her speech broken. When death comes, the head should relax and fall slightly to one side. Sometimes cinematographers will alter the light on the face from a natural skin tone to a grayish hue.

When a western character takes an imaginary .45 slug, the actor should either spin out or topple over backward. One may think the spin has been exaggerated by the movies, but in truth those western bullets crashed into a human being with tremendous force, sometime knocking a man five or six feet. One only has to remember the bloody death scenes on Omaha Beach in Spielberg's *Saving Private Ryan* to realize how far it is possible to go in depicting the horrors of death on screen.

Every actor will appreciate the director's help in devising bits of business to go with dialogue. The average television script has been so hurriedly written that many times the writer only bothers to set down the dialogue, and it is incumbent on the director to provide pantomime action to further characterize the players. When I directed the pilot of *77 Sunset Strip*, I told Edd Byrnes, who played "Kooky," to comb his hair during one of the scenes. Six years later, it was still his trademark and even the subject of a popular recording.

Perhaps the most difficult actors to direct are those who have become directors themselves. Because they know the director's secrets, they are more inclined to have opinions of their own regarding staging, camera treatment and even of the performances of other actors.

Sometimes directors make hit pictures without seeming to direct. For instance, Esther Williams, the famous swimming star of a series of MGM musicals, has this to say in her 1999 autobiography, *Million Dollar Mermaid*: "I had been looking forward to having Mervyn LeRoy's expertise behind the camera. Because of the movies he'd done before, such as *Random Harvest* and *Waterloo Bridge*, I had expected great insight and sensitivity, especially in dealing with the romantic part of the story line. It didn't happen. He wasn't the perceptive director I thought he would be. There's one dramatic sequence near the end of the movie where the glass wall of a diving tank shatters, and my back is broken as I'm pushed through the jagged opening in a surge of water and broken glass. As we got ready to shoot, all Mervyn said was, 'Let's have a nice little scene.'"

According to Williams, she had no idea how that "direction" was supposed to help her performance. No matter whether they were doing a love scene, a fight scene or an action sequence, LeRoy would always say the same thing: "Let's have a nice little scene."

Since Mervyn LeRoy was a highly skilled director, always used to directing highly skilled actors, it may have seemed to the beautiful swimming star that he really wasn't giving any direction, but the truth of the matter lies in the fact that LeRoy considered Esther Williams an accomplished professional.

After the first run-through, the director sizes up the cast. Those who need direction get it. Those who have a clear understanding of their characters may only be told where to stand and when to cross to the window. The finest actors need the least direction.

As a last word regarding the director's relationship with the actors, beware of the "close-up actor." This actor is the one, usually an old-time Hollywood player, who knows all the tricks. He or she has been known to fluff lines deliberately in a group shot when sharing honors with several others, because the actor knows that this is one way to force the director to cover his or her performance in a close-up. Strangely enough, the actor is always letter perfect when the camera comes in close. Fortunately, among the thousands of actors in the movies and television today, the person who stoops to this kind of chicanery is in the minority.

Generally speaking, the director and actors provide a solid super-structure to the foundation of the picture and the story. With mutual admiration and respect, all can work together to create the ultimate in dramatic achievement—entertainment.

THE SERIOUS FIELD OF COMEDY

Years ago when this business was in its infancy, some harried producer uttered the now classic remark, "Our comedies are not to be laughed at!" What the director meant was that turning out comedy film is a serious and exacting affair.

Although my own career started in comedy and I have directed more than 300 comedies, when I think of writing a chapter on the subject I realize how little can be put down on paper on the subject. The director who doesn't already *know* how to do it shouldn't attempt it. Unless it's within his or her unconscious nature to construct the tricky flow of comedy action, perfectly timed and properly staged from the correct angle of approach; unless he or she possesses a personal sense of humor and an appreciation for *all* humor, the director should stay in another field. However, there are several basics that can be passed on to the newcomer.

The pace of comedy is, of course, faster than in drama, but it should never be so frantic that there is no time for reactions. The funniest part of a Laurel and Hardy comedy was Ollie's reactions to Laurel's antics, and vice versa. Laurel scratched the top of his head and Hardy fussed with his necktie while reacting to some nonsensical bit of slapstick.

When an actor reads a funny line, it is funnier if another actor can play off the line, rather than going on with his or her own line. In television comedy, these reactions are mandatory to provide the spaces for laugh tracks.

Normally, a good comedy director avoids long walks by the actors. Instead of the door opening and the actor making an entrance and walking across the room to the fireplace, camera panning, it is better to take one shot of the player coming through the door and exiting the shot.

In directing television comedy, anything goes, just as long as all of Eva Gabor's charms are covered with soap bubbles. A scene from *Green Acres*, directed by Richard L. Bare. (Filmways)

Then set up at the fireplace and let the actor enter this shot. What has been eliminated is five to ten seconds of unimportant movement and a consequent slowing down of the story. A staccato treatment in cutting is helpful in giving the scenes the pace they need, but it should not be so frantic that it shortens the reactions of the people.

An ironclad rule of comedy is that comedians should never laugh at their own jokes. Play it straight, the experts maintain. The ensemble cast of accomplished actors in NBC's delightful sitcom *Friends* are always sincere and never clown around—they believe the situations and take them seriously. And above all, they react. A comic situation in its total construction closely resembles a tragic one, and for the actors to be convincing, they must take it seriously.

Schopenhauer's theory of laughter maintains that we laugh when there is a sudden incongruity between concept and percept. This is important to remember, especially the word "sudden." Almost all comedy depends on the sudden incongruity to tickle our funny bones.

Suppose an actor enters a restaurant, goes to the counter and sees a sign: "Our Food Untouched by Human Hands." The actor then looks beyond the counter and into the kitchen and sees a huge gorilla making hamburger patties. The laughter comes with the *sudden incongruity*. The secret is to not show the gorilla in the long shot that brings the actor into the restaurant.

The degree of ridiculousness of the incongruity determines the amount of laughter. I once shot a scene that had an actor carrying on a conversation with his friend at a lunch counter. He was eating a piece of pie when the waitress came along and cleared the dishes, taking away his partly eaten pie.

"Hey, I've only had one bite out of that!" the actor exclaimed.

With that, the waitress reached in the pie display, took out a fresh piece, took one bite out of it and placed it on the counter. The secret was to not tip off the audience what the waitress was about to do. She had to act like she was going to give the man a new piece of pie. When she took the bite, it had to be done quickly so the incongruity between the concept and percept would be sudden. It was a belly laugh in the theater.

The modern philosopher David H. Monro, in his *Argument of Laughter*, has compiled a list of ten familiar circumstances that will produce laughter:

1. Any breach of the usual order of events, such as eating with chopsticks when one is accustomed to forks.
2. Any forbidden breach of the usual order, such as belching in public.
3. Any indecency, such as a man caught outside his house in his underwear.
4. Any importing into one situation that which belongs in another, such as a drunk at a funeral service.
5. Anything masquerading as something it is not, such as two people in a horse costume.
6. Plays on words, such as puns, spoonerisms, etc.
7. Nonsense, such as television's *3rd Rock From the Sun.*
8. Minor misfortunes, such as a man who slips on a banana peel.
9. Any incompetence, such as the paperhanger who gets tangled up in his paper.
10. Veiled insults (Wife: "To you, marriage is just a word." Husband: "It's more than a word; it's a sentence.").

Schopenhauer's theory of laughter maintains that we laugh when there is a sudden incongruity between concept and percept. In this scene, the incongruity came when the above shot followed the insert of a sign, "Our Food Untouched by Human Hands." (Warner Bros.)

Although Monro can tell us the things we laugh at, he cannot with any accuracy tell us why we laugh. He concedes that to analyze a joke, or to track a comic situation to its source, is to make it disappear.

Often a comedy writer will write a funny line of dialogue and yet when it is delivered by an actor, it fails to get a laugh. This sometimes can be explained by showing that the actual laugh or the high point of the line is buried in the middle instead of at the end where it belongs. Here the director, by inverting the line, that is, placing the word or combination of words that provoke the laughter at the end of the line, can not only ensure the laugh but, in the case of television comedy, prevent the canned laugh track from covering the dialogue.

The full execution of comedy is not a simple matter. The first time that many actors rehearse a scene, they will come up with marvelous nuances of expression or mannerisms. By the time the camera starts to roll, they have already lost some of the freshness they had in the first rehearsal. That is why I never over-rehearse a comedy scene, and if at all possible, I will print the first take. It takes an exceptionally skillful comedy technician to bring spontaneity to the eighth take.

It is important for the director to keep a relaxed atmosphere on the set. The director who goes around scowling and who won't allow some levity among cast and crew has no place in comedy directing. The actors, particularly, must relax and enjoy their work; otherwise the scene will lack the brightness and life so necessary to the playing of good comedy.

I can think of no other comedy director as talented as James Burrows. He has cocreated and/or directed *The Mary Tyler Moore Show, Taxi, Lou Grant, Cheers, Frasier* and *Night Court,* each long running and each very funny. He says: "Situation comedy is a collaborative medium. If there is a creative impact from all sides of a show, the energy will be on the screen. It is about everybody making character relationships real."

Burrows says this about taking chances: "Don't back off, sitcom directors. Go in there with guns blazing, and if you end up dead in the street—you can always try drama."

Jim Abrahams, who directed *Big Business, Hot Shots* and *Hot Shots, Part Deux,* and codirected with the Zucker Brothers *Airplane, Ruthless People* and *Naked Gun,* has this to say about directing comedy: "You have to find a genre that takes itself seriously like cop movies. Then you have to find an actor who has a sense of humor about himself and doesn't take himself too seriously. Charlie Sheen, Leslie Neilsen and Robert Stack don't take themselves seriously. Beyond that, the next step is to ask them to play it like a real movie."

Working with animals is also a part of directing comedy. Almost every television situation show involves a dog, monkey or some kind of animal. For five years, I directed the most difficult, the most temperamental and the "hammiest" animal actor ever to gain stardom in Hollywood—Arnold, the pig. The creation of Jay Sommers, the producer of *Green Acres,* Arnold found his way into the hearts of millions of television fans. His mail, believe it or not, was enormous. And warranted. Arnold signed his name with a crayon. Arnold turned on the television set. Arnold played the piano. He wore dark glasses, a French beret, and a World War I helmet and goggles. He laughed, cried and carried his books to school, where I believe he was in the third grade when the show ended.

Directing animals requires infinite patience and a thorough knowledge of how to trick a performance out of them, in other words, making

Working with animals is not the easiest of the director's multitude of chores, although Arnold of *Green Acres* was one of the most accomplished four-footed actors in Hollywood. "He's a real method pig," said director Bare. (Filmways-CBS)

the animal appear to be giving a human response. I've dangled a live mouse in front of a dog to inspire an alert expression. Other times I've used a small rubber squeaker to make a kitten sit up and cock its head. But, with Arnold, my approach was on a higher level—I baited him with caramels and then whispered two words in his ear, "Oscar Mayer."

chapter eleven

CHAPTER ELEVEN

CREATING A JOB
FOR YOURSELF

FROM STUDENT TO PROFESSIONAL

The aspiring director can read books such as this one, can take courses in cinema and dramatics at a university, can make superb student films and then come to grips with a most perplexing question, "How do I get a job as a director?"

Let's take the case of one film school graduate searching for a place in the entertainment industry. This young person may be armed with a list of contacts, have letters of introduction or be endowed with such an engaging personality that he or she manages to get the ear of an important producer. The young graduate exudes self-confidence while articulately presenting a formidable case for employment, maintaining that he or she will bring rich and imaginative skill to a directing assignment—if only given the chance. The aspiring director will, no doubt, hear a time-worn phrase, "Get a little experience; then come back and see us."

HOW CAN YOU GET EXPERIENCE IF NO ONE WILL GIVE YOU A JOB?

This is the problem and it is a serious one. But, it is not insurmountable, as I found out years ago. In fact, when I made the leap from amateur to professional, it was perhaps at the worst possible time in terms of the economic condition of the motion picture business. Today, with the tremendous output of television films, more directors work every week than ever before, when only theatrical pictures were being made. The opportunity for the director to get that first chance is much simpler today, because of the less rigid demands for perfection that television has brought about. It is one thing to take a chance on a new director by assigning him to an episode of a TV show, and it's another to entrust him with a multimillion dollar movie.

As I outlined in a previous chapter, people become directors in a variety of ways. They are elevated from other jobs within the industry; they come from the legitimate stage; they distinguish themselves in college film productions; or they simply create a job for themselves.

Dennis and Terry Sanders, while in school at the University of California at Los Angeles, produced a twenty-three minute 35-mm dramatic production, *A Time Out of War*. Dennis directed and Terry photographed. When it was completed, the brothers arranged to have it exhibited on television. This led to a theatrical distribution deal with Universal, and, to date, Dennis and Terry Sanders have made more than $20,000 in profit from their labor of love. The film won an Academy Award for best theatrical short subject and won a similar honor at the Venice Film Festival. Since those days, Terry Sanders has received another Academy Award, five Academy nominations and an Emmy for TV shows such as *Maya Lin: A Strong Clear Vision, Lillian Gish, Slow Fires, Four Stones for Kanemitsu* and *To Live or Let Die*.

Paul Wendkos has had a strong interest in films since his days at the University of Pennsylvania. After graduation, he studied film at Columbia University and then started making documentary films for the State Department. His first attempt at commercial filmmaking came when he directed *The Burglar*, which Columbia later acquired. He considers this film a failure resulting from too much ambition combined with too little experience, but from it he began to develop a style that carried him through a score of feature films such as *Guns of the Magnificent Seven* and *Angel Baby*, the latter receiving festival showings at Venice and Berlin.

Sydney Pollack studied acting under Sanford Meisner and then served as his assistant for five years, an apprenticeship that has given him a keen insight into the sensitivities of actors. He appeared in several Broadway productions and the old *Playhouse 90* series. This led to a lasting friendship with director John Frankenheimer, who encouraged him to go to Hollywood, where he got his first chance to direct a television western. He later won an Emmy for *The Game* on the Chrysler Theater program. His first feature assignment was *The Slender Thread*. Sydney Pollack was well on his way to becoming one of the elite, bankable directors after he made *This Property Is Condemned*, with Natalie Wood and Robert Redford; *The Way We Were*, with Redford and Barbra Streisand; and *Three Days of the Condor*, with Redford and Faye Dunaway.

One director who made the transition from student filmmaker to professional came by way of a thorough background in the arts. Irvin Kershner studied painting under Hans Hoffman in Providence, and music at Temple University. After transferring to the University of Southern California (USC), he decided to concentrate his interests in the field of cinema. Already an accomplished still photographer, his work became an integral part of a book illustrating a collection of rare musical instruments. The artistry of the photographs caused more interest than the instruments themselves, and soon young Kershner had a job shooting documentary movies overseas for the United States government. This led to a combined director-cameraman's job on a local television show in Los Angeles called *Confidential File*. But Kershner had higher ambitions, so he and Andrew J. Fenady raised $30,000 and turned out a black-and-white feature picture, *Stakeout on Dope Street*. Warner Bros. promptly bought it outright for a handsome profit to the youthful producer and director. Today, after many films, including the James Bond feature *Never Say Never Again* and George Lucas's *The Empire Strikes Back*, Kershner's films continue to demonstrate his sound, artistic, photographic and musical background.

Mark Rydell was a jazz musician who tired of the night life, so he decided to become an actor. His fellow students at Lee Strasberg's Actors Studio were Steve McQueen and Sydney Pollack. When Rydell came to Hollywood, Pollack introduced him to a producer in television, and soon he had his first chance to direct. After forty television shows, he was given his first feature film, *The Fox*. When Steve McQueen saw what his former classmate could do, he welcomed him as director of *The Reivers*.

John Cluett and Harry Mastrogeorge got together and produced a $60,000 mini-feature called *Cabbages and Kings*, which starred New York model Samantha Jones. Cluett produced and played one of the leading roles, and Mastrogeorge directed, having been Cluett's teacher at the American Academy of Dramatic Arts in New York. They hired a young graduate from UCLA's cinema department as their cameraman and got all the actors and crew members to work for practically nothing. He went on to direct *Hart to Hart* and *The Mary Tyler Moore Show*.

Michael Bay, director of *Armageddon*, went to Art Center Film School in Los Angeles, where he graduated and started making music videos. After creating his own style of shooting, he put together a demo reel of his best work. CAA, the most influential talent agency in Hollywood, saw the reel and took him to see Jerry Bruckheimer and Don Simpson, who browbeat him for six hours and then assigned him to direct *Bad Boys*, his first feature. He says, "I came from wanting to be a photographer as a kid. I like to shoot my own stuff." His next film was the successful *The Rock*, and that led him right into the megahit, *Armageddon*. But Bay still does commercials and has won almost every commercial award during the past eight years.

John Sayles has written and directed eleven films, most of which were low-budget and produced away from Hollywood. A later film, *Men with Guns*, was shot in Mexico and is strong in theme but without a single car crash.

Sayles started writing when he was in the fourth grade. After Williams College (where he took no cinema classes), he got a job in a meat-packing plant, but he continued to write, hoping to augment his meager paycheck. He finally found a publisher for the novel *Pride of the Bimbos* and started acting in summer stock. A friend urged him to write a screenplay, and Sayles tried his hand and found there was nothing mysterious about the screen technique. He sent his first, *Eight Men Out*, to a quickie producer, Roger Corman, who rejected his script but admired his style as a writer. He was hired to write a thriller, *Piranha*, and then Sayles was hooked on the movie business. He raised $40,000 and made *Return of the Seacaucus*, which he directed himself. About his reluctance to compete in Hollywood, he says: "I don't want to be a director for hire. I don't want to make someone else's story. I enjoy making my own movies and I want to keep telling my own stories until I run out of them."

One of the first black directors to make an all-white movie is Forest Whitaker, an ex-actor. His successful *Hope Floats*, with Sandra Bullock and Harry Connick, Jr., is an example of Whitaker's sensitive understanding of the human condition.

In an interview with Darrel L. Hope in DGA magazine, Whitaker comments on rehearsing: "I haven't done a film where I haven't had rehearsals. On *Hope Floats* we rehearsed in the house so the actors knew how to walk from room to room, put something here or there. The cast feels different when they sit on a couch they have already sat on or have smelled a place and touched the walls."

Whitaker, by the way, is a director who thinks that the possessory credit (A Film by _____) is warranted and that it represents the director's vision.

Richard Rush, director of the award-winning *The Stunt Man*, studied cinema at UCLA. After graduation, he worked in Hollywood as a messenger, recording engineer and still photographer. Then he went to an advertising agency, where he got his first chance to work with film on commercials. A few years later he owned his own commercial production company, which led to feature filmmaking. He produced, directed and cowrote *Too Soon to Love*, which was shot in record time and cost only $50,000. When he showed it to Universal, they promptly made a deal that netted Rush and his backers some $200,000.

Rush has this to say to the graduating film student: "If you want to be a director, direct. That's not so difficult nowadays. Working in 35-mm film is expensive, but 8-mm isn't. And the things that cost the most in a studio—the actors, sets, scripts, etc.—are free to the amateur. The only cost is camera and film."

The young director should not shy away from exercising authority just because of youth. There was a time when most actors sought the

Sydney Pollack explains what he wants to Burt Lancaster during the shooting of *The Scalphunters*, a surprisingly good western that was made on a modest budget. Once an actor himself, Pollack came to Hollywood to direct television and made the switch into features after winning an Emmy for his direction on the Chrysler Theatre. (United Artists)

"father image" in their director, and this worked when the director was older or of comparable age. It was rare that a valuable star's reputation was put into the hands of a new, unproved director. But today things have changed . . . considerably. Most theatrical films are made for a youthful audience. It is entirely fitting that they be directed by young directors.

At least one student filmmaker turned his college cinema class into a production center for films with calculated commercial possibilities. Martin Scorsese was too sickly as a child to engage in sports, so his father encouraged him to go into movies. After seeing his first western movie, he was hooked; after seeing *Citizen Kane* on television, he started to understand what a director could do. When Scorsese got to college, he enrolled in every cinema class that New York University (NYU) had to offer and soon was making his own films. His first one was a nine-minute, black-and-white comedy, *What's a Nice Girl Like You Doing in a Place Like This?* The short film won four first prize awards, including the National Student Film Award. His next project, the two-reel *It's Not You, Murray!*, not only won more prizes, including the Jesse L. Lasky Intercollegiate Award of the Screen Producers' Guild, but was distributed commercially. Scorsese, encouraged by the reception given his first two shorts, then decided to make a feature picture. Having graduated from NYU meanwhile, the young moviemaker promptly enrolled in the college's Graduate School of Arts for the purpose of providing himself with a base of operations for his projected film. He wrote a script; then in January 1965 he started shooting in 35 mm, a new milestone in his picture-making activities. Shooting on weekends, Scorsese soon ran out of money, but he had seventy minutes of film in the can.

"The total cost of those seventy minutes was $6,000," says Scorsese. "I got this money by taking out student loans and my father taking out a few bank loans. After we ran out of money, we printed up what we had, even though we knew it wasn't quite ready to be shown. This was an error. I figured I would show the seventy minutes around and raise money to finish the film, but instead many of the people who were excited by 'Murray' were turned off when they saw the half-completed film. The experiment was a total loss, no feature, no jobs, and no money."

For fifteen months Scorsese did odd jobs with New York film companies, including one as a film editor that netted him $350 for two months' work. He had practically written off the idea of ever finishing his feature picture. As he recalls: "Finally, at the end of 1966, my past professor from NYU, Haig Manoogian, formed a movie company with Joseph Weill. They felt that my picture (which was called *Dancing Girls*) had some scenes in it and that if the original script was revised a bit we would have a good picture. We started with $5,000 and finally wound up spending $30,000 in cash. Most of the cast and crew deferred most of their salaries. We began shooting the new scenes in February of 1967 and finished four weeks later. The picture was now titled *I Call First*. While we waited for acceptances from foreign film festivals (which never came), I worked as a news film editor at CBS. Ten months later the picture was accepted into the third Chicago Film Festival."

This was the impetus young Scorsese needed. Roger Ebert of the *Chicago Sun-Times* called the film "A new classic . . . absolutely genuine, artistically satisfying and technically comparable to the best films being made anywhere."

Of course, the title would have to be changed and a few scenes added. The final title became *Who's That Knocking at My Door?*

Finally, in March of 1969, four years and two months after he started shooting at NYU, Martin Scorsese's first feature had its world premiere in Chicago. The press were almost unanimous in their praise. *Time* magazine said that the film ". . . introduces a young director who just may turn out to be one of the brighter talents of this eager new generation." The *Chicago Tribune* added, "Made by 25-year-old Martin Scorsese, the film is sharp, rewarding, often witty, a film highlighted by incredible tuned dialogue." The usually reserved *New York Times* commented, "Scorsese is obviously a competent young filmmaker . . . he has composed a fluid, technically proficient movie, more intense and more sincere than most commercial releases."

One would think that a film that survived the agonies of postponed production and then went on to critical acclaim, would, in turn, recompense its makers for their efforts.

"It didn't," says Scorsese. "The picture opened in New York at Carnegie Hall Cinema and in several other cities. The film got good reviews but didn't make money."

Scorsese went back to NYU as an instructor in cinema. Two years later Roger Corman remembered seeing *Who's That Knocking at My Door* and got in touch with Scorsese and offered him the director's job on *Boxcar Bertha*. Today, Martin Scorsese is one of the most eminent directors among Hollywood's elite.

An outstanding success story of a student turned professional is that of Francis Ford Coppola. He earned his master's degree at UCLA by making a commercial movie as his thesis. He wrote a script called *You're a Big Boy Now*, raised the money to shoot the picture (some $80,000), and

Although he has yet to win the Oscar for Best Director, Martin Scorsese has made many artistic and thoughtful films. He is at the forefront of Hollywood's concerted effort to restore deteriorating old movies that were printed on nitrate stock.

One-time wunderkind Francis Ford Coppola continues to make movies "his way," and he finds that locating his company, Zoetrope, in San Francisco furthers that cause. He has directed three *Godfather* movies as well as *Apocalypse Now* and *The Rainmaker.* (Zoetrope Prods.)

Creating a Job for Yourself   211

produced and directed it himself. The film gained an Oscar nomination for its star, Geraldine Page. Soon after, Coppola was directing *Finian's Rainbow*, an expensive supermusical for Warner Bros. After that he was offered a contract that gave him complete autonomy; he did not have to obtain the studio's approval of stories. He wanted to return to making the "personal" film, and his first was *The Rain People*. He shot his film in *cinéma vérité* style, following the actors across the United States with a company of twenty and a truck that carried all of the highly mobile camera and sound equipment. Coppola says, "I use what you would call a relentless camera—a single shot for as long as eight or ten minutes. The camera just stays and watches; when you are scrutinizing a human thing you don't have to cut."

Truly an exponent of *auteur* theory, Coppola can claim to be the central force behind his films. He is the director of *The Godfather* and the two sequels, as well as *Apocalypse Now*, Bram Stoker's *Dracula* and *The Rainmaker*. He shuns Hollywood and runs his own company, Zoetrope, out of San Francisco.

Then there is the ubiquitous Allen Smithee, who seeks no publicity and never gives interviews but has some advice for those wishing to break into the Hollywood establishment. See "The Smithee Doctrine" on the facing page.

THE BILLION-DOLLAR DIRECTORS

1. Steven Spielberg

Since the measure of a film director's talent is calculated on the box-office grosses of the director's films, there are three directors who stand at the top, because their films each have grossed over a billion dollars.

Steven Spielberg is not only the wealthiest man in the motion picture business, but the most versatile and prolific director in history. The giants of the past—De Mille, Ford, Hitchcock, Stevens, Cukor and the director who replaced him on *Gone With the Wind*, Victor Fleming—pale when compared with Steven Spielberg.

How this young man became the brilliant success that he is today can be understood only when you examine his past.

Steven knew exactly what he wanted to do in life from the moment he borrowed his father's 8-mm movie camera and took his first home movies. He made his first film, complete with story and actors, at the age of twelve after the family moved from Cincinnati to Phoenix, Arizona. He

The Smithee Doctrine

1. Go to college, and if you can't get into film school, get into the drama department. Then only act in leading roles that will attract attention to yourself.

2. Become chums with the classmate who, in your opinion, has the best chance of becoming a top Hollywood star.

3. Graduate somewhere near the bottom of the class, and take revenge by writing a screenplay that is a clone of the most recent money-making blockbuster.

4. Take it to a top agent who will read it and agree to represent you. (This may be time consuming and expect a bunch of rejections.)

5. Have your agent package it with his client Tom Cruise, who has reservations about the story.

6. Rewrite the feminine role for Tom's wife, Nicole Kidman. That brings Cruise aboard.

7. When the studio makes an offer for the package, withdraw your script unless they let you direct the movie.

8. When the studio calls your bluff and assigns Spike Lee to direct, don't go all to pieces—keep your dignity and sell them the script.

9. Move to Malibu and look up your old classmate who has become a top martial arts movie star, thus proving that you knew how to pick 'em.

10. Blackmail your old college chum by threatening to tell *Variety* all about the naughty thing he did backstage during the play you two co-starred in. He agrees to let you direct his Karate film, *A Kick in the Pants.* You are now a film director .

followed this with a five-minute western and got his photography merit badge in the Boy Scouts. By the time he was thirteen, he had copped first prize in a film contest with a forty-minute film, *Escape to Nowhere.*

"I really didn't have any formal instruction," recalls Spielberg. "I just started shooting, making over-the-shoulder shots, dolly shots and everything I had seen on television."

When he reached sixteen and was in high school, his grades went down as his craze for filmmaking went up, for he had gone Hollywood in his ambitions. He turned out a 140-minute epic entitled *Firelight*, which took a year to make and was complete with fancy titles, a music score and a dialogue sound track. Even the budget was of astronomical proportions for Steven, a walloping $500. The film was exhibited at the Phoenix Little

Steven Spielberg made 8-mm films at the age of twelve. He crashed the gates of Universal Studios by donning executive garb and waving at the gateman. By the time he was twenty-two, he was directing Joan Crawford. (Universal)

Theatre with searchlights in the sky and all the hoopla of a Hollywood premiere. When Steven counted the money, he had made a profit of over $500. He promptly put the money in his pocket, for he had financed the production entirely with his own funds earned by whitewashing the trunks of fruit trees.

Later at California State College at Long Beach, the enterprising young filmmaker turned out five more films, one in 35 mm. But he was itching to get inside a Hollywood studio. He had taken a guided tour of Universal Studios but was not allowed to see much in the way of actual moviemaking. So he conceived a daring idea. He had noticed while making the studio tour that the Universal executives all wore basically the same clothing, a Brooks Brothers charcoal suit and a black tie. And they had short, establishment-type haircuts. After a trip to the barber shop and a haberdashery, young Spielberg was the picture of a youthful

214   The Film Director

executive. Armed with a briefcase, he walked right through Universal's main gate and waved at the guard. The guard waved back. Steven nosed around the office buildings and found an unoccupied office that he promptly took over. For months he walked in and out of the studio several times a week. Then, tiring of the long walk to the outside parking lot, he went to a sign shop and had a small sign made which read, "Mr. Spielberg," and placed it on a vacant studio parking space. After that, Steven drove onto the studio lot, the guard on the gate waving and friendlier than ever.

When people on the lot would ask him just what it was he did there, he would reply that he was an "official observer." Studio workers, thinking he might be the boss's nephew or some important stockholder's protégé, warmed up to the personable young man. He watched Universal's biggest pictures being made from close range. He talked with top writers, directors and producers, and everyone gladly answered his questions about moviemaking. Then one day a studio payroll employee walked into his "office" and asked him just who he was, his name was nowhere on the studio records. Spielberg, who had absorbed about as much as he was going to from merely observing, told the payroll man the truth, expecting to be summarily tossed off the lot, if not arrested. When the studio bigwigs heard the full story, they were impressed with the young man's audacity and promptly gave him a bigger office in the Executive Tower. But Steve had seen all that there was to see at the valley studio, so he moved his activities over to Columbia Pictures, where he proceeded to walk in the studio gate, waving to the guard, and looking ever so much like he belonged there.

With his observing days over, Spielberg raised $18,000 and started on his first professional film, *Amblin'*, a twenty-minute short about two hitchhikers. When his former friends at Universal saw the film, they signed him to a director's contract. At the age of twenty-two, Steven Spielberg was the youngest member of the Directors Guild and was directing Joan Crawford in a World Premiere feature film for television. Spielberg says of this experience: "I expected hostility when I started on this film, but no one called me 'Hey kid.' As a matter of fact, the older people on the set were the first to accept me. The only ones I had conflict with were the kids my age who thought maybe they could direct as well as I could."

No doubt about it, young Spielberg had *chutzpa* and confidence in his own ability. It was in no time at all before his talent was fully realized and he was given a movie of the week to direct, the gripping suspense film *Duel*. That led to *Jaws* and you know the rest. He's directed six of the world's twenty-five highest-grossing motion pictures, including number two, *Jurassic Park*, that was nudged from the top spot by James Cameron's *Titanic.*

2. James Cameron

Only one director in Hollywood has made a motion picture that

- was one of the most expensive films ever made;
- went almost $70,000,000 over budget;
- became the highest-grossing movie in history, over one billion dollars; and
- was not a one-of-a-kind movie, having been made at least four times before.

If you have not already guessed it, his name is James Cameron and his film is the stupendous *Titanic.*

Cameron is no stranger to high-budget, blockbuster movies fraught with problems. His impressive list is: *Terminator, Terminator II, Judgment Day, Aliens, The Abyss, True Lies* and *Titanic.*

Even with his reputation as a single-minded director, prone to excesses, Cameron was able to convince 20th Century–Fox to bankroll a production about the most famous sea disaster in history. In the studio's opinion, however, the story not only was old hat but would be much too expensive. Still, Cameron had an angle that would keep his version of *Titanic* fresh and unlike any of the other earlier versions. He would start the story with the real life exploration of the shipwreck, bring in a survivor of the catastrophe as a narrator and add a poignant love story that Cameron was sure would bring freshness and pathos to the well-known narrative.

Twentieth Century–Fox, after budgeting the picture at about $110,000,000, brought in Paramount for a substantial part of the financing. Neither studio imagined that the final cost would exceed $180,000,000. To properly bring the realism that Cameron insisted upon, the studio built a 780-foot-long exterior set re-creating portions of the original ship at the water's edge of Rosarita Beach in Baja California. The set was equipped with hydraulic lifts that raised the stern out of the water. The magic of CGI (computer graphics) did the rest.

When *Titanic* was many millions over budget, Cameron offered to forego his salary and backend participation. Reportedly, once the picture was in the theaters and doing monumental business, the studio reinstated his salary and participation.

When James Cameron took on the immense job of recreating the sinking of the *Titanic* on its maiden voyage, he insisted on total realism. He instructed his art director to get the original blueprints from the ship's builder, and 20th Century–Fox was able to construct a full-scale model of the doomed vessel. (Photograph by Merie W. Wallace, Paramount Pictures/20th Century–Fox)

James Cameron was born August 16, 1954 in Kapuskasing, Canada of a middle class family. His father, Phillip Cameron, was an electrical engineer in a paper mill and a disciplinarian who would take no back talk from his son. This relationship of father and son carried over into Cameron's directing style: He's the boss and everyone better toe the line.

After seeing Stanley Kubrick's *2001: A Space Odyssey*, young Jim was hooked. He immediately got a 16-mm camera and started experimenting with models of spaceships, his attention directed more to the special effects than toward writing a script. The family relocated to Orange County, California, and Jim enrolled in Fullerton College to study physics but dropped out and got married. Still, he couldn't get his fascination for special-effects movies out of his head, and he researched every book and journal that could give him the facts he needed to become a special-effects artist.

Now completely absorbed with the idea of breaking into the motion picture business, James Cameron mustered up the courage to go see the man who was known as the "King of the B's"—Roger Corman, who owned New World Pictures and turned out as many as twelve low-budget films a year. When Corman looked at the young man, his arms full of space models, Corman couldn't help but be impressed because he himself was in the process of making several space age movies now that *Star Wars* had become such a giant hit.

Corman gave Cameron a job as a miniature model maker for a picture called *Battle Beyond the Stars*. Within a year, Cameron was in charge of the special-effects department and was watching and learning from the various directors Corman signed, mainly because he could get them cheaply.

John Sayles had made *Piranha,* and since it did well, Corman decided to do a sequel. James Cameron became the director of *Piranha 2,* and even though he subsequently departed the production, he was on his way. After that he wrote *The Terminator* with Gale Anne Hurd, and when it was completed he sold it to her for one dollar. His only proviso was that he direct. It became his first important film.

How he directed the most expensive movie ever made is a fascinating story, and he answered questions about the making of *Titanic* during a symposium at the DGA that I attended. He recalled: "As a director, I was always cursing that son of a bitch writer [himself] for getting me into this mess. The script evolved while I was writing and wondering how could I do something new and still treat it respectfully. I hit on the idea of a love story with fictitious characters—I could do something with great passion so the personal story could be as strong as the passion of the event. Before I visited the real Titanic at the bottom of the sea, I had written a 160-page 'scriptment,' which means that if I can't think of the exact dialogue for a scene, I don't bog down."

At the symposium, interrogator Jeremy Kagan (himself an award-winning director) asked Cameron if he used storyboards. "For this film we built models of the interior space and a 25-foot-long ship model. We had to figure out what was going to be done with computer graphics and what was real life. Everyone looked at our ship and said, 'My God,' but it would have cost even more to do it in CGI because we had over 100 pages to shoot on the deck of the ship. Also, I believe in shooting as much reality as possible because it benefits everybody, not just the actors."

Regarding rehearsals, Cameron had this to say: "I don't like to over-rehearse. We mostly worked on the chemistry between DiCaprio and Kate Winslet. I like to see what actors come up with. Each take was better than the others. My belief is we've spent all these years to get to this moment and to not get the best everyone can do, I think, is foolish."

Kagan wanted to know what was the best thing and the worst thing about directing. Cameron took no time in answering: "The best is when it's done and it's a big hit. But, honestly, the best part for me is the moment of discovery on the set when the actor creates something magical. The worst is when the lights go down at the first preview."

James Cameron is truly an exceptionally creative director and has the track record to prove it. He shoots for the moon, and if he misses he's still among the stars.

However, I caught what I think was a cinematic blunder. As the *Titanic* is pulling away from the pier on its fateful maiden voyage, a newsreel cameraman is hand-cranking his camera on the *left* side! (The crank is on the right side of the camera.) Cameron, no doubt, had flipped the film over during editing for some reason and hoped no one would notice. I know this because as a kid I hand-cranked my camera, and not with my left hand.

3. George Lucas

On February 10, 1990, The School of Cinema-Television at the University of Southern California had a premiere screening of a documentary that showed scenes from the most outstanding student films of days gone by. Since I had made *The Oval Portrait*, the first student film ever made at USC, it led off the program. The campus theater was packed with present and former students, eager to see the history of student films. In 1966, Lucas had turned out a futuristic film, *THX, 1148EB*, that won him many honors, including the National Student Film Festival.

Lucas was accompanied to the event by Steven Spielberg, and when the program was over and the lights came up, I walked over to Lucas and introduced myself, as we had two things in common. The first was that we were both from the small town of Modesto, California, and the second was that we both sold our student films to Warner Bros. "Hi, I'm Richard Bare," I said.

Lucas got up from his theater seat and extended his hand. "I know you," and turning to Spielberg, said, "This guy showed me my first glimpse inside a major studio."

"I did?" I sure didn't remember.

"Yeah, you were shooting out at Warner Bros., and I called you up and explained that my father told me to look you up. You remember my Dad, don't you?"

"Of course I remember him. He helped me make my high school movie."

Lucas continued to explain to Spielberg that when he was eighteen I had allowed him to watch how I directed, what I said to the actors and how I moved the camera. "Richard here was sort of an inspiration."

By now, I was somewhere between flabbergasted and dumbstruck. All I could mutter was, "What? How's that again?" Still speaking to Spielberg, he continued, "I figured if one kid from Modesto could crash Hollywood, there might be room for two."

Here I was in the company of the two most successful talents in the movie industry, and I couldn't help but compare the difference in our careers, although all three of us made student films that brought us major studio contracts.

George Walton Lucas, Jr., was born on May 14, 1944, and weighed five pounds, fourteen ounces, which may have contributed to the light build he has. His father, George Lucas, Sr., who ran a stationery store, had married Dorothy Bomberger, and together they had three girls and a boy.

When George was a teenager, he began a love affair with comic books that continued well into his grown-up years. Buck Rogers and Flash Gordon were two of his favorites. He did not do well in school and to this day has trouble with arithmetic.

After a short spell at Modesto Junior College, George enrolled at USC. He had no notion of going into the movie business, but when a friend suggested that a couple of cinema classes would be a snap, Lucas signed up. Shortly thereafter, he became fascinated by the nuts and bolts of filmmaking and began to see the movie business as a life's work.

Although his film studies included writing, photography, directing and editing, after a while he started breaking the rules, a habit that would hold him in good stead in the years to come.

Warner Bros. sponsored an amateur film competition, and *THX* won hands down. Lucas was given the opportunity to become a trainee where he could observe the various studio operations. The day that George Lucas showed up for work was the day that Jack Warner moved out, symbolizing the changing of the guard and the ushering in of the new breed of filmmakers. Lucas's first assignment was to shoot *THX* all over again as a feature film.

Francis Ford Coppola, a former film student, recognized Lucas as a "comer" and took him on as an assistant on *The Rain People*. It was not long before the young filmmaker was given the chance to direct *American Graffiti*, which was about high school kids cruising Main Street on Saturday night in Modesto. As they say, the rest is history.

Today, George Lucas presides over a vast campus of filmmaking facilities in Marin County, a testament to the fact that he eschews the film capital of the world and prefers making his films without anyone looking

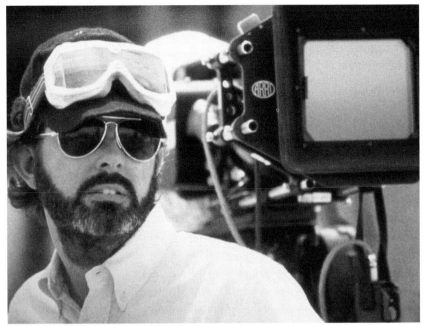

By the time George Lucas directed *American Graffiti*, he was on his way to becoming a director with a firm knowledge of the technology of moviemaking. But as the years went by, he seemed to prefer the job of producer, hiring others like Spielberg to direct the *Indiana Jones* trilogy.

over his shoulder. He even owns his own effects and computer animation house, Industrial Light and Magic.

For some reason, Lucas dropped out as a member of the Directors Guild. Perhaps he thought he could control things better by fully devoting his energies to writing and producing. The fact that he likes to shoot in England may have been a factor, but he did return to directing in *Episode I: The Phantom Menace* after hiring Spielberg and Kershner to direct his earlier *Star Wars* and *Indiana Jones* films. Peter Bart, editor of *Daily Variety*, has this to say about George Lucas: "Next to Stanley Kubrick, he's been the most private of all the major filmmakers. There's Gentle George, the single father, ushering his kids off to school and presiding over his vast empire with the calmness of a proprietor of a cozy little neighborhood bookstore. Then there's Jugular George, demanding ferocious deals with exhibitors, toy companies and everyone else in his path. Indeed, when Jugular George got finished with the theater owners, I was surprised they even retained their popcorn revenues. Whether he's Gentle George or Jugular George, it's lonely out there on that limb—even if you have several billion bucks to show for it."

Steven Spielberg, Richard L. Bare, and George Lucas compare notes at USC's showing of its cinema history film, *The First Fifty Years*. It was the school where Lucas and
Bare got their starts making student films. Lucas told Spielberg that Bare showed him
his first glimpse inside a major Hollywood studio. (Collection of Richard L. Bare)

The cold, hard facts are that George Lucas spent $115 million of his
own money to produce *The Phantom Menace*. It made back its cost, plus
prints and ads, within six weeks. *And* Lucas takes home the lion's share of
all receipts, a deal that harks back to the one he made with 20th
Century–Fox for the first *Star Wars*: He would forego his salary provided
he owned the negative *and* the ancillary rights that include all commercial tie-ins and the vast quantity of toys.

I returned to Modesto a few years ago and had lunch with my old
high school friend, George Sr. "George," I asked, "was your kid anything
like me when he was in high school?"

"What do you mean, Dick?"

"I mean, like, running around with my movie camera, making that
western movie."

George wrinkled up his brow. "Naw, all he ever did was lie in bed and
read comic books."

I wondered where I'd gone wrong.

THE LONG ROAD TO SUCCESS

Since my own entrance into the motion picture business was a result of academic training, and not through any of the other routes, I will recount my own experiences leading up to receiving that first paycheck. Although I had created the most impressive college film of its day and had been honored at a banquet attended by leading luminaries of the film capital who watched me receive an award, it still took me seven years to get a contract with a major studio. Seven long years of frustrating effort to convince a studio that I was the talented young man I thought I was.

My first fascination with the movies came at the age of ten in Modesto, California, when my father bought me a small projector and I proceeded to charge pins as admission to my basement theater. Soon after the first show, I discovered that nickels were as easy to extract from neighborhood kids as pins.

As I matured, and with the principles of projection firmly established, I became the grammar school projectionist, running the study films once a week, and even projecting the religious movies that the Presbyterian Church occasionally presented.

What really motivated me on the way to a chosen profession was when my father presented me with a movie camera on my fourteenth birthday. This was no 8-mm toy, or even a 16-mm outfit. It was a genuine DeVry 35-mm professional motion picture camera, the kind of moderately priced camera that was commonly used by newsreel men.

I wasted no time in mastering its operation, but my exposure left something to be desired. That was when I decided to study motion picture photography by correspondence. Before I had even received my high school diploma, I had sold three newsreel stories to Universal Newsreel at a dollar a foot, and had nearly fallen out of an airplane in the process.

I soon got a job in a gas station so that I could afford my hobby, shooting movies. I convinced the manager of a local theater that a home-produced newsreel would more than pay for itself at the box office. Whether it did or not, I'm not sure, but I had lots of fun shooting the film.

By the time my junior year in high school came around, I was ready to add a dramatic dimension to my amateur filming. With my pal, Bud Shoemake, who was as interested in picture making as I was, I embarked on a two-reel western picture, *West of the Rio Grande*. The cast was recruited from the high school dramatics class, props and costumes were rounded up, and with a borrowed truck we traveled to "location" each

The author (top left) was barely sixteen when he and his high school buddies organized the Cinema Arts Picture Corp. and started shooting the two-reel *West of the Rio Grande*. The 35-mm camera arrived with the last lesson by correspondence from the New York Institute of Photography. (Collection of Richard L. Bare)

No shot was too difficult for the high school filmmakers. When they needed a close-up of the leading lady as she fought to control a runaway horse and buggy, they mounted the movie camera in the rumble seat. When *West of the Rio Grande* was presented at the school auditorium, it made all of its cost back in two nights. (Collection of Richard L. Bare)

weekend. Modesto, being only a few miles from the heart of Mother Lode country, provided easy access to some remarkable and picturesque backgrounds, and for eight months our student group maintained its initial enthusiasm for completing the picture. When it was finally finished and edited, we had spent $480, and now we were ready for the big test. Would anybody come to see it? We had some circulars and window cards printed, put an ad in the *Modesto Bee*, and persuaded a local sign painter to put up a large banner that extended across the main street—all on credit. When the night came for the big show, Bud and I, who were running the projectors, looked through the portholes of the projection room into a jam-packed high school auditorium and received the thrill of our lives. The show went off without a hitch, and at the end of the performance on the last night we counted the money. Not only had we recovered our production costs, but we made enough to cover advertising costs, not always an easy thing to do in professional picture making.

After a summer vacation in Hollywood, during which I managed to get into a studio and get a job as a five-dollar-a-day extra, I returned to school for my senior year all pepped up to somehow make talking pictures. Bud and I spent many hours in our attic "studio" rigging parts from an old phonograph and hooking it in sync with a new camera I had acquired. We selected a part-singing, part-monologue record and had a friend of ours memorize the words to the record. When he was word perfect, we put some makeup on him, then stood him up before the camera and started to turn the crank. The camera mechanism turned the record, and the actor heard the voice. He mouthed his memorized words in perfect sync, and when the film was developed and the record attachment hooked onto the projector, we had accomplished our first talking picture.

After graduating from high school, I enrolled in the University of Southern California. It was the only college on the West Coast that had a cinema department.

My camera, although an inexpensive but professional-looking instrument, was a big hit with the professor of the department as well as the other students, and I was soon chief cameraman for Campus Newsreel. Warner Bros. studio decided to sponsor a film contest and provided a trophy to be awarded to the student who, during the year, made the best amateur film. The contest was open to all colleges, and the studio, seeking to further the career of one of its leading stars, named the trophy the Paul Muni Award.

With this as an inspiration, I was galvanized into action. I adapted an Edgar Allan Poe story, *The Oval Portrait*, and proceeded to gather a student cast and crew to film what I was sure would be the most colossal college film ever made. I found a colleague, Evan Shaw, whose enthusiasm matched mine and who, parenthetically, could hold up his end of the financing side. My new associate, a young divinity student, secretly shared a desire, it seems, to be an actor. He had a classic profile, a deep resonant voice, the body of a young Apollo and was captain of the polo team. After a few hours with me, he was convinced that he should star in *The Oval Portrait* and put up most of the cash money needed as well. I say cash money because I had already talked Metro-Goldwyn-Mayer into lending us stage space, standing sets, wardrobe and so forth. Eastman Kodak Company donated 10,000 feet of negative, and Consolidated Film Laboratories agreed to do our processing at no charge. Later, I was to convince Pacific Title and Art Studio that by providing main and end titles they would further the cause of education at the University, and RKO Studios agreed to make all of our optical effects, fades and dissolves. So, the actual expenditure was small and covered things like gasoline, lunch on location and the few small items of rental that were impossible to promote.

When directors like James Cameron insist that a single point of view makes the best film and that the director should control the production from the inception of the idea to the final editing of the film, they have a champion in me, for I learned early about the practical application of this theory. I had written the script, adapting it from the Poe short story. I owned the camera, so naturally I did the photography. I directed; I produced and edited the film in my room at the fraternity house. I even ran the projector at the banquet when the film was first unveiled. I was not yet twenty.

Filming spanned a three-month period. After shooting our interior scenes at MGM, we labored on weekends shooting outdoor scenes in and around the Palos Verdes hills.

When the big night came at the Roosevelt Hotel on Hollywood Boulevard, *The Oval Portrait* had already been selected as the winner of the college contest and was shown to an audience of Hollywood notables and the Los Angeles press. I was given the Paul Muni award, a handsome plaque, which I was sure would be my *entrée* to any studio in town.

A few weeks later, the picture opened a two-week run at the Egyptian Theatre on Hollywood Boulevard and received glowing notices: "Picture beautiful to look at . . . exquisite proof of the camera's potential art," said the *Hollywood Reporter.*

Daily Variety came forth with, "Production showed sound fundamentals in screen technique and directorial promise by Richard L. Bare."

The now defunct *Los Angeles Post-Record* said, "... a cleverly directed costume drama, and should refresh the jaded appetite for celluloid. Raises the movie to the realm of art."

All this, of course, had its profound effect on me. As I moved about the campus on the few remaining days of the semester, my feet barely touched the ground. At nineteen, I had apparently arrived. My schooling was behind me, and I had the rest of the summer to call on the various studios and to pick and choose the place I wanted to work. I was armed with letters of introduction, a photo of my award, copies of my reviews and an unbridled enthusiasm to crack the business once and for all. One by one, I called on the executives of each studio. Nobody seemed to need a young genius to direct their pictures. They weren't interested in taking on any new assistant directors, or even second assistants. In fact, they didn't need any prop men, furniture movers, or even any messenger boys. How about a job as an observer with no pay? No—not at this time.

When the summer was over, my illusions of fame and success in the movie business had been replaced with more practical appraisals of the situation, and I took the first offer that came my way in three months of hounding the studios for a job. A director I had met arranged for me to pile lumber on the back lot at Paramount for twenty-one dollars a week. Admittedly the job was a letdown, but I was nevertheless grateful and plunged into my duties as a laborer with virgin zeal, hoping that someone in the production office would notice that I was obviously superior to the job I was doing.

I piled lumber harder and faster than any other man on the gang. This seemed to upset the foreman, and I was told to slow down as it made the other men look bad.

I would work for eight hours, then drop into my bed at the YMCA completely fatigued. The phone would ring at eight o'clock, and a voice would say, "You want to work the night shift?" When I began to hedge, the voice announced they could easily take me off the list since I was a new man. One night in particular, after having worked a day shift, I got up, put on my clothes and trudged into the studio to answer a call for night work. I was herded onto a truck with a gang of other souls, and driven to the Paramount Ranch at Calabasas.

There we shoveled all night long to level the side of a hill so that Josef von Sternberg's grips could lay a dolly track for a shot he would be making for *The Scarlet Empress*. I was bawled out for working too fast. The next day I quit.

USC students shot *The Oval Portrait* at the Metro-Goldwyn-Mayer Studios in Culver City. Producer Walter Wanger arranged for the students to film on the lot. Eastman Kodak donated the film; Consolidated Film Lab donated the processing. (Collection of Richard L. Bare)

My next employment was as an assistant cameraman on a six-day "quickie," and although elated at my good fortune, I soon found out why I had been selected over more experienced men. I had agreed to defer my twenty-five dollar salary until after the picture was completed. I deferred and I waited. I never got paid.

With my funds depleted, I went home to Modesto somewhat in defeat. It looked like I was never going to get a job in Hollywood. Then something came into my life that was to renew the spark and even kindle the old flame again.

I ran across an ad in the classified section of the *San Francisco Examiner* that read, "ASSOCIATE WANTED. Film director wants to meet party with small amount of capital to produce western picture. Box 616-A."

When a battered old Lincoln drove up to my father's house, and an unimpressive looking fellow introduced himself as Denver Dixon, I was

The Oval Portrait was the first University of Southern California film production. The author, at the age of nineteen, is shown with script in hand, directing fellow student Evan Shaw, in full character makeup. This early venture won the Paul Muni Award. (Collection of Richard L. Bare)

frankly disappointed in what I saw; but then I was not about to let slip away any chance to become involved in the making of a Hollywood movie.

Dixon explained that he was actually Art Mix, the silent movie western actor, and had recently made a contact with a New York distributor who was interested in releasing a series of westerns in which Dixon would star as well as direct. All he needed to get the first picture made, which was to be a two-reeler, was the small sum of $2,500. He explained that he had many friends in Hollywood who would help him and that he could get a cast and a cameraman who would wait for their money, and he knew a laboratory that would extend him credit. He already owned the story, so that was no problem.

I rose to the bait like a hungry trout and told Denver, as he preferred to be called, that I could get him the money provided that there was a responsible position for me. Eagerly, he offered me the position of producer, an equitable arrangement, I thought.

Remembering my money-raising abilities with such amateur projects as *West of the Rio Grande* and *The Oval Portrait*, I tackled some good friends in Modesto. Within a week, we had formed a company and I was headed for Hollywood, this time, I was certain, for good.

Denver had gone ahead and rented a small studio on Santa Monica Boulevard, and had lined up a flea-bitten cast of old western cronies who had worked in the old Art Mix silents. I soon got better acquainted with Denver. He was a one-man outfit, a pioneer along Poverty Row, which was the area around Gower Street and Sunset Boulevard, and a promoter who took a backseat to no one. He had for years managed to raise the capital to make westerns, exacting his livelihood out of the production money in the form of salary, for very little ever came back from the distribution of Art Mix westerns. His screen credits were a classic deception. They always read, "Victor Adamson presents - - Art Mix starring in - - Directed by Denver Dixon." But they were all the same man.

Years before, he had acquired the name of Art Mix during the period when Tom Mix was the giant of all western stars. Knowing the value of a name, he always controlled his billing on the posters outside the theaters, so that the name "MIX" was oversized, while the name "Art" was infinitesimally small.

A few years before I met Denver Dixon, Fox Film Corporation filed a large damage suit against this man who was capitalizing on the name of one of their top stars and who, they claimed, was misleading the public. Denver, never a man to run from a good scrap, frantically looked around for a legal loophole. His agile mind soon came across one. He had learned from a lawyer friend that if Art Mix was his legal name, the Fox people wouldn't have a leg to stand on. Quickly, Denver sprang into action. He looked in the phone directory until he found an Arthur J. Mix. He called Mr. Mix for an appointment and went out to see him. A half hour later, and with the promise of a fifty dollar payment, Arthur J. Mix agreed to adopt the middle-aged western actor, and thereby legalize the name Art Mix. Fox Film Corporation dropped its suit, probably deciding that it wasn't worth their time anyway.

My first professional screen credit as a producer was on a two-reel western entitled *The Double Cross*, starring Art Mix, but nobody ever got a chance to see it. It was never released. I guess it was a new low even for Adamson-Dixon-Mix.

Again, I went back home, this time more sure than ever that I was a perpetual failure. It seemed the only films I could make that people would pay to see were amateur ones. So, temporarily, I shifted my energies toward another direction in show business. I found a vacant theater in Carmel, California, signed a lease, and started showing foreign films. The venture was an instant success.

This theater was to sustain me for the next three years, while I was carefully studying the work of the world's leading picture-makers, secretly making plans for another frontal assault on Hollywood.

I formed a corporation in Carmel and raised capital to make a color short subject based on Robert Edgren's newspaper syndicated cartoons, *Miracles of Sport*. The picture cost $5,000, and we sold it to Warner Bros. for $2,500. But it was a good film, and people saw it in theaters, even if the stockholders didn't fare so well. I was moving up.

The theater business was getting so good in Carmel that my fame as an entrepreneur of foreign films spread to Southern California. I was invited to run a newly proposed art film theater in Claremont, with the capital to be supplied by local citizens. Knowing that I would be closer to Hollywood, I made the move from Carmel to Claremont and invested all my savings in the new project. In one year, I was broke again—a combination of underfinancing and poor clearance, which means the pictures I could get were only old ones.

Determined never again to go home to Modesto, I slipped into Hollywood and, by a stroke of good timing, managed to get a job as assistant cameraman with George Pal, who was then hiring nonunion cameramen for his Puppetoon shorts.

This was the turning point in my then young career. After a year of experience as a cameraman actually being paid to do the job, I was ready to pursue photography as my life's work. I applied to the cameraman's local 659, I.A.T.S.E., and was summarily turned down. As I look back, I can only be grateful, for it pointed my energies toward a more lucrative profession—directing.

About this time I had made the acquaintance of Warren Scott, who had succeeded Boris Morkovin as head of the Cinema Department at USC. News of my mild flurry of campus fame a few years previous had sifted down to Scott, who was in need of additional instructors in the art and techniques of filmmaking, so I became an addition to his staff. For the first semester, I taught photography; then I joined forces with William Keighley in a class in film directing.

Although I had come quite a way from my lumber piling days at Paramount, I was still far from my goal, which was to have a studio contract in a creative position. Even my close association with Keighley opened up no doors, for there was still no established route for an

The evils of tobacco made an appropriate subject for a university-financed student production, so Richard L. Bare wrote, produced and directed *So You Want to Give Up Smoking* for USC. When Warner Bros. saw it, they wanted to buy it and did. That was the start of Bare's professional career. (Collection of Richard L. Bare)

academically trained picture-maker to become a major studio employee. I knew—I had tried everything. It was at this time that I formulated the plan that inspires this chapter. If there were no jobs, I would create one.

Two years before in Carmel I had written a short subject script entitled, *So You Want to Give Up Smoking*, and had sent it to Pete Smith, who was then making his short series at MGM. Pete sent it back with a note saying he had enjoyed it very much and had even tried to get it passed by the studio. But, since it dealt with methods to eliminate the smoking habit, he felt that it would alienate too many powerful tobacco companies.

Now I had a script. Warren Scott needed projects, actual productions that could be made at the University that would serve as practical training grounds for the students. It took little persuasion on my part to get Scott to see the obvious benefits of shooting such a moral script as one that dealt with the evils of nicotine.

With ample funds available, I gathered together some of the best students from the photography and directing classes and turned out a professionally slick two-reel short. For the smaller roles, friends and university students were used, but for the major part, a professional actor was persuaded into donating his services for the cause of education. His name was George O'Hanlon, and he never suspected that this was the start of a fifteen-year association with the fellow who at that time was known to him as "Teach."

When the film was completed, and the students had received the benefit of experience gained from working on a production, it worried me

With the success of *So You Want to Give Up Smoking* behind him, Richard L. Bare went on to make sixty-five more subjects, each titled *So You Want to . . . .* Most theatergoers knew the series by the title *Behind the Eightball*, since that was the trademark for the series of one-reelers. Here, in one called *So You Want to Get Married*, the bride's mother raises her daughter's hand in victory as the minister pronounces Joe McDoakes a married man. (Warner Bros.)

Creating a Job for Yourself   233

that all this effort in turning out a genuinely entertaining picture was going to repose quietly in a can, unappreciated by millions of theatergoers throughout the world.

So, one day, acting completely on impulse, I took the film out to Warner Bros. studio and showed it to Norman Moray, then head of short subject distribution. When the lights came on after the screening, he asked me what I wanted for it. Completely off guard, I stammered out a price, "Twenty-five." Moray, without batting an eyelash, wanted to know whether I was referring to hundreds or thousands. Hundreds, I assured him.

Without any more small talk, he stood up and asked me to come with him to the legal department where contracts would be drawn right away. As I walked down the corridor, a horrible thought occurred to me. Here I was about to sell something that really didn't belong to me. I could tell Moray the whole story, confess how the film was made to educate students, and explain that the negative belonged to the University and that in all likelihood it would frown on any such commercial exploitation of the film. And, if I did tell him all this, he, being a very busy man, would turn his attention to other available shorts on the market and buy up the year's quota of outside product. I could see my big opportunity for a studio affiliation postponed another seven years.

So, I took a chance. I went through the preliminary motions of getting the contracts started and then dashed out to the University to see Scott.

I hedged for five minutes, trying to present to him what I had done in a way that wouldn't make him think of me as some scholastic Ponzi. Just when I thought he would veto the whole thing, he came up with a solution to my dilemma.

"Now, in your opinion, did the students get practical experience in filmmaking?"

I assured him that they did, indeed.

He pondered the situation for a moment. "Now, we don't have any fireproof vaults here at the University, do we?"

I ventured that certainly we didn't. Again he pondered. "What did you say you got from Warner Bros.?"

"Twenty-five hundred dollars."

Scott moved to the window and peered out as if some University sleuth might be lurking. "Well, I suppose if we turned over the negative to you for safekeeping—and you donated a thousand dollars to the University—we might consider the matter closed."

I quickly agreed that this was, indeed, a wise solution. I delivered the negative to Warners, picked up the twenty-five-hundred-dollar check and then endowed USC with one thousand. Not bad for all concerned.

So far as is known, it has never happened before or since: a student-made film sold to a major company and becoming the prototype for a series that ran for ten years. Here director Bare and star O'Hanlon pose in their first personal chairs, symbol of Hollywood success. (Warner Bros.)

A month later, Warner Bros. asked me to make another; and this time it was, *So You Think You Need Glasses*. I hired O'Hanlon again, and this time he was paid for his services, as well as brought up to date on the smoking picture. When *Glasses* was completed, I signed O'Hanlon to a personal contract, calling for seven years of service with options, of course. Warner Bros. looked at my second picture, and I was invited to join the short subject staff under Gordon Hollingshead as a writer.

Seven years had rolled by since I had received the Paul Muni Award. I was now in the door. Under contract! It wouldn't be long before I'd be a studio director.

CHAPTER TWELVE

chapter twelve

THE DIRECTOR'S REQUIREMENTS AND RESPONSIBILITIES

THE DIRECTORS GUILD OF AMERICA

Now that I had a studio contract, I knew that I had to become a member of the Directors Guild of America (DGA) to impress the front office that I possessed full requirements for a position as a staff director. The Guild at that time was composed of only a few hundred members and the initiation fee was nominal. The bylaws defined just what a director was: "A director is one who directs the production of motion pictures as the word *direct* is commonly used in the industry, and the fact that he may also render services as a producer and/or writer shall not take him out of the classification of director."

A director who worked for the minimum scale in those days got $312 per week, and he worked on Saturdays as did all shooting crews. For membership in the Guild, a director paid $250 in initiation fees and nominal yearly dues. To join the Directors Guild of America today, the cost is $6,500 in initiation fees if you are employed in major studio and network TV, or $3,500 for low-budget films under $1,200,000. Annual dues for all members are $50 per quarter plus 1.5 percent of DGA income over $10,000.

With over 5,000 directors currently on the membership list, the man or woman who works for union scale receives approximately $10,000 per week in feature films. If the director works by the episode in TV, the minimum salary is $16,000 for a half-hour sitcom, and $28,000 for an hour show; for a two-hour movie, the salary is $77,000.

The minimum amount of preparation time and cutting time that the director must give to an employer is spelled out. A starting date, with one-week's latitude either way, must be given to the director at the time of employment, and any location travel must be in transportation "first class or the best obtainable."

If the production of a motion picture, after having closed down, is resumed again, the director may be called back but paid only for the actual time worked, in contrast to the actors who must be paid "carry time" if they have not completed their roles. Elizabeth Taylor's much publicized illness on *Cleopatra* resulted in many hundreds of thousands of dollars paid to actors as carry pay.

On a *term contract*, a period of employment not less than twenty-six weeks, a director may be given *layoff*, usually not more than six weeks in each twenty-six week period. During layoff, the director is, of course, not paid. A director under contract can be *loaned out* to another company, even for more money than is called for in the contract, and the difference is pocketed by the director's employer.

A director may be *suspended* for reasons that run the gamut from mental or physical incapacity to *force majeure (literally "superior power," or events and circumstances that cannot reasonably be anticipated)*. Naturally, the director agrees to conduct himself with due regard to public convention and morals, and, in the word's of one studio's contract, ". . . not to commit any act that will tend to degrade him in society or bring him into public hatred, contempt, scorn, or ridicule, or that will tend to shock, insult, or offend the community."

The director, according to the Guild Agreement, is to be consulted regarding the cast before the assignments are made, with the exception of any cast members who were assigned prior to the director's signing.

With regard to editing, the director is entitled to prepare the "director's cut," but the production company retains the right to re-cut the film. It is the producer's obligation to notify the director of the time and place of all "sneak" previews.

Further clauses relative to editing give the director the right to express his or her editorial ideas directly to the company executive in the event that the director and the producer don't see eye to eye. However, all final decisions are to be the producer's: "The producer's decision as to all cutting and dubbing shall always be final, and nothing herein contained shall be so construed as to prohibit the making of such changes as the producer may deem fit."

There is nothing in the Basic Agreement to prevent a Spielberg or a Cameron from making other arrangements with the studio, and, of course, they always do. Like all union agreements, the Director's Basic Agreement is to protect the average director, not the giants whose services are sought and paid for at premium prices and working conditions.

Screen credits have always been a controversial subject in Hollywood, and the Guild has covered it this way: "The director shall be given credit on all positive prints in type not less that 50 percent of the size of the title, and no other credits shall appear on such card, which shall be the last title card appearing prior to principal photography."

In television and on some features, the director's credit may be as outlined above, or it may come at the end, being the first credit to appear on the screen.

There is an additional compensation to directors of television, and the Basic Agreement states:

> *The salary paid to the director for his services in a television motion picture shall constitute payment in full for the telecasting of such motion picture once in each city in which any television broadcasting stations are now located.*

WHY JOINING THE GUILD IS SO IMPORTANT

The director's salary is payment for the first network prime-time run. If the network gives the film in question a second run, it will pay the director 100 percent of his initial salary. All subsequent syndication runs are calculated using a base figure as shown in the following table.

Additional payments are due on all films shown on television in foreign countries. There is also a rather complicated arrangement whereby a small percentage of the "producer's gross" is paid to the director for home video shown in both foreign and domestic markets.

These generous rerun payments, referred to as *residuals*, are the popular topic of conversation among Hollywood television groups. Residuals are paid to writers, directors and actors who are lucky enough to work on television shows that get more than one showing. I knew one director who fondly named his boat *Residual*, since it was from this source that the cost and upkeep of his hobby came.

Syndication Run Payment Schedule

Run	30 Minutes	60 Minutes	90 Minutes	100 Minutes
Base	9,381	17,661	26,498	43,996
2nd	4,690	8,831	13,381	42,070
3rd	3,752	7,066	10,599	13,998
4th	2,345	4,416	6,624	8,749
5th	2,345	4,416	6,624	8,749
6th	2,345	4,416	6,624	8,749
7th	1,407	2,650	3,974	5,249
8th	1,407	2,650	3,974	5,249
9th	1,407	2,650	3,974	5,249
10th	938	1,766	2,649	4,399
11th	938	1,766	2,649	4,399
12th	938	1,766	2,649	4,399
13th	938	1,766	2,649	4,399

All runs over 13 pay 5 percent of base.

The theory of rerun payments, as established by the leading talent guilds, maintains that every time a film is reshown it has taken a creative job away from someone. The residuals are a form of penalty to the producer and sometimes turn out to be a windfall to the Guild member.

The many feature films butchered by television stations have caused the inclusion of a clause in the Basic Agreement that ensures that the director will be consulted before any cutting is done on the film when shown on television.

The Directors Guild was one of the first union organizations to recognize the danger of a producer's making a motion picture for one medium and then exhibiting it in another. Strict regulations are in effect now, but I can remember when I directed the first hour-long television film ever made in Hollywood and for a very small fee, since television was just getting started. A month or so after its showing on a leading network, I saw the picture advertised in a downtown Los Angeles theater. All my protests and those of my attorney could do nothing to persuade the producer that he had done anything illegal or immoral. But, when bargaining time came around again, the Guild put teeth in the language that would prevent this from ever happening again. Parenthetically, when I directed the pilot film of *77 Sunset Strip*, which was made as a ninety-minute theatrical feature, I was paid a theatrical salary under the terms of the Basic Agreement. Later, when the film was rerouted from the theaters directly to its premiere as an ABC Network program, I was paid again, this time for directing a television film.

Many years ago, the practice of *deferring* salaries got started in Hollywood, and in some cases, it is still around today. The Directors Guild Basic Agreement specifically prohibits its membership from postponing their salaries, but it allows them to make better terms for themselves if they can.

With the proliferation of ultralow-budget films, the Guild in its desire to staff these films with union members has offered independent producers a "side letter" agreement, greatly reducing its members' salaries.

Yes, directing is a rewarding business from many standpoints. The Directors Guild of America provides many so-called fringe benefits to its members through its liberal pension plan and group insurance program. Retirement for the director may come at age sixty or sixty-five, at the director's election, provided he has 180 or more months of credited service as a director.

One of the most controversial points ever discussed in Hollywood labor meetings has been a demand by the three talent guilds (directors, writers and actors) for additional payment for the members' services on those theatrical motion pictures made after 1948 that were shown on television. As a result of years of negotiations, on feature pictures made after April 30, 1960, the producers have agreed to contribute to the DGA 2 percent of their gross television receipts, after deducting a flat amount of 40 percent of total gross receipts for distribution fees.

Through the Guild's Benevolent Fund, members may receive financial aid in time of stress, and many contributions are made to nonindustry charities through this branch of the Guild's activities.

Each February the membership gathers, usually at the Beverly Hilton Hotel in Beverly Hills and the Waldorf-Astoria in New York, to have a social evening and applaud the winners of the Directors Guild Achievement Award for the year. The feature picture director who has, in the opinion of the members, distinguished himself during the year, is presented a gold medallion, and similarly the best television director of the year receives equal honors. The awards have a true significance, since the winners have been adjudged by other directors who are in a position to evaluate a director's contribution to a film.

Housed in its own handsome building on Sunset Boulevard in Hollywood, the Directors Guild of America has combined with the New York Directors Guild and the Radio and TV Directors Guild. The objectives of the Guild are stated, in part, in its bylaws: "To represent and coordinate the activities of the various individuals now or hereafter engaged or employed as directors in the motion picture and television industries—to help its members secure equitable compensation and better working conditions—to establish and enforce standard minimum contracts—and to adopt, promulgate and encourage the observance of a code of ethics for its members and those similarly engaged or employed."

A new member will be admitted upon the payment of the initiation fee and first-quarter dues, provided he or she has obtained the written recommendation of three director members and can qualify as having landed a job.

Although the Guild may take strict disciplinary action against a member who, in the opinion of the board, may be guilty of any act that may be prejudicial to the welfare of the Guild, there has been a conspicuous absence of directors or assistant directors who have behaved in a notorious way or have brought discredit upon themselves or the motion picture and television industries. In the main, the men and women who have chosen directing as their life's work have brought a dignity and stature to their profession that has few parallels among the guilds and unions of the vast entertainment industry.

THE DIGITAL WORLD OF FILM

Ever since Woody Allen placed himself beside Hitler and Roosevelt in real stock footage in *Zelig*, Hollywood has been scrambling to push the envelope of computer animation. Now, John Wayne can be seen in beer commercials, cleverly stuck in shots he never would have allowed were he living.

Natalie Wood died in a tragic boating accident in Catalina before she could finish the MGM picture, *Brainstorm*. The picture shut down and was stalled for months while the studio tried to figure out how to finish it without the star. After much shifting and "cheating," the film was eventually released, but Wood's absence in some scenes hurt the narrative. Had this unfortunate accident happened today, the studio would merely call on ILM or James Cameron's company, Digital Domain, who would take the actress's likeness from other scenes in the picture and through CGI let her animated image complete her role.

Up until the advent of video assist, the technique whereby the director monitors the action as the camera records it, not much in the way of new technology changed the way movies were made. That is, until CGI (Computer Generated Images) arrived on the scene, bringing with it a new word to be added to the lexicon of the cinema—*pixel.* Pixels are small blocks of color that form the hundreds of lines necessary to make a picture, and are the basic units that make up the digital frame.

While this book does not profess to delve into the complexities of computer animation, let it be known that whatever directors can conjure up in their heads, the magic of CGI can make a reality.

According to Kevin Rafferty, computer graphics supervisor on *Episode 1: The Phantom Menace,* the special effects on that film is on a magnitude never seen before. He says that over 2,000 FX shots were made, compared with fewer than 200 straight, or undoctored, shots.

Explosions, miniature train wrecks and burning buildings have traditionally been shot with a high-speed camera that conversely produces slow motion. On *Top Gun,* to depict an aerial dogfight, Jim Williams shot a collision of six-foot-long F-14 models with a camera that burned up film at the rate of 300 frames per second. The effect, when projected at 24 frames per second, was unbelievably real.

Andre Bustanoby, visual effects supervisor for James Cameron's Digital Domain, uses a 3-D camera to store an actor's facial and body movements in a digital library that is later composited into a shot. Who is to say that the next step won't be a movie made with all the characters done by CGI? That would be one way to break the $20,000,000 salaries of some movie stars today.

RECOGNIZING NEW TALENT

One of the requirements of a director is to possess the ability to recognize new talent. Hollywood and New York are literally stock pens of undiscovered actors just waiting for someone to come along and give the needed boost. The director is able to react somewhat emotionally to this situation, since he became a director through the same process—someone took a chance on him.

One director I know met a young girl at a lunch counter on Sunset Boulevard. He was immediately struck by her long, honey-blond hair, unmarred by harsh bleaches. She had a wholesome, natural beauty, wore practically no makeup, and what she did wear was in excellent taste.

My friend introduced himself to the girl, telling her that he was a director at a major studio and inquiring whether she had thought about picture work. She replied that she had, indeed, thought about it, was in fact an actress from the East and had recently arrived in town. The director took her to the studio and arranged to give her a screen test. The head of the studio heard about the girl and, although he didn't meet her in person, ordered the red carpet treatment.

When word got around the studio that "the chief" had ordered the finest possible test, the various department heads got busy. The makeup people swarmed around her, deciding that her face could be remodeled by the right application of shadowed makeup. Oversized false eyelashes were added, and her eyebrows were shaved and then painted on to give her a more "provocative look." The hairdressing department decided that her natural honey-blond locks were too dark and wouldn't photograph right and that a glamorous new hair style would enhance her chances. The wardrobe department disdainfully rejected the idea of her wearing the appealing sweater and skirt she wore to the studio the first day. Her dress must be a tight-fitting, sequined evening gown. The studio dentist looked her over and made a porcelain jacket to fit over a small space between two of her teeth.

When the director made the test, he hardly recognized her as the same girl he met at the lunch counter. When the head of the studio ran the test, he hotly demanded to know why the director and talent head had wasted his time and money. "She looks like just any other Hollywood starlet," he said.

One night I was in a small, rather "divey" bar on Sunset Strip that was a familiar hangout of bit players and stunt men. I was introduced to a young man by the name of James Bumgarner and learned that he was a new actor in town having just come off the road in *The Caine Mutiny Court Martial*. There was much levity and libation in the place that night, and little consideration was given to the future of the motion picture business.

The next day, TV head Bill Orr of Warners' suggested that we find some new faces for some of the smaller parts in the first episode of

Cheyenne. We had already signed Clint Walker, an unknown, for the lead, and now Orr wanted more unknowns. I remembered the tall, handsome fellow in the bar the previous evening, so I called the place and got the bartender. No, he didn't remember the fellow. Then, I remembered that actor Bob Lowery had introduced us, so I rang the bar again, this time for Lowery's number. The bartender didn't have his number but said he'd probably be seeing Lowery that night and would give him my message. I told him to be sure to have Lowery call me at the studio. Three days went by, but finally Bumgarner called. I told him if he wanted a job in television he'd better get out to the studio right away. Within an hour, he arrived at my office and I gave him a scene to read, the part of a young army lieutenant.

Bill Orr, who listened in on the reading, agreed with me that this handsome fellow was no Barrymore but that he did come across with some personality. Was he good enough for the part? Orr decided to take a chance with me, and so I shot the one-day bit with Bumgarner. The next day, Jack Warner viewed the dailies with Bill Orr. When the young actor's scene came up, Warner said, "Who's that guy?"

Orr said, "His name is James Bumgarner."

"Well, take the bum out and give him a seven-year contract." And that's how I discovered James Garner.

While on the subject of having an instinct for talent, I must admit that it hasn't always been this way. I missed picking one bigger than Garner.

I was testing six actors a day, looking for an actor to play a part in a Technicolor western. One of the candidates was an unknown actor, Rock Hudson. I thought he was the worst of the lot. I missed out on the opportunity of being able to claim that I was responsible for Hudson's success.

Another time I was having dinner alone in the Cock N' Bull on Sunset Strip. I noticed a beautiful young lady at a nearby table. I gathered my courage, moved over her way and introduced myself, wanting to know if she was interested in getting into pictures.

"Not anymore," she cooed. "My name is Kim Novak."

At that time, she had starred in at least two important films. And I was ready to "discover" her.

THE DIRECTOR'S RESPONSIBILITIES

From the time a film is scheduled for production until the final shot is in the can, the director's life is one decision after another—all under the tremendous pressure of time and temperament, of budgets and

To Richard—
The cause of it all
Thanks a million
Sincerely
Jm Garner

The author met James Garner in a bar one night and gave him a small part in a television film at Warner Bros. Within a year Garner was starring for Warners' in *Maverick*, which was also directed by the author. (Warner Bros.)

blueprints. Before shooting begins, the director is called on to be a master strategist, planning the production with all the skill of a military chief of staff. Once on the stage, the director must become an instant tactical expert, confidently meeting an infinite variety of daily problems while calling all signals with the flexibility of a major league quarterback.

Although there will always be many different kinds of directors, no one should attempt this profession without possessing infinite patience and the stubbornness of a bull; you must be strong of heart and body, schooled in the use of words, lest you misunderstand the author and mislead the actor.

The director must be decisive, yet cooperative; imaginative, yet truthful in his art. The director must be a psychologist, analyst, teacher; captain, teammate, baby-sitter; artist, craftsman, bookkeeper; thinker, dreamer, workhorse; storyteller, magician and *showman.*

The film director has many responsibilities:

To the author—to augment, to strengthen and give life to the written word.

To the players—to guide and inspire them in interpreting the story in terms of their personalities, not the director's.

To the producer—to use the money he or she has been entrusted with wisely, striking a delicate balance between quality and cost.

To the audience—to tell a story with honesty, neither talking down from lofty heights nor underestimating the perception and taste of the public—and, above all, to *amuse* and *entertain.*

A LAST WORD TO THE ASPIRING DIRECTOR

Where can the student filmmaker, when his or her academic training is complete, go to find employment in a chosen field?

There was a time when the talented student seeking employment stood face to face with a wall as impregnable as the Rock of Gibraltar. The old-guard studio establishment, while proclaiming a never-ending search for youthful talent, offered few opportunities for the amateur who was ready to turn professional.

Fortunately, a new and more youth-oriented regime is in control of Hollywood's film companies, and they are more receptive to the aspiring director, especially if he has made a short film that shows off the film-maker's talent. Steven Spielberg did it, George Lucas did it, and I did it. In my case the amateur film became the pilot for a series of sixty-three short films called "Joe McDoakes" that for ten years was in the top-ten box office short subjects and garnered three Oscar nominations. I am not saying that I became the giant director that Spielberg and Lucas became; all I mean is that we started out on the same level playing field. We made films that showed off our talents, and we were justly recognized.

Roger Corman, at one time the most prodigious producer of B movies (*Fall of the House of Usher, Bloody Mama*) actually sought out graduates from cinema schools, although he has confessed it was basically to save money.

It was Corman who first employed Francis Ford Coppola while he was still at UCLA. Coppola sold Corman a script for $250 and then became his assistant at $400 per week doing odd jobs such as dialogue director, cameraman and assistant director. Corman later financed Coppola's first solo film, *Dementia 13*, which launched the ex-student as an innovative director. Corman has also financed Bruce Clark, a former UCLA cinema graduate, in a film called *Naked Angels.* Such fairly well-known names as Bernie Kowalski, Curtis Harrington and Irvin Kershner all at one time or another in their halcyon days received both guidance and financing from Corman.

Even Irvin Kershner himself, the ex-cinema student, has lent a helping hand to trainees, his most notable being Mathew Robbins, who observed the director firsthand on *Loving.*

It is not difficult to find an agent who, after viewing a young filmmaker's movie, might take an interest in furthering his career. There are also several concerns that specialize in handling experimental films.

The Directors Guild of America is doing its part to help the new directors. Every other Friday afternoon, the Guild screens unreleased feature films. The showings are well attended by distributors looking for product. Guild member Mitch Matovich took advantage of this opportunity and screened *Deadly Delusions*, his latest film.

Black director Tim Reid also screened his thriller *Asunder* at the Guild, hoping to entice a distributor. Chances are that he found a release for his film because it was exceptional.

The late director George Seaton, who directed *Miracle on 34th Street* and *Airport*, was one of the first in the industry to bring students on the set while he was shooting, assigning each trainee a rotating task from the variety of jobs connected with actual production. Ex-protégé Daisy Gerber got her start with Seaton and is now a top Production Manager with many solid credits.

There is no question that the combined efforts of the film industry and the more than 600 college cinema departments have provided an atmosphere for the novice director unparalleled in the history of motion pictures. It is left to the student to accept the invitation extended by making the finest, most original and technically excellent film he or she can possibly create. When that is done—if the aspiring director has achieved his or her goal—somebody will roll out the red carpet of opportunity.

If you want to be a director—*be one.* Find ways to prove your worth. Master your craft before attempting art. Rules must be learned before they can be effectively broken. Prepare yourself for the job of directing; then *stick to your goal,* no matter how many disappointments come your way. For, with this philosophy, you must succeed. Talent will win out, and you will be given the chance to guide the production of a motion picture—you will have arrived; you will be the *director.*

APPENDIX A

DIRECTORS GUILD OF AMERICA AWARD WINNERS FOR THEATRICAL DIRECTION

1948   Joseph Mankiewicz, *A Letter to Three Wives*
1949   Robert Rossen, *All the King's Men*
1950   Joseph Mankiewicz, *All About Eve*
1951   George Stevens, *A Place in the Sun*
1952   John Ford, *The Quiet Man*
1953   Fred Zinnemann, *From Here to Eternity*
1954   Elia Kazan, *On the Waterfront*
1955   Delbert Mann, *Marty*
1956   George Stevens, *Giant*
1957   David Lean, *The Bridge on the River Kwai*
1958   Vincent Minnelli, *Gigi*
1959   William Wyler, *Ben-Hur*
1960   Billy Wilder, *The Apartment*
1961   Robert Wise/Jerome Robbins, *West Side Story*
1962   David Lean, *Lawrence of Arabia*
1963   Tony Richardson, *Tom Jones*
1964   George Cukor, *My Fair Lady*
1965   Robert Wise, *The Sound of Music*
1966   Fred Zinnemann, *A Man for All Seasons*
1967   Mike Nichols, *The Graduate*
1968   Anthony Harvey, *The Lion in Winter*

1969 John Schlesinger, *Midnight Cowboy*
1970 Franklin J. Schaffner, *Patton*
1971 William Friedkin, *The French Connection*
1972 Francis Ford Coppola, *The Godfather*
1973 George Roy Hill, *The Sting*
1974 Francis Ford Coppola, *The Godfather, Part II*
1975 Milos Forman, *One Flew Over the Cuckoo's Nest*
1976 John Avildsen, *Rocky*
1977 Woody Allen, *Annie Hall*
1978 Michael Cimino, *The Deer Hunter*
1979 Robert Benton, *Kramer vs. Kramer*
1980 Robert Redford, *Ordinary People*
1981 Warren Beatty, *Reds*
1982 Richard Attenborough, *Gandhi*
1983 James Brooks, *Terms of Endearment*
1984 Milos Forman, *Amadeus*
1985 Steven Spielberg, *The Color Purple*
1986 Oliver Stone, *Platoon*
1987 Bernardo Bertolucci, *The Last Emperor*
1988 Barry Levinson, *Rain Man*
1989 Oliver Stone, *Born on the Fourth of July*
1990 Kevin Costner, *Dances with Wolves*
1991 Jonathan Demme, *The Silence of the Lambs*
1992 Clint Eastwood, *Unforgiven*
1993 Steven Spielberg, *Schindler's List*
1994 Robert Zemeckis, *Forrest Gump*
1995 Ron Howard, *Apollo 13*
1996 Anthony Mingella, *The English Patient*
1997 James Cameron, *Titanic*
1998 Steven Spielberg, *Saving Private Ryan*

As to be expected, Steven Spielberg has won three DGA awards, more than any other feature director.

Only four times has the winner of the Academy award for best director not gone on to win the DGA award. Those directors are:

1968 Carol Reed won the Oscar for *Oliver!*
1972 Bob Fosse won the Oscar for *Cabaret.*
1985 Sydney Pollack won the Oscar for *Out of Africa.*
1995 Mel Gibson won the Oscar for *Braveheart.*

appendix b

DIRECTORS GUILD OF AMERICA AWARD WINNERS FOR TELEVISION DIRECTION

1953 Robert Florey, *The Last Voyage*

1954 Roy Kellino, *The Answer*

1955 Don Weis, *The Little Guy*

1956 Herschel Daugherty, *The Road That Led Afar*

1957 Don Weis, *The Lonely Wizard*

1958 Richard Bare, *All Our Yesterdays*

1959 Phil Karlson, *The Untouchables*

1960 George Schaefer, *Macbeth*

1961 Ernie Kovacs, *A Study in Silence*

1962 David Friedkin, *The Price of Tomatoes*

1963 George Schaefer, Shaw's *Pygmalion*

1964 Lamont Johnson, *The Oscar Underwood Story*

1965 Dwight Hemion, *My Name Is Barbra*

1966 Alex Segal, *The Death of a Salesman*

1967 George Schaefer, *Do Not Go Gentle Into That Good Night*

1968 George Schaefer, *My Father and My Mother*

1969 Fielder Cook, *Teacher, Teacher*

1970 Lamont Johnson, *My Sweet Charlie*

(In 1971, the DGA began giving more than one award.)

1971   John Rich, *All in the Family*
       Buzz Kulik, *Brian's Song*
       Daniel Petrie, *Hands of Love*
1972   Gene Reynolds, *M.A.S.H.* pilot
       Lamont Johnson, *That Certain Summer*
       Robert Butler, *Dust Bowl Cousins*
1973   Gene Reynolds, *M.A.S.H.*
       Joseph Sargent, *The Marcus/Nelson Murders*
       Charles Dubin, *Kojack*
1974   Hy Averback, *M.A.S.H.*
       John Korty, *The Autobiography of Miss Jane Pittman*
       David Friedkin, *Kojak*
1975   Hy Averback, *M.A.S.H*
       Sam Osteen, *Queen of the Stardust Ballroom*
       James Cellan-Jones, *Jenny, Lady Randolph Churchill*
1976   Alan Alda, *M.A.S.H.*
       Daniel Petrie, *Eleanor and Franklin*
       Glenn Jordon, *Rights of Friendship*
1977   Paul Bogart, *All in the Family*
       Daniel Petrie, *Eleanore and Franklin—The White House Years*
       John Erdman, *Roots*
1978   Paul Bogart, *All in the Family*
       Marvin Chomsky, *Holocaust*
       Gene Reynolds, *Lou Grant*
1979   Charles Dubin, *M.A.S.H.*
       Michael Mann, *The Jerrico Mile*
       Roger Young, *Lou Grant*
1980   Noam Pitlik, *Barney Miller*
       Jerry London, *Shogun*
       Roger Young, *Lou Grant*
1981   Alan Alda, *M.A.S.H.*
       Herbert Wise, *Skokie*
       Robert Butler, *Hill Street Blues*
1982   Alan Alda, *M.A.S.H.*
       Marvin Chomsky, *Inside the Third Reich*
       David Anspaugh, *Hill Street Blues*
1983   James Burrows, *Cheers*
       Edward Zwick, *Special Bulletin*
       Jeff Bleckner, *Hill Street Blues*

1984 Jay Sandrich, *Bill Cosby Show*
Daniel Petrie, *The Dollmaker*
Thomas Carter, *Hill Street Blues*

1985 Jay Sandrich, *Bill Cosby Show*
John Erman, *An Early Frost*
Will McKenzie, *Moonlighting*

1986 Terry Hughes, *Golden Girls*
Lee Grant, *Nobody's Child*
Will McKenzie, *Moonlighting*

1987 Will McKenzie, *Family Ties*
Jud Taylor, *Foxfire*
Marshall Herskovitz, *Thirtysomething*

1988 Steve Miner, *The Wonder Years*
Lamont Johnson, *Lincoln*
Marshall Herskovitz, *Thirtysomething*

1989 Barnet Kellman, *Murphy Brown*
Dan Curtis, *War and Remembrance*
Eric Laneuville, *L.A. Law*

1990 James Burrows, *Cheers*
Roger Young, *Murder in Mississippi*
Michael Zinberg, *Quantum Leap*

1991 Peter Bonerz, *Murphy Brown*
Stephen Gyllenhaal, *Paris Trout*
Eric Laneuville, *I'll Fly Away*

1992 Tom Cherones, *Seinfeld*
Ron Lagomarsino, *Picket Fences*
Rob Thompson, *Northern Exposure*

1993 James Burrows, *Frasier*
Michael Ritchie, *The Positively True Adventures of the Alleged Texas Cheerleader Murdering Mom*
Gregory Hoblit, *NYPD Blue*

1994 David Lee, *Frasier*
Rob Holcomb, *ER* pilot
Charles Haid, *ER*

1995 Gordon Hunt, *Mad About You*
Mick Jackson, *The McMartin Trial*
Christopher Chulack, *ER*

1996 Andy Ackerman, *Seinfeld*
Betty Thomas, *The Late Shift*
Christopher Chulack, *ER*

1997 Andy Ackerman, *Seinfeld*
        John Herzfeld, *Only in America*
        Barbara Kopple, *Homicide*
1998 Michael Cristofer, *Gia*
        Paris Barclay, *N.Y.P.D. Blue*
        Thomas Schlamme, Pilot *Sports Night*

APPENDIX C

appendix c

GLOSSARY OF
MOTION PICTURE AND
TELEVISION TERMS

A

action   The business or movement by players or objects within a scene. The command given by the director to start acting.

Arriflex   The most popular handheld camera used today. A reflex-type camera that allows the operator to view the action as it is being filmed through the lens.

angle, camera   What the camera takes in. This angle may be drawn by projecting two straight lines from the center of the lens to the two outside edges of the scene as photographed.

angle of approach   The point from which the director allows the audience to view the film.

animation   1. Screen cartooning that is photographed frame by frame to give the illusion of movement.   2. In acting, to give life to; make lively, gay or vigorous.

answer print   The first trial composite (sound) print of a completely edited, dubbed and scored motion picture.

aperture   In a camera, the lens, or round iris diaphragm, that allows light to pass through to the film. Also, the square opening that frames the picture being taken.

aspect ratio   The shape (not the size) of the frame of a motion picture. From the old standard of 1.33 to 1, to Cinemascope's 2.35 to 1.

assistant director   The person who handles strictly production matters, rather than matters concerning the art of directing.

B

back light   The so-called Rembrandt lighting, a technique in which strong light is thrown on the actors from the back of the set, rimming them in a kind of halo that gives the appearance of relief to the picture.

balance   The relationship of the light and shade in a picture. The cameraman usually measures the brightest portion of the light with a meter and then balances the shadowed portion by eye.

Barney   Soundproofing blanket used when shooting sound with a silent camera.

blowup   1. An enlargement of a scene magnified on the optical printer. 2. The "fluffing" (misstatement) of a line by an actor.

BNC   Once the standard sound camera manufactured by Mitchell Camera Company.

boom, mike   The adjustable pole that holds the microphone and extends out over the actors' heads.

break it up   The filming of other angles of a master scene, usually close-ups.

bridge   A close-up, insert or other angle, which is made to be placed between two sections of the same scene and camera angle.

business   A definite bit of action, as "business of unpacking suitcase."

C

camera boom   The cranelike device that holds the camera and gives it completely vertical, horizontal and diagonal mobility.

camera left   The left side of the camera. Opposite of stage left.

camera right   The right side of the camera as the cameraman stands looking toward the action to be photographed. Opposite of stage right.

center of attention   In motion pictures, that which the camera is focused upon.

CGI   Computer-generated images that make impossible shots look truly real.

clap sticks The black-and-white sticks that are attached to the slate and that are clapped together to make both a visual and a sound impression for the purpose of facilitating the "syncing" of the scene by the editor.

close-up An individual shot of an actor, usually taking in the head and shoulders, and not showing anything below the top button of a suit.

composition The arrangement of various objects; also, the choosing of a point of view in a picture so that the whole will be pleasing.

continuity The detailed plan of a motion picture containing action and dialogue in the order in which they are to be shown.

contrast The degree of difference between the shadows and highlights of a photograph.

coverage The number of close-ups or other angles the director shoots in addition to the master scene.

crab dolly The camera perambulator that eliminates the use of metal tracks and that permits the camera to be moved in any horizontal direction. It has a vertical movement of approximately five feet.

crane *See* **camera boom.**

credit titles The announcements at the beginning or the end of a film that give the names of the various artists and craftsmen.

cut 1. Stop the camera. 2. Stop the action. 3. To edit or shorten a scene by cutting the film. 4. The end of the scene.

cutaway A shot that filmically shifts to another subject.

cutback Where two lines of action take place simultaneously, the secondary action is shown in cutbacks. A shot that alternates between two parallel pieces of action.

cut-in Any close-up or insert that is added between the beginning and end of the scene.

D

dailies The film of the previous day's scenes just as they have come from the laboratory. Also known as rushes.

day for night Shooting in the daytime but resulting in a nighttime quality on the film. Accomplished with filters.

definition The sharpness or clearness with which objects are photographed by a lens.

density   1. The degree of darkness of a negative determined by the amount of opaque silver deposit on the film.   2. The brightness of the light in a scene.

depth of field   The range in which objects are sharply in focus for a particular lens.

diffusion screen   A screen or spun glass placed in front of a light source to reduce the harshness of the lighting.

discovered   A term used to denote the fact that an actor or object is already in the scene when the scene commences.

dissolve   The gradual transition, or melting, of one scene into another. Accomplished by overlapping a fade-out with a fade-in.

documentary   A film that depicts actions or events as they are, with no attempt toward dramatization. Usually made in natural locations with nonactors.

dolly   The camera perambulator.

dolly shot   A moving shot accomplished by pushing the camera dolly about the set.

double exposure   A composite picture made by exposing the same piece of film twice, either in the camera or in the optical printer.

down shot   A shot taken from a high point looking down.

drive motors   The motors that operate the camera and sound recorder in synchronization.

dubbing   The process of re-recording several soundtracks onto one composite track.

dupe negative   A duplicate negative made from a fine-grain print.

E

empathy   The complete understanding by an audience of a character's feelings.

exposure   The length of time the light is allowed to act upon the film emulsion, or the amount of light allowed to pass through the lens.

exposure meter   An instrument that determines exposure by measuring the intensity of light.

exterior   Any scene shot outside the stage.

extras   The nonspeaking actors who usually perform in the background.

eyelight   A small light used near the camera to bring out a sparkle in an actor's eyes.

F

fade-in   The beginning of a scene that gradually comes from complete black to full in.

fade-out   The end of a scene that gradually disappears to complete black.

feet per minute   Pertaining to standard film travel speeds. Sound speed is 90 feet per minute; slow motion is 180-plus feet per minute.

fill light   The weaker light used to balance the shadow side of a subject.

filter   Any glass or gelatin used in the camera to change color values, to balance or to create night effects.

final cut   The final polished and reedited film, ready for dubbing and scoring.

finder   An accessory that shows the approximate field embraced by the lens used by the director and cameraman in lining up a shot.

flare   A fogged spot on the film due to reflection of a strong light on the lens surface.

flatness   Lack of brilliance or contrast in a print or negative. Also, in lighting, the effect caused by having the key light close to the camera.

focus   The plane in which a lens produces a sharp image.

fog   A veiling of the image that is caused by unwanted light falling upon the exposed film.

frame   1. An individual piece of film or one separate exposure.   2. To compose a scene.

frames per foot   Thirty-five-mm film has 16 frames per foot of film. Sixteen-mm film has 40 frames per foot.

frames per second   Silent movie speed is 16 frames per second; sound speed is 24 frames per second.

f-system   The former method of calibrating lens diaphragms in terms of exposure; replaced by the t-system.

full shot   A comprehensive shot that shows either the actors in full figure or all of the set.

G

gate   The two metal plates that hold the film in place as it receives its exposure in the camera.

glass shot   A scene in which the camera shoots through a glass on which is painted a part of the background. Replaced by CGI.

gobo   Black boards that are used either to shade light off of walls or to keep light from hitting directly into the camera lens.

grain   Visible granules of metallic silver in a negative.

grips   The carpenters on a set who move wild walls, handle gobos and operate the camera dolly.

H

halation   A kickback of reflected light that shines too strongly into the lens of the camera.

half tones   The various tones between highlight and shadow.

hard light   The arcs used to approximate sunshine on a set.

head   The top of a piece of film. When film is wound and ready for projection, it is referred to as being "heads out."

high key   Lighting with few dark tones. Used in comedies and light entertainment.

highlights   The lightest part of a scene or print. The darkest part of a negative.

I

illusion of reality   The quality of a scene that purports to be real or actually happening.

imaginary line   A location, corresponding to the proscenium in the theater, over which the camera should not move when making close-ups in order to maintain a consistent direction of looks.

infinity   A distance setting of the camera lens beyond which everything is in focus.

insert   A close-up of a letter, gun and so on used to call attention to or identify the object.

interior   Any scene photographed inside a building or stage.

interlock   A condition arising out of perfect synchronization between the camera and the sound recorder.

intermittent movement   The mechanism that pulls down the film, one frame at a time, in a camera or projector.

J

juicer   A slang name for electrician.

jump cut   The effect of splicing together two pieces of film that have been photographed from the same angle, without bridging them with a close-up or other angle.

K

key   A length of background film that is projected from the rear onto a process screen (also plate).

key light   The main, and usually most intense, light in a scene.

L

lap dissolve   Same as **dissolve**.

leader   The blank portion of film that precedes the actual photography on a reel.

lens mount   The device that holds a lens onto the camera.

line cutting   The act of eliminating speeches through editing, either on paper or on film.

locale   A locality or environment in which a scene takes place.

location   Any place away from the studio used as a setting.

long focal-length lens   A lens at least 75 mm in length that shortens perspective and tends to make the background appear out of focus.

long shot   A shot that is made a considerable distance away from the subject.

looping   The process whereby an actor re-creates his or her dialogue on the sound stage in sync to the picture. This is done to replace faulty dialogue recorded under noisy conditions in such places as factories, airports or busy streets.

low key   Photography in which lighting is held to a minimum; also, lighting with many dark tones.

M

magazine   The light-tight container that feeds and takes up the film in a motion picture camera.

master shot   A continuous take that covers all, or a great part, of a scene.

matching action   In cutting, the act of selecting two pieces of film that contain an overlap of action and then selecting the spot where the cut will be smoothest.

matte box The device that extends forward of the camera lens and that is used to hold filters and mattes.

medium shot A shot that shows a figure from the waist up or that has two or more people in it; somewhere between a close-up and a full shot.

meter reading Measuring the intensity of the key light in order to determine the t-stop to be used on the lens.

method acting A style of acting introduced by Stanislavsky of the Moscow Art Theatre that helps the actor to *be* the character, not *play* the character.

miniature Small-scale sets or props used to represent actual settings; often used to reproduce train wrecks, ship sinkings, explosions and the like.

Mitchell The motion picture camera formerly the standard of the film industry. Replaced by Panavision.

montage A series of individual shots that, when viewed together, form a unified story impression.

movement 1. In a camera, the intermittent mechanism in the camera that pulls down the film a frame at a time. 2. In dramatics, changing the place or position of the actors, the background or the camera. Also accomplished in editing.

moving shot Any shot made while the camera is in motion, either on a dolly or on another moving vehicle.

Moviola A linear viewing machine that plays both picture and sound. Used in the cutting rooms. Largely replaced by flatbeds.

N

negative The raw film that receives its exposure through the camera and that, when developed, has its images reversed, light for dark.

neutral density filter An optical glass or gelatin that reduces the amount of light reaching the film.

night for day Shooting that is actually accomplished under night conditions but that is lighted to give the effect of day.

O

opticals Fades, dissolves, blowups or other trick effects made in the optical printer.

outline A synopsis of a story, usually what the writer starts with before developing characters or scenes.

outtake   A take that was completed but not printed either because of mechanical error or because of low-quality performances.

overcranks   Operating the camera at above-normal speed to produce a slow motion effect, sometimes at 300 frames per second.

overexposure   Allowing too much light to travel through the lens and onto the film, resulting in a light, washed-out print.

overlap   1. When shooting a scene from two or more angles, the intentional overlapping of action to facilitate making a smooth cut during editing.   2. When shooting a close-up of one actor and the actor off camera picks up his cures too quickly, the accidental overlapping of dialogue on the soundtrack.

P

Panavision   The superbly engineered camera favored by all filmmakers who can afford its high rental cost.

pan shot   A shot made while the camera swings on its tripod in a horizontal arc.

pantomime   Action in which the actors express themselves by means of gestures, without using any words.

parallel action   Two lines of action that occur simultaneously, shown to the audience via a cutback.

pick it up   In an incomplete scene, the order to continue with the action from the same spot at which it went bad, with or without changing the camera angle.

pixel   The small, discrete units that make up a digital picture in computer animation.

P.O.V., point of view   1. Usually a view of the action as seen by an actor. 2. The intellectual interpretation that an actor brings to a character.

print   The order given when a take is satisfactory. Also, the positive film.

processing   The developing and printing of motion picture film.

process shot   A shot made by photographing foreground action against a translucent screen, upon which another background has been projected from the rear. Also, front projection.

projection   1. In acting, a technique of voice control in which the actor speaks loudly enough to be heard at a distance.   2. In film, throwing an enlarged image upon a screen.

R

raw stock   Unexposed negative available in 400- or 1,000-foot rolls.

reading   Trying out for a part; the interpretation of a line of dialogue.

rear projection   *See* **processing.**

reflex   A camera that allows the operator to view the scene being filmed through the lens.

rough cut   The first viewing of a picture after it has been put together.

rushes   Same as **dailies.**

S

scene   A unit of action. A succession of one or more shots within a sequence.

score   The music for a motion picture.

screenplay   A script containing dialogue and action in continuity.

scrims   Diffusion screens placed over the lights to soften their effect.

sequence   A unit of action in which there is no lapse of time; a sequence sometimes encompasses several scenes.

short focal-length lens   A lens that gives the feeling of depth from a 35-mm to a 9-mm "bug eye."

shot   A single piece of film within a scene; a take.

shutter   The device inside the camera that rotates before the film, intermittently allowing it to receive exposure. The shutter opens while the film is stationary and closes while the film is being moved to the next frame.

slate   The numbering board that is held up by the assistant cameraman before a take is made. The slate number is used to identify the film in the laboratory and cutting room.

slow motion   The effect obtained by speeding up the camera, or overcranking.

sound speed   The speed of a sound recording—24 frames per second, or 90 feet per minute.

soundtrack   The magnetic tape that is the result of a sound recording. In projection, the optical area located at one side of the picture on the positive print.

special effects   A general term referring to almost any unusual effect used to create an illusion in a film.

speed   1. The state occurring when the camera and the recorder have reached their proper operating rate. This is the point at which the director can now say "Action." 2. The sensitivity of film.

splice   The place where two pieces of film are joined together.

split focus   When two objects, one near to the camera and the other farther away, are both critically sharp.

split screen   A procedure used to duplicate an actor in a scene. This technique is used when creating the illusion of identical twins, or when one actor plays two parts.

stock shot   A scene taken from a previous picture and placed in the film library. Stock shots are usually film of scenic locales or hard-to-duplicate action.

stop   The lens aperture in t.values.

stop motion   The process of exposing one frame at a time, as in animation.

sync   The point at which the picture and the soundtrack are properly aligned.

T

tail   The end of a reel of film after it has been projected.

take   An individual piece of film with no cuts. A shot.

takeup   The mechanism that winds the film onto the spool in the magazine after it has received its exposure.

tape   The soundtrack or the picture in video.

technical   In acting, playing a scene with limited emotion or with genuine feeling on the actor's part, but not necessarily giving that impression to the audience.

teleplay   A television screenplay.

thread   To place the film in the camera and make ready for shooting.

tilt   Moving the camera on its tripod in a vertical arc.

titles   The credit announcements that accompany a motion picture.

tone deaf   Said of an actor who cannot imitate another's reading of a line.

treatment   A more detailed version of the story after the outline, but before the screenplay is started.

t.system   Method of calibrating exposure. The t.system has replaced the f.system.

U

undercrank   To slow down the speed of the camera in order to give the illusion of speeded-up action.

underexposure   Not allowing enough light to reach the film.

universal focus   When all objects, near and far, are in sharp focus.

up shot   A shot made from a low position with the camera angled upward.

V

video assist   A TV camera attached to the movie camera so that the director can replay the take on the set.

W

whip   To quickly pan from one object to another.

wide-angle lens   Same as **short focal-length lens**.

wild camera   A silent camera, not in sync with the sound recorder.

wild track   A soundtrack made independently from the camera.

wild wall   A removable wall from a set.

wipe   An optical effect that allows one scene to merge with another by moving a sharp line across the frame.

Z

zoom lens   A lens that can change its focal length from short to long, or from long shot to close-up.

APPENDIX D

appendix d

BIBLIOGRAPHY

Abbott, Denise. "Martha Coolidge." *On Magazine,* 1993.

Azinoff, Eliot. "John Sayles." *DGA Magazine,* 1998.

Bart, Peter. "Open Letter to George Lucas." *Daily Variety,* 1999.

Berger, Warren. "The Ad Guys Take Charge." *Los Angeles Times,* 25 July 1999.

Black, Noel. "George Romero at Directors' Retreat." *DGA Magazine,* 1998.

Burrows, James. "The Comedy Director Knows Best." *DGA Magazine,* 1998.

Carrol, Tomm. "Sir Alan & the Round Table." *DGA News,* 1994.

Clarke, Charles G. "Professional Cinematography." *American Cinematographer,* 1968.

Coleman, Hila. *Making Movies—Student Films to Features.* New York: New York World Publishing Company, 1969.

Corliss, Richard. "George Lucas." *Time,* 12 April 1999.

Deutch, Joel. "Directors in Dialogue—Clint Eastwood." *DGA News,* 1993.

Elrick, Ted. "Interview with Robert Zemeckis." *DGA News,* 1995.

———. "Martha Coolidge." *DGA Magazine,* 1998.

———. "Wes Craven Screams Again." *DGA Magazine,* 1998.

Emmons, Steve. "Interview with Phillip Creager." *Los Angeles Times,* 20 May 1999.

Fisher, Bob. "Aspect Ratio for HDTV." *On Magazine,* 1994.

Gessner, Robert. *The Moving Image.* New York: E. P. Dutton, 1968.

Hardesty, Mary. "Spielberg, Hanson & Brooks." *DGA Magazine,* 1998.

Heard, Christopher. *Dreaming Aloud.* Toronto: Doubleday, 1997.

Hodapp, William. *The Television Actor's Manual.* New York: Appleton-Century-Crofts, 1995.

Hope, Darrel L. "Interview with Forest Whitaker." *DGA Magazine,* 1998.

Iorio, Paul. "Sleuthing Chinatown." *Los Angeles Times,* 8 July 1999.

Jacobs, Lewis. *The Movies as Medium.* New York: Farrar, Straus & Giroux, 1970.

Kantor, Bernard R.; Irwin R. Blacker; and Anne Kramer. *Directors at Work.* New York: Funk & Wagnalls, 1970.

Lewis, Colby. *The TV Director-Interpreter.* New York: Hastings House, 1968.

Levy, Andrew. "Michael Bay." *DGA Magazine,* 1998.

Lindgren, Ernest. *The Art of the Film.* New York: The Macmillan Company, 1968.

Lopez, Steve. "Sundance Summer." *Time,* 19 July 1999.

Malkiewicz, Kris. *Cinematography.* New York: Simon and Schuster, 1989.

Mascelli, Joseph V. *The Five C's of Cinematography.* Hollywood: Cine-Grafic Publications, 1968.

Millerson, Gerald. *The Technique of Television Production.* New York: Hastings House, 1969.

Natale, Richard. "Interview with David Cunningham." *Los Angeles Times,* 13 June 1999.

Perry, George. *Steven Spielberg.* New York: Thunder's Mouth Press, 1998.

Pizzello, Stephen. "Spike Lee's 70s." *American Cinematographer,* 1999.

Pollock, Dale. *Skywalking* (George Lucas). New York: Da Capo Press, 1999.

Redman, Nick. "Alan Smithee." *DGA News,* 1992.

Reiz, Karel, and Gavin Millar. *Techniques of Film Editing.* New York: Hastings House, 1968.

Rilla, Wolf. *A–Z of Movie Making.* New York: The Viking Press, 1970.

Schmidt, Rick. *Feature Filmmaking at Used Car Prices.* New York: Penguin Group, 1988.

Smallman, Kirk. *Creative Film-Making.* New York: The Macmillan Company, 1969.

Sorenson, Peter. "Hot Pixels." *Special Effects,* 1998.

Spottiswoode, Raymond. *Film and Its Techniques.* Berkeley: University of California Press, 1970.

Troy, Patricia. "Mimi Leder." *DGA Magazine,* 1997.

Yonover, Neal. "Deux or Die." *DGA News,* 1993.

INDEX